BRITISH POLITICAL BIOGRAPHY

JOHN W. DERRY

CASTLEREAGH

ALLEN LANE

British Political Biography
Edited by Chris Cook

Copyright © John W. Derry, 1976

First published in 1976

Allen Lane
Penguin Books Ltd
17 Grosvenor Gardens
London SW1

ISBN 0 7139 0838 6 (cased edition)
ISBN 0 7139 0839 4 (paper edition)

Printed in Great Britain by
T. & A. Constable Ltd
Hopetoun Street, Edinburgh

Set in Monotype Modern Extended No. 7

The title page caricature by W. Heath is reproduced with
the kind permission of the Trustees of the British Museum

CONTENTS

        In writing this study of Castlereagh I have not attempted either a conventional biography or a complete narrative of events. I have kept the aim of the series firmly in mind, and though the interest is kept focused on Castlereagh throughout, I have endeavoured to show how his career reflected the assumptions and circumstances of a particular period, how he represented a certain style of political behaviour, and how he contributed to the development of a distinctive political tradition. I hope that what I have written will do something, however modest, to rescue him from the abuse of posterity and from the caricature that presents him as inhuman in his personal character, rigid in his thinking, and inflexible in his conduct.

A brief book such as this would have been impossible without the specialist work of other historians. I have indicated my principal debts in the references and bibliography, but two names call for special mention: Sir Charles Webster and Mr H. Montgomery Hyde, whose works are the foundation upon which all modern appreciations of Castlereagh rest. I should also like to thank the staff of the Durham County Record Office, whose courteous efficiency made the consultation of the Castlereagh Papers contained in the Londonderry Collection a pleasant and enjoyable task.

The author and publishers wish to thank G. Bell & Sons Ltd for permission to quote extracts from Sir Charles Webster, *The Foreign Policy of Castlereagh 1812-1815* and from the same author's *The Foreign Policy of Castlereagh 1815-1822*, and Macmillan & Company Ltd for permission to quote material from H. Montgomery Hyde, *The Rise of Castlereagh*.

JOHN W. DERRY

1

MYTHS AND REALITIES

Few statesmen have served their country so
faithfully and so selflessly as Robert Stewart, Second Marquess of
Londonderry, who was best known to his contemporaries by his
courtesy title of Viscount Castlereagh, but none of comparable
eminence has been so wantonly abused during his lifetime or so
viciously misrepresented after his death. Despite the vindication of
Castlereagh, both as man and as minister, which has been the
cumulative effect of historical research over the past fifty years, his
reputation still suffers from the false image projected by radical
journalists, romantic poets and defunct popular historians. The
sneers of Byron and Shelley count for more than the labours of Sir

Charles Webster and Mr Montgomery Hyde, while the tragic circumstances of Castlereagh's mental collapse and suicide are irresponsibly
exploited to throw doubt upon his mental stability at earlier stages of
his career. In Ireland the destruction of the Union of 1801, which he
toiled so hard to create, assists the perpetuation of the myth that he
betrayed his country, while the romantic glamour which so per-
versely surrounds the rebellion of 1798 allows the cruel lie that he
was bloodthirsty and vengeful, during and after the rising, to be
diffused and believed. The contrast between the professional
historian's view of Castlereagh, summed up in Mr C.J.Bartlett's
judicious study which was published in 1966, and the popular
misconceptions surrounding his name, confirms the persistence of
credulity and the slowness with which historical truth dispels the
crudities of legend.

Castlereagh's reputation reveals as much about the vagaries of
historical writing as his career tells us of the complexities of politics
and diplomacy in the first twenty years of the nineteenth century.
The criteria by which self-confident Victorians misjudged him were
as inappropriate as their assessments were inept. Harriet Martineau's
four-volume work, *A History of the Thirty Years Peace*, gave vigorous
expression to the conventional liberal view of Castlereagh. He was
jeered at as 'an enemy to his race', a man of narrow-minded
obstinacy who had thrown away the opportunity of elevating 'the
better impulses of Europe'. He was 'the screw by which England had
riveted the chains of nations', and his death was celebrated as 'a ray
of hope in the midst of thickest darkness'. Even when it was conceded that he was an amiable and generous man in private life, there
was no relaxation of the relentless insistence that, more than any
other British statesman of the time, he was the strong-willed
instigator of repression at home and abroad.[1] But Castlereagh could
not be fitted into any of the fashionable historical mythologies of the
nineteenth century. Lacking apologists on all sides of the political
spectrum, he suffered from the neglect of specialist historians until
the twentieth century. To the liberal he was an obvious foe, the ally
of Metternich and a stern symbol of reaction. To the nationalist,
whether in Britain or Ireland, he typified the eighteenth century's
distrust of nationalism as a force disruptive of order within established societies and of any stable equilibrium between states. But he
was just as unattractive to those seeking to construct a Tory version
of democracy with which to challenge the monopoly of liberalism.
He could not be portrayed as a Tory who had identified himself with
the masses against the classes. His clear-sighted and sober political

realism could not be assimilated into the poetic rewriting of history in a Young England style. He had defended the country's institutions, but he was no advocate of an alliance between Crown, Church, aristocracy and working people against the dominance of the middle classes.

Similarly, despite his decisive contribution to the defeat of Napoleon, he was no imperialist. He bequeathed no ringing phrases or memorable gestures to those who invested ideals of empire with glory and purpose. His indifference to ideas of imperialism offended imperialists, while his involvement with Europe appalled isolationists. As a practitioner of traditional diplomacy he was hated by those who presumed that international relations were best conducted in the spirit of a handful of platitudes resonant of John Bright's most unctuous style. But the very restraint with which Castlereagh managed Britain's relations with her continental allies and with the United States of America ensured that his handling of foreign policy lacked the appeal of Canning's jaunty anticipation of Palmerston's disdain for foreigners and despots.

As Leader of the House of Commons during Lord Liverpool's ministry Castlereagh had come to be popularly associated with ideas of systematic repression, and his defence of the magistrates after the Peterloo affair was cited as further evidence of his hardness of heart. Those who expected a politician to be first and foremost an orator argued that his speeches in the House of Commons were further confirmation of his sluggish and pedantic mediocrity. Lord Salisbury was right in claiming that if Castlereagh had coined a few striking phrases his reputation would have been transformed out of all recognition, but, unlike Canning, Castlereagh had no desire to pose, either for his contemporaries or for posterity, and his self-control and integrity made it easier for received misconceptions to carry conviction with all those who were too lazy to question the popular caricature.

Castlereagh was also unfortunate in that his defenders were less agile than his detractors. His half-brother's edition of his correspondence was little more than a diligent compilation, with little historical explanation or analysis throughout its twelve volumes, and Alison's three volumes could not undermine the dominance of more nimble writers. Despite the inaccuracy of their judgements, and the prejudice which compounded their ignorance, Byron and Shelley embodied a thriving tradition of vivid misrepresentation in what they wrote about Castlereagh, and there was no one of comparable gifts to challenge their hold on the popular mind. In *The Masque of Anarchy*

Shelley showed great skill in character assassination. Eldon represented fraud and Sidmouth hypocrisy, but Castlereagh typified something worse:

> I met Murder on the way –
> He had a mask like Castlereagh –
> Very smooth he looked, yet grim;
> Seven bloodhounds followed him:
>
> All were fat; and well they might
> Be in admirable plight,
> For one by one and two by two,
> He tossed them human hearts to chew
> Which from his wide cloak he drew.

Memories of 1798 were cleverly mingled with reminiscences of Peterloo. The sly reference to Castlereagh's proverbial self-control added to the impression of sleek, heartless cruelty. For those who liked to personalize their politics, reducing matters of great complexity to a simple clash of personalities, lines such as these were conveniently memorable.

Shelley chose to depict Castlereagh as a murderer, but Byron's savage lines in the dedication to *Don Juan* summed up everything that radicals liked to believe about Castlereagh. The legend of his apostasy and bloodthirstiness in Ireland was combined with jibes about his courage, his self-discipline and his lack of children (which had been used in a vicious debating thrust in the Dublin Parliament many years before). After asking, somewhat redundantly, whether a resurrected Milton would have obeyed 'the intellectual eunuch Castlereagh', Byron warmed to his task:

> Cold-blooded, smooth-faced, placid miscreant!
>   Dabbling its sleek young hands in Erin's gore,
> And thus for wider carnage taught to pant,
>   Transferred to gorge upon a sister shore,
> The vulgarest tool that Tyranny could want,
>   With just enough of talent, and no more,
> To lengthen fetters by another fixed,
> And offer poison long already mixed.
>
> An orator of such set trash of phrase,
>   Ineffably, legitimately vile,
> That even its grossest flatterers dare not praise,
>   Nor foes – all nations – condescend to smile,
> Nor even a sprightly blunder's spark can blaze
>   From that Ixion's grindstone's ceaseless toil,
> That turns and turns to give the world a notion
> Of endless torments and perpetual motion.

A bungler even in its disgusting trade,
    And botching, patching, leaving still behind
Something of which its masters are afraid –
    States to be curbed, and thought to be confined,
Conspiracy or Congress to be made –
    Cobbling at manacles for all mankind –
A tinkering slave-maker, who mends old chains,
With God and Man's abhorrence for its gains.

If we may judge of matter by the mind,
    Emasculated to the marrow *It*
Hath but two objects, how to serve, and bind,
    Deeming the chain it wears even men may fit,
Eutropius of its many masters, – blind
    To worth as freedom, wisdom as to wit,
Fearless, because *no* feeling dwells in ice,
Its very courage stagnates to a vice.

These stanzas sum up a complete mythology – the legend of the heartless Irish renegade, who connived with reaction abroad and who initiated repression at home, whose courage only reflected his inhumanity and whose political career was as sterile as his marriage. But *Don Juan* did not contain all that Byron had to say about Castlereagh. He heard the news of his death with venomous gloating, expressing his feelings in vituperative doggerel:

    So he has cut his throat at last! He? Who?
    The man who cut his country's long ago.

His friend John Cam Hobhouse urged Byron to be more careful in how he dealt with Castlereagh's death, but Byron returned to the subject in some lines which were even more meretricious:

    Posterity will ne'er survey
    A nobler grave than this:
    Here lie the bones of Castlereagh:
    Stop, traveller, and —!

The lurid caricature of 'carotid-cutting Castlereagh' had received its final form.

When Castlereagh died there was universal glee among radicals. Cobbett, for example, urged the imprisoned Joseph Swan to keep up his spirits by brooding on the news that Castlereagh had cut his throat: 'Let that sound reach you in the depths of your dungeon . . . and carry consolation to your suffering soul!'' But not all comments, even by political opponents, were so unfair or so exultant. When the heat of political controversy cooled, Castlereagh's virtues were admitted, although somewhat grudgingly. Brougham, who was especially obnoxious to Castlereagh's half-brother because of his misrepresentation of his character and policies, nevertheless conceded that if all the other members of Liverpool's administration were placed in one scale and Castlereagh in the other he would singly weigh them all down. 'One can't help feeling a little for him, after being pitted against him for several years pretty regularly . . . Also, he was a *gentleman*, and the only one amongst them.'[2]

The attitudes of the period's two most famous diarists were more mixed. Creevey could bring himself only to admit that Castlereagh had managed a corrupt House of Commons 'pretty well'. He confessed that he had been a brave man, but he criticized his limited understanding, arguing that his life had been spent 'in an avowed, cold-blooded contempt of every honest public principle'.[3] Greville was more magnanimous and more just. He believed that Castlereagh's talents had been great and his character even greater. He recognized his qualities, even when they had been offset by other defects:

His appearance was dignified and imposing; he was affable in his manners and agreeable in society. The great feature was a cool and determined courage, which gave the appearance of resolution and confidence in all his actions, and inspired his friends with admiration and excessive devotion to him, and caused him to be respected by his most violent opponents.

Greville thought Castlereagh a prolix and monotonous public speaker except when he was provoked by something which had been said in debate. Nevertheless, he was always heard with close attention. 'He never spoke ill; his speeches were continually replete with good sense and strong argument and though they seldom offered much to admire, they generally contained a great deal to be answered.' Greville shared Creevey's high opinion of Castlereagh's excellence as a parliamentary manager. 'He was', he wrote, 'one of the best managers of the House of Commons who ever sat in it.' He achieved this distinction because he had the good humour and the agreeable manners which were essential for winning the confidence of the House. Greville thought that these qualities were more important than eloquence for a Leader of the House of Commons, and the majority of his contemporaries agreed with him.[4]

But the arts of political management are less comprehensible than oratory for later generations. A brilliant speech can retain something of its magic even on the printed page, and even those who know little of the context in which it was delivered can thrill to its invective or laugh at its humour or be swept along by its passionate grandiloquence. A few sparkling phrases impress themselves more easily on the public memory than a lifetime of patient political negotiation. To understand why Castlereagh appealed so powerfully to the majority of the House of Commons it is necessary to have some comprehension of the structure of politics at the time, of the nature of party conflict, and of the reasons for the formation of certain ministries or the persistence of particular political rivalries or alignments. The House of Commons may often produce great orators, but it never wholly trusts them. Despite his brilliance in debate Sheridan was always regarded with suspicion by the majority of M.P.s. Edmund Burke's speeches have made a bigger impact upon posterity than they did upon contemporaries. Castlereagh lacked eloquence, but he possessed a fund of common sense, a feeling for the mood of the House and the ability to carry conviction as much by strength of character as by force of argument. He bore the chief burden of defending the government's actions in the House of Commons, and a close examination of his conduct as Leader of the House reveals why Liverpool valued his services in this regard so highly, even when this responsibility occasionally conflicted with his duties as Foreign Secretary. The respect shown to Castlereagh by the backbenchers of his day helps in discerning the real man who lay behind the legend and in appreciating more correctly the reasons for his dominance within the government and his primacy within the House of Commons.

Castlereagh never lacked tributes from his contemporaries, although they usually came from men who were uncongenial to the self-appointed guardians of public enlightenment. The Duke of Wellington owed much to Castlereagh's patronage and support and he had, in his turn, a high opinion of his friend's merits. Wellington especially admired Castlereagh's clear judgement and calm courage, and he thought that he possessed most of the essential political skills, but he shrewdly recognized where the weak spot lay – 'he could do everything but speak in Parliament, that he could not do'.[5] Nor were tributes lacking from other public figures. The Earl of Ripon had accompanied Castlereagh to the continent in 1813. Many years later he recalled his mastery of the diplomatist's art and the tribute paid to Castlereagh by the House of Commons when he returned from the peace negotiations in Paris: 'the whole body of the Commons of England rose from their seats upon his appearance, and greeted him with cordial acclamations'. In Ripon's opinion no one was better suited than Castlereagh for the conduct of international affairs. 'The suavity and dignity of his manners, his habitual patience and self-command, his considerate tolerance of difference of opinion in others, all fitted him for such a task; whilst his firmness, when he knew he was right, in no degree detracted from the influence of his conciliatory demeanour.'6 This is far removed from the popular picture of a harsh and unbending reactionary whose icy intransigence repelled those who sought to deal with him.

It is significant that three of the warmest tributes paid to Castlereagh came, not from the Ultra-Tory faction, but from Sir Robert Peel and two eminent Peelites. Peel had a deep respect for Castlereagh. He wrote appreciatively of his 'high and generous feelings', his 'courteous and prepossessing manners', his 'warm heart and cool head', his great moral and personal courage, his industry and, by no means least, his good temper. Lord Aberdeen always remembered the encouragement he had received from Castlereagh at the beginning of his political career, and in his opinion few men ever deserved more highly of his country than Castlereagh had done. Sir James Graham was another who emphasized Castlereagh's generosity of spirit, even towards his political opponents. 'I can never forget the charm of his amiable manners and of his noble nature. I . . . should be ungrateful if I did not recollect his kindness . . . History, I am persuaded, will be more just than his contemporaries, and he is not the first great man over whose tomb has been written – "*Ingrata Patria*".'7 These tributes are a reminder of the general respect in which Castlereagh was held throughout the Tory party during the years after the war against Napoleon. Like Pitt he was always eager to encourage promising political talent whenever he discerned it, and while he possessed the confidence of older Tories such as Sidmouth and Eldon he had the trust and affection of many of the younger men whose careers were just beginning.

Foreign diplomatists admired Castlereagh's poise and command. His sheer professional expertise compelled their esteem. Richard Rush, the American minister in London, with whom Castlereagh shared a desire for friendly Anglo-American relations, had a deep regard for the British Foreign Secretary. He recognized that he was 'British in all his policy and projects', but he appreciated the undeviating integrity and unflinching honesty which informed all his political conduct. 'Always self-possessed, always firm and fearless, his judgement was the guide of his opinions, and his opinions the guide of his conduct, undaunted by opposition in Parliament or out of it.'8 Metternich's estimation of Castlereagh's qualities was unlikely to commend the Foreign Secretary to liberal opinion in England, but, despite their disagreements, Metternich had a shrewd insight into Castlereagh's character, describing him as 'absolutely straight, a stranger to all prejudice, as just as he is kind'. Metternich especially admired Castlereagh's ability to distinguish truth from falsehood, though he might also have reflected that on occasion he had himself been inconvenienced because of it.[9]

Nor were favourable impressions of Castlereagh limited to those who had experience of office. Samuel Bamford, the radical, was struck by the contrast between the image and the reality when he was examined before the Privy Council in 1817. He discovered that the King's ministers were very different from their popular caricature. Lord Sidmouth was affable and friendly, and Bamford described Castlereagh sympathetically as 'a good-looking person in a plum-coloured coat, with a gold ring on the small finger of his left hand, on which he sometimes leaned his head as he eyed me over'. He discovered that their lordships had a sense of humour, and he concluded that much of the prevalent discontent sprang from misunderstanding and mutual ignorance rather than from any malice aforethought on the government's part.[10]

The contrast between popular error and private truth is all the more evident when the testimony of those who knew Castlereagh well is taken into account. Croker's admiring tribute is well known. 'Londonderry goes on as usual,' he wrote on 21 December 1821, 'and like Mont Blanc continues to gather all the sunshine upon his icy head. He is *better* than ever; that is, colder, steadier, more *procurante*, and withal more amiable and respected. It is a splendid summit of bright and polished frost which, like the travellers in Switzerland, we all admire; but which no one can hope, and few would wish, to reach.'[11] Yet, perceptive though it was in some ways, Croker's description is somewhat misleading. The emphasis on frost and ice and glacial self-control helped to perpetuate the notion that Castlereagh was some bloodless phenomenon, and since both friend and foe used the same pattern of metaphors they overlooked the cost of Castlereagh's self-control and the passionate feelings which lay beneath his calm and lofty public face.

Mrs Arbuthnot was one of Castlereagh's most ardent admirers. She loved and respected him deeply and in her *Journal* she wrote of him in tender and affectionate language. However bitter his political opponents were she could not believe that he could have any private enemies. He was 'loved to adoration' by his family and friends. She admired his personal beauty, his commanding presence, his grace and courtesy, his kindness and generosity. She went so far as to say that he was 'excessively agreeable, a great favourite amongst women', and on at least one occasion his wife's jealousy was roused.[12] But he was also an adoring and exemplary husband: indeed, his devotion to Lady Castlereagh was the cause of much amusement, for her social indiscretions were often acutely embarrassing for her husband, the most notorious instance being when she wore his Order of the Garter in her hair. But Castlereagh's letters to his wife were touching in their affection, and though Lady Castlereagh could not claim to be her husband's intellectual equal she gave him the understanding and unwavering loyalty his sensitive nature craved.

Mrs Arbuthnot was too deeply involved with Castlereagh to be other than prejudiced in his favour, but much of what she said is borne out by less partial witnesses. There can be no doubt that Castlereagh possessed considerable personal charm. His domestic life was happy, and he enjoyed the company of friends and children. He liked nothing better than spending time on his farm at Cray in Kent, where he took a keen interest in growing flowers, often pruning them himself, and in looking after the animals in a small menagerie which he had established for his wife's amusement. He was a kindly master to his servants, and he was charitable to the poor of the parish. He was a good churchman in a characteristically unobtrusive way: at the Congress of Vienna his fondness for singing hymns to the accompaniment of a harmonium caused as much wry comment as his determination to improve his dancing by regular practice. He was passionately devoted to music. Although his technique as a 'cellist was limited he liked to play instrumental and chamber music with musically gifted friends. His musical ear was excellent, and whenever music was being made he eagerly joined the party.[13]

His habits were abstemious. He drank little wine and he liked to go to bed early. During the summer he got up at five o'clock in the morning; in the winter he stayed in bed until seven. As a young man his health had been considered delicate, and when, with the onset of middle age, he suffered from attacks of gout, he bore them with considerable patience. During parliamentary sessions he worked between twelve and fourteen hours a day. He tried to keep fit by taking walks before breakfast. Three or four hours spent in his library were unalloyed delight, wrested from a busy and burdensome world. Because he had chosen to leave St John's College, Cambridge, without proceeding to a degree it was often forgotten that he had been a bookish undergraduate. He had done well in college examinations, and like so many others of his class he retained a love for classical literature throughout his life. Although he was more sceptical about the merits of Greek nationalism than many others who had been similarly saturated in the classics he could not help remarking that one's education taught one an admiration for the Greeks. But unlike many contemporaries he had a shrewd appreciation of the difference between the Greece of classical and Hellenistic times and the Greece of the early nineteenth century.

It would be absurd to claim that Castlereagh's agreeable nature in private life ought to compensate, in some sense, for the alleged harshness of his conduct in public life. Any sustained examination of his attitudes of mind and his public conduct is enough to demonstrate the falsity of the familiar caricature. But the myth can be exploded in terms of his personality. Here was a man endowed with the power to win and keep friends, whose character was both more complex and more attractive than legend suggests. Despite Castlereagh's integrity it would be foolish to construct a favourable glacial image, which would be little more than an inversion of the unfavourable one. Self-control is a desirable quality in a politician: the heart ought to be subservient to the head. But for all his self-control Castlereagh was not immune from intense and vehement feelings. He was usually capable of resisting them, but there were times when his self-restraint lapsed. The most dramatic example of his emotions getting the better of him was his duel with Canning, when his passionate and unrelenting ferocity shocked many of his contemporaries, including those who were generally sympathetic to him because of the provocation he had endured. Similarly he was sensitive to the humanitarian considerations which moved others, as over the abolition of the Slave Trade, even when he was dubious about their political practicability. He ignored neither the dedication of the abolitionists nor the obstacles to translating their principles into action. Because he recognized the constraints within which politicians had to work he found appeals to unalloyed principle embarrassing and exasperating, but, pragmatic though he was, he was no cynic, however frankly he faced the more selfish aspects of human behaviour and the elements of conflict within society and between states.

The legend of Castlereagh as a man of ice is, therefore, unacceptable, and so is any suggestion that his foreign policy was inflexible and intransigent. At one time it was fashionable to decry Castlereagh as little more than a dupe of Metternich, the simple-minded tool of subtle and devious reactionaries. But the researches of Sir Charles Webster and Dr Henry Kissinger have exploded this misrepresentation. Similarly, the contrast between the foreign policy of Castlereagh and that of Canning was exaggerated, Castlereagh being labelled as reactionary, Canning as liberal. But this convenient juxtaposition has been shattered by historical research. Canning's policies may now be seen as, in some ways, a continuation of Castlereagh's, expressing more provocatively a change of emphasis which had already been taking place before Castlereagh's death. It might also be thought tempting to contrast Castlereagh's 'European' policy with Canning's more obviously 'British' one, but while Canning always distrusted the Congress system, and the degree to which it involved Britain with the affairs of the continent, in no sense did Castlereagh ever neglect to safeguard vital British interests. He valued the Congress system, but he never allowed wishful thinking to blind him to the realities of power, and whenever there was a clash between British interests and the demands of the European system he placed British interests first. Unlike Canning he believed that the Congress system had great potential for the purpose of securing international peace, but he did not assume that all conflicts of interest would thereby be painlessly resolved. He thought that British interests were best secured by a judicious involvement with Europe, but there was nothing starry-eyed about his approach, and although in the immediate aftermath of the Congress of Vienna he talked enthusiastically of the prospects for diplomacy by conference he had no intention of imposing some speculative conception upon the management of foreign policy.

He was no isolationist. He remembered the Revolutionary and Napoleonic Wars too well ever to forget that however powerful Britain was at sea she needed a continental ally to win her major wars. But he had no desire to become implicated in any alliance which was pledged to persistent intervention in the internal affairs of sovereign states. Non-intervention was as much a principle of Castlereagh's diplomacy as it was of Canning's, but Canning gave the idea a more active and bellicose twist. Nevertheless, flexibility was as much a part of Castlereagh's conduct of foreign policy as firmness. Recognizing that Britain had an interest in the maintenance of the balance of power in Europe he hoped that conference diplomacy would enable an equilibrium to be achieved and sustained, but he had no wish to be drawn into too firm an alliance with one *bloc* of European Powers, despite his mistrust of Russia, and he knew that there would be occasions when British interests differed from those of her European allies, as over the struggle of the Spanish and Portuguese colonies in Latin America against their traditional overlords.

It was once fashionable to criticize the diplomatists of 1815 for ignoring the principles of liberalism and nationalism. This standpoint has been substantially revised in recent years. One recent writer on the history of international relations has commented that to expect the Congress of Vienna to have applied the principles of liberalism and nationalism in the peace settlement is about as realistic as suggesting that in 1945 the victorious allies ought to have made the principles of Nazism the basis of their own attempts at European reconstruction.[14] But though Castlereagh has been rescued from nineteenth-century misrepresentations on this score it would be equally misleading to exaggerate the internationalist aspects of his approach to the relations between the Powers. Fashions in interpretation consequent upon British entry into the European Economic Community ought not to justify an undue emphasis on the Europeanism of Castlereagh's foreign policy. He was not trying to unify Europe. He was attempting to minimize the inevitable tensions between the Powers, rather than exacerbate them. Throughout the negotiations of 1814 and 1815 he was sensitive to potential disagreements between Britain and Austria, on the one hand, and Russia and Prussia, on the other. The protracted negotiations over Poland and Saxony reflected serious clashes of interest between the allies, even before the final victory over Napoleon had been won. Castlereagh favoured a generous peace settlement with France because he realized that once the Bonapartist régime had been replaced Britain and France might well be drawn together in common opposition to the policies of the central and eastern Powers. But he also sought to strengthen Prussia on the Rhineland as an insurance against any resurgence of French aggression, and he persisted with Pitt's scheme for the unification of Holland and Belgium in a stronger kingdom of the Netherlands in order to thwart French expansionist designs in the Low Countries. Castlereagh contemplated an alliance between Britain, France and Austria in order to challenge Russian domination, but despite this he was usually cautious about anything which would divide Europe into two hostile alliances. A foreign policy as subtle and sophisticated as this, with its sober recognition of the transient alignments governing relations between the powers and of the essential interests which it was the duty of any British Foreign Secretary to secure was not the product of a crude and unimaginative mind. Poise, balance, determination and flexibility were the hallmarks of Castlereagh's approach to foreign affairs.

Castlereagh valued the Quadruple Alliance, not as a means of imposing a rigidly reactionary régime throughout Europe, but as a reasonable insurance against the outbreak of precipitate war. The

Powers had a common interest in stability and peace, but inevitably
they would from time to time find themselves in conflict over various
issues. Although Castlereagh was sceptical about the likelihood of
many of the new constitutions established after 1815 working out in
practice he was reluctant to allow intervention to take place unless
some real threat to European peace had been proved beyond all
reasonable doubt. Purely domestic upheavals did not justify intervention on the part of the Powers, acting collectively. Collective
security was a necessary insurance against any renewal of French
aggression, especially if this were once again to be linked with
revolutionary ideology, but this did not constitute a *carte blanche* to
meddle in the internal affairs of the various states of Europe.
Eventually Castlereagh came into conflict with Metternich on this
point. Even when he could not prevent Austrian intervention in
Naples – even when he came to accept such action as necessary – he
was eager that such intervention should be taken on Austria's
initiative and responsibility, and not by the alliance as a whole. He
admitted that Austria's special interests in Italy were threatened by
the disorders in Naples, but British interests were not involved, nor,
in his view, were those of the other members of the alliance. Nor was
Britain a member of the Holy Alliance. Castlereagh regarded it as 'a
piece of sublime mysticism and nonsense' (one of the few quotable
phrases he left to posterity). He distrusted vague appeals to generalized moral principles as a guide for the conduct of international
relations. Ultimately his unease about Metternich's growing tendency to invoke a theory of interventionist conservatism in as
dogmatic a fashion as a revolutionary appealing to notions of
liberalism and enlightenment compelled Castlereagh to dissociate
himself from the actions of those Powers with whom he had hoped to
collaborate in the cause of peace.

But even here there was a more subtle, possibly even an ambivalent, aspect to his conduct. Sceptical as he was about the ideas of
Christian paternalism and benevolence which the Emperor Alexander I had originally advocated as the principles of the Holy
Alliance, he could still appeal to such principles when seeking to
convert the Russian Emperor to a more cautious policy over the
Greek revolt. No one could be more pragmatic, more distrustful of
theoretical speculation, than Castlereagh, but this did not mean that
he was incapable of appreciating the powerful appeal ideology could
make, however deceptive he believed it to be. Cool and controlled,
and unconvinced by much that passed for political wisdom, he was
not unaware of the attractiveness of political ideals, but he was

persuaded that they were all too frequently dangerous and delusory, and no one who had lived, as he had lived, through the Irish rebellion of 1798 and its aftermath could be ignorant of the impact of emotion, rhetoric and nationalist fervour on the politics of a divided and embittered people. Castlereagh's Irish experience was fundamental to his political attitudes. It explained his profound appreciation of the contrast between romantic oratory and political reality. He had seen how much fine talk of an Irish republic had led to savage slaughter and civil strife, with the deluded peasantry paying the price for smooth-tongued proclamations and rousing calls to arms. Much the same thing had happened in France in the 1790s. Castlereagh's distrust of ideals divorced from practicalities was the result, not of purblind prejudice, but of chastening experience. He had seen what revolution meant at first hand, and he was more appalled by the sufferings endured by the innocent than impressed by the allegedly splendid future that was said to lie beyond the tumult, the violence and the treachery which were endemic accompaniments of social unrest.

Just as Castlereagh's foreign policy can now be placed in a more comprehensive context, so the achievement of the Liverpool administration can be more fully appreciated. It is still possible to come across denunciations of the Liverpool ministry as reactionary and repressive, but such manifestations reflect the persistence of legend rather than the measured conclusions of research. No other contemporary government was as successful in coming to terms with unprecedented social change, although those who feel a psychological compulsion to romanticize pre-industrial England find it necessary to seek out historical villains and are impelled to assert that Liverpool, Sidmouth and Castlereagh wantonly and brutally repressed the mass of the people. Ironically, Liverpool and his colleagues were preoccupied with preserving as much as they could of a familiar way of life. They believed that the country's established institutions had given Britain unparalleled peace and stability, and they therefore wished to preserve the constitution as a security for the national well-being. They had no desire to strengthen the powers of central government, or to undermine traditional liberties. They restricted the rights of public meeting and free expression only when they were convinced that these were being abused and that a real threat to public order existed. The old criticism of Liverpool and Castlereagh was that they over-reacted to rumours of a revolutionary threat that never existed. The current charge takes a different form. Working-class radicalism is now depicted in less respectable colours.

It is claimed that there was a genuine revolutionary tradition in England, and that men such as Jeremy Brandreth and Arthur Thistlewood deserve to be honoured as some species of folk hero. These claims are hotly debated among historians, and there is much scepticism about the prevalence or potential effectiveness of such a revolutionary tradition. But it can at least be suggested that when Cabinet ministers were the intended victims of plots to cut their throats and to parade their severed heads through the streets of London they did not act unreasonably in seeking to curb sedition and crush conspiracy.

Much of the problem stems from the tradition which gives an exaggerated place in the history of post-Waterloo England to the Peterloo affair, and which assumes that parliamentary reform and the repeal of the corn laws were the primary themes of British politics after 1815. Of course there was a vocal, though not particularly effective, lobby urging measures of parliamentary reform, though with little agreement about exactly what such a reform should entail. When work was short and food prices were high the cost of bread became the obvious and understandable focal point of heated controversy and agitation. The bewildering impact of industrialization stimulated unrest in periods of economic recession. But it is difficult to see how the reform of Parliament would have lessened the sufferings brought about by the industrial revolution, or how any early nineteenth-century government could, in any significant sense, have guided the process of industrial innovation and technological change into more amenable channels. The government lacked both the will and the means to intervene in the economic development of the country. The experience of the recent past seemed to confirm that government intervention had usually meant inefficiency, higher taxes, an increased cost of living, and greater popular resentment and social strife. The new science of economics emphasized that there were forces at work which governments were powerless effectively or intelligently to control. Economic progress was seen as the consequence of economic freedom. The notion of government regulation was as discredited as the old mercantilist system, and it was widely regarded as an outmoded relic of monarchic absolutism and aristocratic privilege. For most Englishmen, central government was not the real centre of authority. Authority was best represented by the squire or the magistrate, and many of the new men who were investing their capital and their skills in the novel processes of industry saw both the central and local patterns of authority as little more than hangovers from the burdensome past.

To attack established privilege implied the assertion of economic as well as political freedom.

It was, nevertheless, usual for governments to respond to particular demands for security on the part of threatened interests. The notorious Corn Law of 1815 was an attempt to meet the legitimate anxieties of the agricultural interest about the dangers of foreign competition in undermining the prosperity of British farming. There was nothing new about a law to control the import of foreign corn. It was a traditional safeguard, and it illustrated the way in which Liverpool and his colleagues liked to follow precedent in their response to events. They had also to be sensitive to the mood of the House of Commons. In 1815 the ministry abolished the income tax, not because it was convinced that the time was right to honour the promise that it would be of wartime duration only, but because the House of Commons insisted that the hated tax should go. Castlereagh complained, rightly though indiscreetly, of the Commons' ignorant impatience of taxation, but on a matter as fundamental as parliamentary confidence in the government's management of the national finances the ministry had to defer to the wishes of the House of Commons. Far from defying the feelings of the House, Liverpool and Castlereagh consistently recognized their obligation to defer to them.

Liverpool and his colleagues were poised uneasily between the rural world of the eighteenth century and the industrialized world of the nineteenth. They sensed that the old order was changing, but they clung to familiar landmarks as long as they could. They knew that they could not prevent change, but whenever they were apprehensive about what it would mean, they sought to slow down its pace. Within Parliament Liverpool complained that he lacked the resources of patronage which had been available to eighteenth-century ministers for the strengthening of the government's base of support in the Commons. It was ironic that the disciples of Pitt lamented the consequences of those administrative and financial reforms which had been the great achievement of Pitt's peacetime ministry. Liverpool also lacked the means which later nineteenth-century administrations possessed for maintaining their control over the House of Commons: party organization, parliamentary discipline and a tighter hold over the procedure of the House. Broadly speaking Liverpool's government was conservative in political matters and in everything pertaining to the institutions of the country, and liberal in economic and commercial policy. The government was not dogmatically committed to *laissez-faire*. Though most ministers believed that commerce, agriculture and industry would prosper without arbitrary government interference, they reserved the right to act whenever important interests needed to be safeguarded. Nevertheless, even while making due reservations for special cases, they assumed that merchants, bankers, businessmen and manufacturers had a better sense of what made for prosperity than politicians had.

When Liverpool said that the greater part of the miseries of which mankind complained were beyond the control of human legislation he was not speaking heartlessly: he was stating what the majority of his contemporaries believed to be the facts of the case. Sidmouth shared the same sentiments: 'Man cannot create abundance where Providence has inflicted scarcity,' he had written in 1812, and five years later he was repeating his warnings that 'the alleviation of difficulties' could not come from the intervention of the government or from Acts of Parliament. But it would be false to imply that Liverpool, Sidmouth and Castlereagh were unmoved by distress. During the post-war labour troubles on Tyneside, for example, Sidmouth made it plain that he appreciated that the seamen had genuine grievances, which it was the duty of their employers to meet. But voluntary agencies and voluntary action would be more effective than the interference of the central government, and it was not part of the government's responsibility to meddle in the normal relations between masters and men.[15]

Liverpool, Castlereagh and Sidmouth were more concerned with the exploitation of distress and hardship by radical agitators, who were manipulating those who were the victims of unemployment and industrial change. They knew that the roots of much seemingly political discontent were economic, but they believed that only when discontent spilled over into overt political agitation was the central government involved. Even here they had no desire to depart from established constitutional practice. They saw themselves as the guardians of the constitution, and although they were prepared to take extraordinary action to defend it against subversion they had no wish to pioneer new ways of asserting governmental authority. Rather they sought to strengthen the real source of authority in the 'face-to-face' society of market towns and villages. The famous Six Acts of 1819 did little more than give additional powers to local magistrates when dealing with sedition and riot, and even when they went beyond this they were far less dramatic than radical mythology claimed. Those found guilty of writing or publishing seditious libels could be transported for seven years – on the second conviction.

Magistrates were empowered to search for and confiscate arms, and the training of persons in military evolutions and the exercise of fire-arms was prohibited. These were reasonable securities for public peace, not arbitrary outrages against common sense. Castlereagh, who was responsible as Leader of the House of Commons for carrying the Bills through Parliament, told the Commons that in some parts of the country the spirit of disaffection bordered on rebellion. Even so, he was eager to assure the House that nothing in the Acts would curtail the 'real right of meeting to deliberate on public affairs which is the inherent right of Englishmen', and which he believed to be 'essential to the exercise of our free constitution'. The Acts, Castlereagh argued, were meant only to prevent the right being abused by those seeking to prepare for open rebellion. When the situation changed the Acts would be amended or repealed. This was not the language of extreme repression. Given the type of information on which the government had to act, and the experience of the previous twenty-five years which was in the minds of the King's ministers, what was striking was the restraint of the government, not its extremism. The Acts abridged the activities of agitators; for the mass of the population life went on as before. The government's attitude to these matters had been well summed up by Sidmouth when speaking to Samuel Bamford during the latter's examination before the Privy Council. Sidmouth stated that he felt great pleasure in restoring Bamford to his family, and he would not ask him to meet conditions which any good and honest men would find objectionable.

We are not averse to the subject petitioning for a redress of grievances; it is the manner in which that right has been exercised which we condemn; a right may be exercised in such a way that it becomes a wrong, and then we must object to it. Mr Bamford, there are three things which I would have you to impress seriously on your mind. The first is, that the present distress of the country arises from unavoidable circumstances; the second, that His Majesty's ministers will do all they can to alleviate such distress; and thirdly, no violence, of whatever description, will be tolerated, but it will be put down with a very strong hand. I wish you well; I assure you I wish you well; and I hope this is the last time I shall ever see you on an occasion like the present.[16]

All this is resonant of a vanished pre-Keynesian world, in which governments intervened only within a very restricted range of social and economic issues. Anyone accustomed to sustained government intervention in the management of the economy probably finds the mood astonishingly passive, even when it reflects a mild paternalism. The confession that, at best, a government could only alleviate distress, rather than prevent it, echoes the assumptions of a distant and almost innocent age. But while the conservatism which dominated the British ruling class precluded the government from tackling the problems of industrial change in a bold, original spirit, it also ensured that there would be no wholesale abandonment of traditional parliamentary procedures and familiar political practices, and no widespread acceptance of reactionary dogma or totalitarian repression. The government was as reluctant to initiate any 'White Terror' at home as Castlereagh was to support the interventionist policies of the Holy Alliance abroad.

The Peterloo incident, shocking as it was, can now be seen as a tragic accident, for which responsibility must be shared among magistrates, yeomanry and the organizers of the demonstration, rather than the expression of a considered policy of ferocious repression on the part of the government. Historical research has shattered the myth that Peterloo represented the culmination of premeditated savagery by a tyrannical government. The ministry had neither the desire nor the intention of initiating a series of military actions to disperse public gatherings. Even so far as the sequence of events in Manchester is concerned the evidence is much more conflicting than older historians admitted, even if the outcome reflects little credit on the local yeomanry.

But for Castlereagh the Peterloo affair was doubly unfortunate. It was his responsibility to defend the conduct of the Manchester magistrates in the House of Commons, but he knew from his own experience how authority could be embarrassed or even discredited by the excessive zeal and extreme partisanship of those vested with the duty of maintaining order. He had personal knowledge of the type of excesses of which an inexperienced and poorly disciplined yeomanry were capable. But there was no doubt in Castlereagh's mind that the magistrates had to be supported, whatever criticisms were being voiced of their handling of the situation. For a government spokesman to add his own criticisms to those which were being bandied about so freely would undermine the confidence of the men on whom the government depended for the preservation of public order throughout the country. Though the responsibility for dealing with agitation had been delegated to the local magistrates the government still had to accept ultimate responsibility, even for actions which it had been unable in any significant sense to control, and which it might well regard with a measure of private misgiving.[17]

Castlereagh's attitudes to the issues of the day were not obscurantist. He did not believe that it was possible to preserve the *status quo* without making necessary changes and judicious concessions. He rejected any idea of remodelling the representative system from first principles, and he thought it unwise to introduce measures of parliamentary reform when times were unruly or public order disturbed, but in certain circumstances he was prepared to condone the cautious disfranchisement of boroughs which were guilty of excessive or notorious malpractices or corruption. On these matters he was sensitive to the feelings of the House of Commons. In November 1819 he stated that he was willing to accept Lord John Russell's proposal to disfranchise Grampound, although he favoured an amendment which insisted on a franchise qualification of £20 if the seats were transferred to Leeds. He was not opposed in principle to all reforms: after all, Pitt's reform proposals in 1785 had envisaged disfranchising thirty-six of the most corrupt boroughs (thwarted though the scheme had been) and in this area of controversy Castlereagh was, as in many other things, Pitt's disciple.

It is often forgotten that for contemporaries the politics of the 1820s were dominated, not by the reform of Parliament, but by the issue of Catholic emancipation. Castlereagh died before the Catholic question erupted as a major public controversy as a result of Daniel O'Connell's intervention in the Clare by-election, but throughout his career Castlereagh was sympathetic to Catholic relief. He had been convinced that the Union with Ireland should have been accompanied by Catholic emancipation and commercial concessions, and although he accepted the realities of the political situation after Pitt's resignation in 1801 he never lost either his interest in Catholic relief or his willingness to be identified with the Catholic cause. But he had no wish to see the Catholic question dominate British politics to the exclusion of everything else. He knew that it was an issue which would inflame prejudice and embitter debate, and he was therefore uneasy lest Catholic emancipation should be the consequence of a prolonged and heated public agitation. His own preference was for a carefully negotiated compromise settlement, and he was always eager to try to collaborate with the Catholic bishops in order to devise a mutually acceptable agreement. He knew that one of the greatest obstacles to emancipation was the fear that it would undermine the established church in Ireland, and partly to meet this anxiety he argued that it was desirable that the Catholic clergy in Ireland should be paid out of public funds. If the Catholic clergy could be assimilated, at least to some extent, to the established order, and if an agreement could be reached on the appointment of Catholic bishops which would recognize the legitimate interests of both the

Pope and the British Crown, then the risks of Catholic extremism would be minimized. It is ironic that a man who has been frequently criticized for allegedly ignoring the wishes of the House of Commons, and for failing to take the House into his confidence over the conduct of foreign policy, should be decried as a reactionary, simply because on two important issues – parliamentary reform and Catholic emancipation – he deferred to the wishes of the House of Commons and accepted restraints on his own freedom of action. On the Catholic issue he stood firmly on the liberal wing of Liverpool's Cabinet.

Unhappily for Castlereagh's reputation he was associated with three topics which inspired much in the way of historical mythology: the Irish Act of Union, the post-Waterloo reaction in domestic politics and the Holy Alliance. On each of these his attitudes were more complex and his behaviour less simple-minded than was once assumed. It is significant that on each of these subjects the main tendency of historical research over the past forty years has been distinctly 'revisionist'. The passing of the Irish Act of Union was not merely 'an orgy of corruption'; the Liverpool administration was not wholly reactionary or repressive; and the policy associated with the Holy Alliance was not one which Castlereagh endorsed. Castlereagh must, therefore, be placed firmly in the context of his own time, and if he is judged by the standards appropriate to his career, and not by the assumptions and expectations of a later age, then his qualities are evident and undeniable. His contribution to the politics of an era was massive and decisive, and though radical mythology erred in the specific meaning with which it endowed the figure of Castlereagh it did not err in seeing him as a symbolic figure who had impressed himself upon the pattern of British politics over a generation.

Castlereagh's career throws light on the nature of the Pittite heritage, and on that balance of political preferences which Pitt had bequeathed to the men who had learned the skills of government under his tutelage. Pitt's influence upon Castlereagh was all-pervasive. He had been Castlereagh's major political benefactor, and Castlereagh always regarded himself as Pitt's disciple. This conviction heightened the rivalry between himself and Canning. It also meant that Castlereagh's priorities were those of a man who believed that politics was best understood as a sober craft rather than an intoxicating ideology. Like Pitt, Castlereagh saw politics in terms of the art of government, and government was seen, not as the implementation of speculative ideals, but as the patient reconciliation of conflicting interests and the judicious conduct of public administration. This did not exclude improvement or reformation, but it meant that both were best understood and most successfully accomplished within the framework of a received pattern of political behaviour.

If one may adapt a phrase of Mr Henry Fairlie's, Castlereagh envisaged politics, not merely as the art of the possible, but also as the 'art of the necessary'.[18] Government had a limited function, but that did not mean that it was ignoble. In domestic policy the government's duty was to preserve those essential securities which ensured that men could live their own lives within the freedoms prescribed by the constitution, and defended by the rule of law. In foreign affairs, peace was to be preserved, not by the invocation of abstract principles, but by the recognition that conflicts of interest, while being inescapable, were to be resolved within the context of a European equilibrium, the preservation of a diplomatic order being itself more important than the gratification of the national interests of any one of the European states. Like Pitt, Castlereagh did not see politics in party terms. The expressions Whig and Tory appear remarkably rarely in his correspondence, although his attitude towards the opposition Whigs was disdainful and sardonic, and with good cause, since he could not forget their defeatism and irresponsibility during the Napoleonic War. Like Pitt he disliked the practice of systematic opposition, and like Pitt he spent most of his public life in office.

Mrs Arbuthnot exaggerated, however, when she claimed that throughout his career Castlereagh always held a post of major significance. Nevertheless, it was astonishing that a young Ulsterman should so speedily push himself into the forefront of national politics. He did so because he was always capable of seeing political events and decisions against the background of the great issues of the time, and because he handled difficult assignments with skill, prudence and courage. He grew in stature with each new test of his judgement and capacity, and his thinking was always attuned to the magnitude of the problems with which he was dealing. Nor was his greatness limited to his achievements as one of the greatest of Foreign Secretaries: two historians, Sir John Fortescue and Professor Richard Glover, both of them specialists in the history of the British army in the early nineteenth century, have claimed that he was also a great Secretary for War. Indeed, Professor Glover has written of his 'ever-growing admiration' for 'that ogre of the Whigs', affirming after his detailed study of military administration, 'In capacity for hard work, in grasp of reality (both as to needs and to difficulties), in indifference to uninformed or otherwise foolish criticism, in the *tact des choses possibles* – in all these things Castlereagh was first-rate.'

Wellington won the victories and the glory in Spain, but it was Castlereagh who had provided him with the men and the means with which to fight.[19]

Castlereagh's career is uniquely interesting because it reflects not only the experiences of a man attuned to the mature exercise of power but also the political structure and conventions of the age. His personality continues to fascinate because despite his self-control and restraint his character was more complex than his enemies and all but the most intimate of his friends realized. He accomplished much in the service of the state, but had he not died at the time and in the way he did his reputation might never have suffered so much at the hands of the prejudiced and the ignorant. He was only fifty-three when he died, and he was well-fitted to dominate the politics of the 1820s as emphatically as he had dominated those of the previous decade. As a politician he was still capable of further development. In economic and financial matters he had always been identified with the more liberal section of Liverpool's Cabinet. Although he was not at ease with economic or fiscal theory he was generally in sympathy with ideas of freer, if not of absolutely free, trade. Neither on parliamentary reform nor on Catholic emancipation had he anything to fear by comparison with his colleagues.

Had he lived he might well have been associated more publicly and more prominently with the more liberal period of Tory rule in the 1820s, and like Peel he might then have been identified with the transition from the older Toryism to a more up-to-date Conservatism. By both conviction and experience he was better equipped than either Wellington or Peel to handle the Catholic question, and had that issue been more skilfully managed the history of early nineteenth-century party would have been very different. Castlereagh's appeal was to all sections of the Tory party, and he would have been a good choice to succeed Liverpool as Prime Minister. Had he been at the head of the ministry the Tory party might not have split up in the way it did in the years 1827 to 1830. In dealing with the question of parliamentary reform Castlereagh might well have been more pragmatic than Peel. The crowning irony was that Castlereagh's suicide helped fortuitously to perpetuate his over-identification with the troubles of the immediate post-war years, suggesting as it did that only in 1822 did the liberal element in Liverpool's ministry become dominant, with Canning's conduct of foreign policy apparently marking a departure from that of Castlereagh. Yet both F.J. Robinson and Robert Peel – two men thought to typify the new liberal Toryism – were close to Castlereagh, Robinson especially being a protégé of Castlereagh in his early years in public life. The tragedy of Castlereagh's suicide was, therefore, more than a private catastrophe. It contributed to the formulation of myths which essentially misrepresented, not only the man, but the tenor and significance of his long and distinguished career.

B

THE IRISH UNION

Robert Stewart was born in Dublin on 18 June 1769. He was the second son of Robert Stewart and his wife, Lady Sarah Frances Seymour-Conway, a daughter of the First Earl of Hertford. In the same month that Robert Stewart the younger was born his elder brother, Alexander, died, and Robert became his father's heir. His mother died in 1770, his father marrying again in 1775. His second wife, like his first, belonged to the English aristocracy. She was Frances Pratt, the eldest daughter of the First Earl Camden. These contacts were important for the Stewarts. They marked the family's assimilation, stage by stage, into the Anglo-Irish aristocracy and they established significant political links with influential English families.

Like so many Ulstermen the Stewarts were of Scots descent. The eighteenth century saw their emergence into a place of distinction in Irish society and politics, but only during Castlereagh's own lifetime was the transition from commerce and provincialism to aristocracy and political power completed. From 1769 to 1783 his father was M.P. for County Down in the Irish House of Commons. In 1789 he was created Baron Londonderry in the peerage of the kingdom of Ireland. Thereafter promotions in the Irish peerage came at regular intervals: Viscount Castlereagh in 1795, Earl of Londonderry in 1796 and Marquess of Londonderry in 1816. After the Irish Union of 1801 he sat as a representative Irish peer in the House of Lords. Since it was often felt that his son symbolized aristocratic pride at its most forbidding it is interesting to note that the Stewarts were not aristocrats with a long history of privilege and eminence behind them. Rather, they were tough, hard-working, unromantic Ulstermen, realistic in their approach to the problems confronting them, whether in business or politics, and with a shrewd understanding of the value of intelligent marriages in advancing the fortunes of the family. In religion they were Presbyterians. The younger Robert Stewart was baptized a Presbyterian, only conforming to the Church of England when entering St John's College, Cambridge, and his father remained a Presbyterian throughout his life. This is another reminder that Castlereagh was in many ways a new man, and like other young men of ability he benefited from the patronage of the Younger Pitt. But he had to fight for his pre-eminence: he did not inherit it. The mixed background from which he emerged contributed to the mythology of apostasy which later clouded his reputation. Ulster Presbyterians were saddened to see him attach himself to the established Church and the English connection. But there was nothing discreditable about his behaviour in either case. Castlereagh's political development was marked by an impressively quick maturity. He learned much from his early experiences, and he soon responded to an acquaintance with a wider world than that represented by the local rivalries of Ulster politics or the limited vision of the Dublin Parliament. He was soon questioning many of the assumptions which underlay the passions of Irish public life, and from the beginning of his political career he showed that he was capable of thinking on a scale which transcended the parochial limitations of denominational prejudice or family rivalry.

Castlereagh's earliest surviving letter demonstrates his determination to succeed. Writing to his uncle, Alexander Stewart, on 6 October 1777, he proudly told him that he was at the top of his

class – 'no boy shall get above me'. He was 'resolved to study very
close when at my book, and to play very briskly when disengaged'.
He was relieved that his sister was unmarked by the smallpox,
wished that she could understand how much he loved her and all his
friends, and was longing to see his parents again. He ended by
avowing, 'I am still a true American.'[1] Like many Irishmen the boy
sympathized with the cause of the American colonists. Those who
yearned for the legislative independence of the Dublin Parliament to
be wrested from Britain naturally supported the struggle of the
Americans against the supremacy of the Westminster Parliament.

However, it would be foolish to read too much into the political
loyalties of a boy of eight. He was doing little more than reflect the
attitudes prevalent among his family and their friends. More
significant was the depth of affection he showed for his father and
stepmother. Castlereagh always thought fondly of the mother he
had never really known. Until he died he wore a lock of her hair in a
locket around his neck. But his relations with his stepmother and her
children were happy: he always referred to his half-brother Charles,
who eventually succeeded him as Marquess of Londonderry, as his
brother, and there was a strong emotional bond between them. All
the evidence suggests that Castlereagh's childhood and upbringing
were serene and untroubled. He was educated at the Royal School of
Armagh and at a private school at Portaferry. In 1786 he was
admitted to St John's College, Cambridge. Though he went down
without a degree he was not idle. He did well in those college
examinations he sat, and the reputation he had as an undergraduate
was that of a reading man, something which at least partly refutes
disparaging remarks about the defects of Castlereagh's education
which were common at one time.

His youth was enlivened by one sensational incident which
illustrated both his courage and his presence of mind. On one occasion
when he was out sailing with the twelve-year-old son of a local
schoolmaster their boat sank and the boys escaped drowning only
because Robert Stewart remembered that the human body was
lighter, bulk for bulk, than water, and that they would be able to
float safely if they kept their heads above their bodies and avoided
disturbing the water. Robert was a poor swimmer, and his young
friend could not swim at all. They survived for an hour, and were
rescued only in the nick of time, but for a boy of seventeen Robert
had shown that he had a cool head in a crisis.

There was little doubt that he would enter politics, and that meant
finding a seat in the Dublin Parliament. The American War of

Independence had enabled the Irish to achieve the repeal of Poyning's Act and the other pieces of legislation which had subordinated the Dublin Parliament to that at Westminster. During the most critical years of the war the Irish Volunteers had demonstrated that they were just as willing as the Americans to fight for their rights. They had organized themselves to resist a possible French invasion, but they had frightened the British government into recognizing their claims to be treated as a nation, not a dependency. The Rockingham administration persuaded an embarrassed British Parliament into conceding what the Irish had demanded. The settlement of 1782 meant that the Crown still linked Ireland with Britain, but the Dublin Parliament had won legislative independence. It seemed that a decisive victory had been gained, but, despite its apparent success, the settlement of 1782 was deficient in effectiveness and it was doomed to ultimate failure.

The independence of the Dublin Parliament left untouched several of the most crucial problems facing the country. Ireland was a divided society. The Dublin Parliament, however much it sang the praises of Irish freedom, represented only the Anglo-Irish ascendancy, chiefly Anglican and wholly Protestant in religion, and determined to hang on to its privileges for as long as possible. The majority of the Irish peasants were Catholics, and as such they were excluded from sitting in Parliament. Until 1793 they did not even share in the 40-shilling freehold franchise. But the division was more complicated than a simple antagonism between Protestant and Catholic would suggest. The Presbyterians of Ulster resented the virtual monopoly of power exercised by the Anglican establishment and the extent to which they, too, were regarded as second-class citizens.

The country also suffered from acute economic difficulties. Deficient in mineral resources, backward in farming techniques, excessively dependent upon the potato and fearful of British competition in trade and industry, Ireland was the poor relation of the British Isles. Many landlords were absentees, and outside Ulster tenants had neither security of tenure nor the assurance of adequate compensation for any improvements they might make to their holdings. Rack-renting was common, and a growing population meant that living standards remained pitiably low. At times of scarcity even subsistence was jeopardized, especially if the potato crop was threatened with blight. Religious suspicion, political frustration and economic misery combined to create a situation which called for the highest political skills, if tragedy were to be averted.

But the Protestant ascendancy was divided within itself. There was no comprehensive agreement, even among the ruling *élite*, about the best means of tackling the problems which were so glaring and so terrifying. The more liberal Protestants, led by Henry Grattan, hoped that a measure of Catholic relief would alleviate the most burning grievances that afflicted the majority of Irishmen, but even here Grattan and his friends, despite their vision of a revitalized Irish nation, assumed that the Catholics would accept the political leadership of the Protestant ruling class, if only it showed itself to be capable of enlightenment. They under-estimated the intensity of the estrangement which separated the two communities. What they offered to the Catholics was insufficient to meet Catholic claims, but more than enough to rouse Protestant fears. The majority of Protestants regarded concessions to the Catholics as being fraught with danger. To admit the Catholics to the franchise or to allow them to sit in Parliament were seen as steps which would certainly undermine the Protestant ascendancy. Property and political status would both be threatened. Though the majority of Irishmen were eager to demonstrate their independence of Westminster they were nevertheless bitterly divided about how to deal with the problems facing their country. The legislative independence of the Dublin Parliament had rallied national sentiment, but it did nothing to cure the ills of the Irish nation.

Political opinions were not only divided, they were divided in a confused and perplexing manner which defied reason. Many of those who claimed to be radical in their attitudes towards the British connexion were intransigently conservative in everything pertaining to the Protestant ascendancy in Ireland itself. Even among the Ulster Presbyterians the last twenty years of the eighteenth century saw the beginnings of a shift to a more conservative position which ultimately – given the later benefits of industrialization – led them to value the British connexion as their chief security against the rule of a Catholic-dominated Dublin Parliament. Many Presbyterians had been involved with the Irish patriotic movement, and many were to be active in the United Irishmen during the 1790s, but a distrust of Catholicism was never eroded simply by a sense of common hostility towards the Anglican aristocracy or a patriotic resentment of British dominance. One of the gravest obstacles facing progress in Ireland was the Dublin Parliament itself. Even after the triumphs of 1782 and the concessions wrung out of the Rockinghamite government in London (an administration with which Irish Whigs found it easy to identify) the Irish Parliament was unfitted to carry the reforms necessary to prevent continued social tension, persistent religious bitterness and eruptions of agrarian violence. For the more thoughtful among the Irish ruling class the question was posed in an especially agonizing form: how could reform be achieved without sacrificing either the independence of the Dublin Parliament or the continuation of the Protestant ascendancy?

The situation was further complicated by potential conflicts between the British and Irish Parliaments. The government of Ireland still centred round the Lord Lieutenant, appointed by the current administration in London, and who was usually as determined as George III himself to maintain intact the conventional prerogatives of the office, especially as these related to the appointment and dismissal of officials. Legislative independence did not, of itself, make the Dublin Parliament either representative or responsible. Many Irishmen had no sense of identity with it, but the determination of the most reactionary members of the ascendancy to exploit the Dublin Parliament to the full in order to assert their own privileges as against Westminster meant that every crisis was soon compounded with special difficulties. Lord Lieutenants feared an alliance of the Irish with the opposition in the British Parliament and during the Regency Crisis of 1788 Pitt saw the Irish Parliament deliberately and provocatively take up a Foxite position on the controversial question of the appointment of a Regent during the illness of George III. The recovery of George III prevented a situation of grotesque political confusion materializing, but, coming as it did on top of the defeat of his plans for Irish free trade, the truculence of the Irish Parliament confirmed Pitt's doubts about the quality of political judgement prevalent in Dublin. While, like most British statesmen, he preferred to let Irish problems lie dormant if he could possibly do so he was profoundly anxious about the constitutional relationship between the two countries.[2]

Thus, although they were bitterly divided in their attitudes to the claims of Catholics and Presbyterians for civil and political equality, both reactionaries and liberals among the Protestant political nation in Ireland clung desperately to the independence of the Dublin Parliament. The French Revolution added new ingredients of conflict to the Irish scene: an ill-judged idealism and a heady republican ideology were injected into an already feverish political situation.

It was against this confused background of communal mistrust and religious strife that young Robert Stewart challenged the supremacy of the Marquess of Downshire by standing for election for the County of Down in 1790. He was supported by an alliance of

Irish Whigs, Presbyterians and Independents, and in contesting the seat he was also standing forth as the family champion. During the campaign he behaved as his supporters expected him to behave. He drank toasts to President Washington and the United States of America, to the happy establishment of a constitution in France, and – most dramatically of all – to our sovereign lord the people. These slogans reflected the hopes of the hour. Irish patriots had long thought of themselves as comparable with the Americans, and in 1790 opinion was favourable to the constitution-making that was taking place in France. In both Britain and Ireland Whigs hoped that the French would succeed in setting up a moderate constitutional monarchy. As yet few shared the suspicions and fears of Edmund Burke. Even Pitt himself was convinced that sooner or later the upheavals in France would terminate in the establishment of a constitutional monarchy. It was, therefore, possible for a young Irish Whig to praise our sovereign lord the people without the phrase carrying overtones of riot and butchery.

It would have been more surprising if Robert Stewart had not conformed to the habitual postures of Irish political controversy. He was expressing what upbringing and circumstance had made it natural for him to accept as the sentiments appropriate for someone who was critical of the government in Dublin Castle, and who was defying the wishes of a powerful local magnate and titled representative of the Anglo-Irish ascendancy. What may be doubted is the depth of his commitment to the sentiments that came so readily to his lips. It was all too easy for him to accept the clichés of opposition. He had no experience of political life, and he was being thrust forward without any personal awareness of the complexity of the issues with which he would soon have to deal. What is astonishing is not that he abandoned these youthful postures, but that he matured so quickly after entering Parliament. He saw that most of the slogans on which he had been reared had little meaning and that others grossly oversimplified the needs of the hour. He did not give up his belief in the necessity of reform in Irish affairs, but he appreciated that it was difficult to decide which reforms were to have priority and how they were to be carried in existing circumstances. His apprenticeship in the Irish House of Commons coincided with the French Revolution's plunge into its violent phase and the assimilation of Jacobinical ideas into the already embittered Irish political consciousness. These two factors reshaped his political outlook and cast his political future into a new mould.

The County Down election was rowdy and spirited and it was

marked by extravagant expenditure on both sides. The Stewarts spared no expense in securing Robert's election. The family spent £60,000 on the campaign, and the family fortunes never really recovered from this immense outlay. But at least Robert's father had the satisfaction of seeing his son elected. With 3,114 votes he came second to Downshire's son, Lord Hillsborough, and thus shared the return for the double-member seat. By eighteenth-century standards the poll was heavy.

During the campaign Robert Stewart pledged himself to supporting a Place Bill, the reform of Parliament, the disfranchisement of revenue officers, and a Bill to prevent arbitrary and excessive bail. All of these were conventional Whig proposals, reflecting the Rockinghamite mythology transferred to the Irish context. His commitment to parliamentary reform referred to the Irish, not the British, legislature. But neither his Whig principles nor the exhilaration of victory made him forget the fact that some of his supporters' tenants had not voted as they should have done. When thanking Lord Moira for his support Robert told him that it might even be necessary to make those who had defied his wishes feel his resentment: 'Such conduct when overlooked serves to increase . . . inattention to the landlord's recommendation.'[3] No Whig could afford to ignore the realities of eighteenth-century electioneering. Even reformers relied on influence and patronage for their political success. So, inevitably, Robert praised the electors of County Down in effusive language. He thanked his supporters warmly for their hard work and for their votes; he affirmed that he loved the cause of the people; and he promised to maintain the constitution he revered. As yet he did not suspect that these two priorities might come into conflict, and that to secure the constitution might imply abandoning the popular party.

Other influences were already at work upon his mind. His stepmother's father, Earl Camden, was giving him advice which heightened his growing sensitivity to considerations other than those which sprang from Irish politics. Camden had spotted Robert Stewart's abilities and potential, and he was anxious lest he should be wasted in Irish squabbles. There was a greater political arena for a man of promise than the Dublin Parliament. A young man of political gifts would be foolish to embroil himself in provincial disputes. Camden was uneasy about Londonderry's anxiety to push his son into the Irish House of Commons at the first opportunity. He suspected that one motive might be to ensure that Robert took up permanent residence in Ireland. But Camden believed that this was the worst possible thing for Robert's prospects. Being confined to Ireland would mean frustration. It would do little for his political career, and it might, over a period of years, breed a feeling of discontent and futility.

Camden saw that too forthright a commitment to the Irish Whigs would seriously prejudice Robert's political future. The links between the Dublin opposition and the Foxite Whigs were too close for comfort. In the aftermath of the Regency Crisis they would obstruct any promising opening in British politics. As Lord President in Pitt's administration Camden's advice to young Robert Stewart was subtle and thoughtful. He suggested that on all matters on which he was not pledged he would be wise to reserve his judgements. He warned him of the need for discretion: too many political secrets were betrayed and too many political reputations were undone over the dinner table or while sharing a convivial bottle of wine. He would be wise to insist on a true independence, avoiding all embarrassing political entanglements, and he should speak only on subjects upon which he had taken the trouble to prepare himself. The shrewdest advice was posed as a query: 'Would there be any harm in professing yourself a friend of the Pitt administration in England, though you are in opposition to the Castle?'[4]

This was to give a personal twist to the already idiosyncratic loyalties of Irish politics, but it was no more absurd than many of the postures habitually adopted in Dublin. A reformer and a Whig could oppose the Castle, could plead for Irish reforms (especially in administration), and could argue the case for a reform of Parliament, but these very issues could be put to Pittite uses in England. Pitt had tried to reform Parliament, and he had implemented significant improvements in public administration. He represented both a respect for the constitution, as understood by the majority of his contemporaries, and an ostentatious regard for probity in public affairs. If Robert Stewart could make a name for himself as an independent in the Irish Parliament, without prejudicing his prospects in English politics, then he would be putting independence to the sort of purpose that experienced political campaigners such as Camden understood. It was essential to show that a commitment to improved administration and parliamentary reform in Ireland did not necessarily lead to an association, however indirect, with the Foxite Whigs at Westminster. There was no irresistible logic about Irish independency leading to a Foxite commitment. Camden's advice was acute and perceptive, and what is more it was acted upon.

It was, therefore, not surprising that in his first speech in the Irish

House of Commons Robert Stewart was cautious, eager to demonstrate his objectivity, and careful not to offend any major interest. He called for a thorough inquiry into Irish trade in India and the East Indies: the House would be able to act more effectively on the basis of full and accurate knowledge. An inquiry could do no harm and it might do some good. But even here he let slip a phrase which indicated that his mental horizons and political vision were less restricted than were those of the majority of Irish M.P.s. 'His wish was that the subject should be fully investigated, and afterwards he hoped the House would determine, not with a spirit of local partiality, but as a member of the British Empire.'[5] This must have sounded strange to many of those Irishmen who had noted his pledges and promises during the County Down election, but those who were fond of arguing that the Crown afforded an adequate security for the link with Britain could hardly object to the sentiment. Everyone knew that Irish prosperity could not be divorced from British commerce and industry. The dispute over Pitt's free trade resolutions in 1785 had already shown that. Robert Stewart could argue that he sought to exploit the British connexion for the good of Ireland. Such an objective was not in conflict with the desire for improvements in Irish administration or a reform of the Irish Parliament. There were interests which bound the two nations together, whatever objections might be made to British dominance or subservience to the Castle. British monopolies affected Irish trade, and the most dramatic example of a trading monopoly was the British East India Company. It was surely better to settle such matters on a foundation of full and sound information, a sober recognition of common interests and a willingness to drive a hard but realistic bargain, rather than allowing the opportunity for improvement to slip by while indulging in emotionally satisfying but politically futile rhetoric.

Robert Stewart's conduct was noted in London, not least by Camden. He had taken an independent line. No one objected to his voting against the administration on matters on which he had been forced to commit himself during the election, but it was unusual to have an Irish Whig, critical of the Castle and eager to sustain a reputation for independence, making a practice of prefacing his speeches with tributes to the skill and sagacity of William Pitt. In some ways the respect which Robert Stewart had for Pitt manifested the deepest of those political feelings which were absolutely his own, rather than the inheritance of his family or the products of circumstance. Even before Camden had suggested that he should publicly

state his support for Pitt, Robert had confided to him that he was
prevented by circumstances from expressing the regard and sympathy for Pitt which he had come to feel. There was already a
tension between what his upbringing had imposed on him and what
his own inner convictions demanded of him. Temperament and
intelligence were at odds with habit and convention.

In any case his own reactions to the experience of sitting in the
Irish House of Commons were mixed. He had no illusions about the
virtues of the Dublin Parliament. Rich in debating talent and
distinguished by brilliant oratory, it was deficient in most of the
other political skills. Although they prided themselves on their
independence most M.P.s impressed Robert Stewart with their
servility, their lack of original thinking and their fondness for
familiar platitudes even when the times called for bold initiatives.
He was disgusted by those who slavishly obeyed the dictates of the
Castle, but he was just as repelled by those who followed the great
parliamentary patrons. He believed that the influence of the Irish
boroughmongers and political magnates was more dangerous to the
vitality of Irish public life than the influence of the Crown. He could
not forget that the majority of Irishmen played little or no part in
the election of the House of Commons, and that even the respectable
and propertied classes had little control over the conduct of their
representatives once they were elected. But he was also sensitive
towards the ignorance and violence of Irish popular feeling, whether
Catholic or Protestant. He found it impossible not to confess that the
constitution suffered from glaring defects. To refuse to do so was to
live in a cloud-cuckoo land, far from political reality, and Robert
Stewart found the realities of politics more fascinating, more compelling and more satisfying than any romantic day-dreams or
fanciful speculations. It was in the real world that he sought to test
his skills and prove his worth, and so, even when he criticized the
status quo, he rejected popular fallacies and fashionable mythologies.
He despised the suggestion that Britain was to blame for every one
of Ireland's ills, but he also denied that reform in Ireland was
impossible because the Irish were incapable of being entrusted with the
freedom Britain enjoyed. He valued the link with Britain, but he did
not want to see it maintained merely by corruption. Where others
saw only subordination he saw partnership as the secret of progress;
where others dreamed of independence he urged co-operation.

His dislike of corruption has a touch of irony about it, when the
means which Cornwallis and Castlereagh adopted to carry the Act
of Union are recalled. But what is impressive is that, unlike most

other Irish Whigs, young Robert Stewart applied a reformist critique to the conventional postures of Irish patriotism as well as to the blemishes of the political system. He had already sensed the limits of the 1782 settlement. It was not a lasting solution. Despite the complacency with which English Whigs congratulated themselves upon it, it was merely an interim arrangement. Neither conservatives nor reformers were satisfied with it. It would have to change; the only question was when and how. Though Robert Stewart was only beginning to grope uncertainly and unsurely towards an answer to the problems of the Anglo-Irish relationship he approached the British connexion in a different spirit from that which dominated much Irish thinking. There was a clear-eyed willingness to face the truth about his earliest political experiences. For a man of his youth and his background his boldness and his intellectual courage were remarkable.

He confided many of his hopes and fears to his uncle, Lord Bayham, who was soon to become the Second Earl Camden. In 1793 Robert Stewart told him that Ireland would either have to be governed by reason or united to Britain by force. There was no middle way. He was troubled by the conviction that the behaviour of the Irish and the conduct of the British government made a reasonable solution unlikely and impracticable. He sensed the dangers to the Protestant establishment, both in Church and State, if Catholic relief were granted without institutional reform. If the British government thought that by granting the franchise to Catholics they would solve the Irish question they were deceiving themselves. While the Irish Dissenters might be conciliated with constitutional reforms this was not true for the Catholics. It could hardly be doubted that if the Catholics gained political power they would seek to use it to undermine the Protestant establishment. He made this point in the most emphatic style:

I believe that reform will effect itself either now or in a few years. If that be the case, and the election franchise is given to that body, a few years will make three-fourths of the constituency of Ireland Catholics. Can a Protestant superstructure long continue supported on such a base? With a reformed representation and a Catholic constituency, must not everything shortly follow? Can the Protestant Church remain the Establishment of a State of which they do not comprise an eighth part, which will be the case when the Catholics are co-equal in political rights? At present they form the half, being as numerous as the Dissenters. This makes all the difference in the world; for enemies within and without the State tell very differently. The one destroys by *legislation*, the other by *rebellion*. You observe that we paint too strongly the danger of Protestant resentment and underrate Catholic anger. Although inferior in numbers, I consider the Protestants infinitely the more formidable body. They have thought longer on political subjects, and are excited to a higher pitch than the Catholics; besides, I do not think you are likely to appease the latter by any concession you are about to make to them. Nothing short of co-equal rights will satisfy them, and these you cannot yield if you wish to preserve your Church and State; for in order to preserve the Church, the patronage of the Crown must be employed in its support. Therefore, although the Catholics may have equal rights, they cannot have equal enjoyments . . . Give them anything rather than the franchise, for it forces everything else. Property will feebly resist a principle so powerful.[6]

The Dissenters had no interest in destroying the established Church, for they had no desire to set up their own in its place. Furthermore, the government exaggerated the common ground between Dissenters and Catholics. If the claims of the Dissenters were met they would lose interest in the grievances of the Catholics. Far from being united the Protestants and Catholics were "by the ears in four counties", and Catholics had broken into many houses in their search for arms.

Castlereagh was making no claim to possess the secret of any easy solution; he was exploring the magnitude of the problem, and giving free expression to the anxieties which he shared with many Irish Protestants and which he believed were being seriously neglected by the government in London. He had seen through much of the rhetoric with which Irish Whigs deceived themselves, and when Pitt's government pressed on with the enfranchisement of the Catholic freeholders he opposed the measure. But this did not mean that he ignored what he considered to be the legitimate aspects of the Catholic case. He approved of the civil rights which were now made available to Catholics – the right to sit on juries, take university degrees, serve as junior commissioned officers in the army and navy, become magistrates, and own land without special disabilities – but he believed that enfranchisement would provoke further resentment. He was anxious about the situation in those constituencies where the majority of the electorate were Catholics and were possibly ill-disposed to the political preferences of their Protestant landlords. But if some political or constitutional security could be found for the Protestant establishment, then he saw no objection to the Catholic freeholders having the vote. As on a number of other issues his attitude was more complex than many of his contemporaries realized. He did not condemn the enfranchisement of Catholics on principle: he feared what its consequences would be.

In 1791 Robert Stewart spent some time in France and Belgium. Despite his early sympathy with the revolution he was uneasy at what he saw, and, even more, at what he sensed. He was probing for the real meaning of the political catchphrases of the day, and he became convinced that the French were expecting too much from their new constitution. This was understandable: when men had lived under despotism for so long it was natural for them to exult in the idea of liberty, but disillusionment would breed more discontent. 'The novelty', he told Camden, 'of possessing freedom, even in the abstract, to them is perfect happiness.' But once the excitement had died down, what would count would be the practical merits of the new system, not the metaphysical speculations on which it was based. If the new constitution produced tangible results which would happily stand comparison with conditions under the *ancien régime* then things would settle down. But he was disturbed by the state of public opinion in France. Men seemed blind to reality, their minds being heated by ideas which were intoxicatingly novel. He doubted the ability of the French to show the cool judgement which was necessary in their situation, and he was saddened by the failure of the new French régime to provide the three essentials of good government: the adequate protection of personal liberty, the public recognition of individual property rights, and a modest level of taxation.

But his anxieties did not lure him into romanticizing the *ancien régime*. He took up neither a straightforward conservative position nor a naïve revolutionary one:

> From what I have said you will not rank me amongst the enthusiastic admirers of the French Revolution as the noblest work of human integrity and human wisdom. I really am not. I discover in what they have done much to approve and much to condemn. I feel as strongly as any man that an essential change was necessary for the happiness and for the dignity of a great people, long sunk in a state of degradation. I lament that those into whose hands the fate of their country devolved aimed at accomplishing so much more than could be effected at once without introducing confusion, from a suspension of civil government, and more, I am inclined to think, than ever can be realized in such a kingdom as France without perpetually risking her tranquility.

He believed that France desperately needed reform, but he distrusted the speculative principles on which change had been based. 'I do not', he assured Camden, 'wish their principles to gain ground anywhere. I am convinced they are unsafe, and I trust that no country in which I have either stake or affection will follow their example.'[7] He watched the French situation with mounting disquiet, and his

sense of misgiving was intensified by what he saw of the condition of
Ireland in the same year. He was learning fast. Those boisterous and
thoughtless youthful toasts about the sovereignty of the people
seemed centuries away, lost in a happier and more serene past. He
still deplored the scandalous defects of the Irish constitution, but
however objectionable the régime in Ireland he preferred it to a
revolution. There was need for amendment, and he believed that
reform would strengthen rather than weaken the British connexion.
But he was coming to dread an alliance between the Catholics and
the more extreme and disaffected Protestants. If such a combination
ever took place there would be widespread tumult and disorder.
There were times when he wondered whether Ireland would have to
endure the sort of ordeal that was afflicting France. To avoid it
Ireland needed the help of Britain. He was more and more convinced
that, whatever the complications of British government policy or the
delusions which fed Irish discontent, Britain and Ireland needed each
other. He hoped that a recognition of their interdependence would
ensure that Britain and Ireland would remain attached by affection
as well as political interest, and that some way forward would be
found to a just solution of the problems of their relationship.

He was still far from seeing his way clearly. Although he had
learned to scan the received conventions of Irish political life with a
critical eye he was torn by conflicting emotions and contending
loyalties. He tried to honour his commitments to his constituents,
and to those who had worked so enthusiastically for his election, by
voting with the opposition whenever he believed himself pledged to
so doing. Some of his confusion was mistaken for a subtle Machia-
vellianism, but nothing could be further from his fundamentally
straight and honest nature. His confusions were the reflections of the
attempt he was making to think his way through a number of
complex and interrelated problems. There were times when he
thought that reform would strengthen the British connexion; there
were others when he was not so sure. It was not surprising that his
conduct baffled the Lord Lieutenant. Westmorland regarded Stewart
as a promising young man, but he distrusted protestations of
admiration for Pitt when they were allied with votes and speeches in
the Irish House of Commons which were critical of the administration in Ireland. Not only the government was perplexed by Stewart's
behaviour. His own friends and supporters found it difficult to
follow and hard to explain. He was more and more an enigma. He
defied the rules of the game. The Castle thought him too rebellious:
his Presbyterian friends thought him too fond of praising Pitt and of

avowing his loyalty to the links with Britain. In a word, they were coming to distrust him as being much too 'English'.

His response was to claim that he sought to sacrifice neither his Irish convictions to his English principles, nor his British sentiments to his Irish convictions. He argued that Irish problems had to be placed within the larger context of the British Empire: only then could they be fully understood and only then would any lasting solutions be found. Writing to Dr Alexander Haliday, the Secretary of the Northern Whig Club, he was forthright and vehement:

> As to my propensities being *quite too English*, my reply is that I should feel exceedingly degraded in my own estimation were I selfish or base enough in any instance to sacrifice the one to the other. Infinite as my attachment is to Ireland, I trust that, when reasoning upon their relative duties and common concerns, my heart is sufficiently enlarged to discuss every question with the feelings which become a member of the Empire. I trust I never shall be an Irishman in contradistinction to the justice due to Britain, nor an Englishman as opposing and betraying the interests of this country.[8]

He warned against exaggerating the faults of the Irish constitution, since this could lead to experimenting with more objectionable extremes. It was one thing to denounce excessive corruption; it was another to deny to the executive the influence within the House of Commons which was necessary to make effective government possible. The Irish Parliament should act as a deliberative assembly, with a mind and conscience of its own. It ought not to be a gathering of delegates, supinely obeying the orders of their constituents.

Most of all he deplored irresponsible attacks on Britain. If the internal stability and external security of Ireland were to be preserved it was imperative for the country to retain its links with Britain. The British fleet was Ireland's greatest protection, the charter by which Irish commerce was sustained. Talk of a complete separation from Britain was nonsense. If the British connexion was shattered Ireland could not remain wholly independent, and it was deplorable to envisage any link with France, 'that melancholy example of misapplied philosophy, of political excitement and popular delirium'. He was distressed by the signs of disaffection in Ireland, and he reaffirmed his conviction that Ireland was attached to Britain by ties of interest, affection and blood as well as by purely constitutional arrangements. He lamented that the Irish political spirit was warped by a narrow and unworthy nationalism, an outlook which was pernicious for those very reforms it was supposed to favour.

He did not ignore the dangers of risking unpopularity, but he could not sacrifice his own judgement to the demands of popularity.

'There is a feeling in my breast which disclaims and despises applause, let it proceed from whom it may, when persuasion cannot sanction the incense. If popularity (which I very much suspect) is of that fleeting nature that it expires upon the slightest contradiction, is it not an illusion too visionary to administer gratification to the most susceptible imagination?' He reiterated his detestation of the practice of imposing instructions upon M.P.s. He would honour the obligations he had entered into, but the more he reflected upon the practice the more his reason condemned it as repugnant to the principles of the constitution. It saddened him to have such an important difference of opinion with someone he respected and to whom he owed so much, but he found it impossible to write or act in any other way. He assured Dr Haliday that his friendship was invaluable and he sought to sweeten their disagreements by stating that he would welcome the opportunity to resolve their differences in discussion.

It is apparent from all this that Castlereagh was essentially an inner-directed politician. It was to his own conscience that he looked for the validation of his standpoints. His independence had become a more virile and more questioning characteristic than either Camden or Haliday had anticipated. He was emerging as a politician in his own right sooner than anyone had expected. But his development was a complex and intense affair; there was no smooth transition from one political viewpoint to another. Robert Stewart's robust mind could not defer to what he was rapidly coming to despise as mere prejudice, and he was discovering that he did not share the deceptions and delusions afflicting so many of his contemporaries.

His early years demonstrated the true independence of his position. Nothing is further from the truth than the suggestion that he took up Whig postures, only to abandon them in order to achieve office. Those attitudes which he had merely inherited, or which he had casually adopted because they represented the outlook prevalent among those who dominated his Ulster background, were being exposed, not to the wilful demands of heartless ambition, but to the searching scrutiny of a tough-minded and intelligent young man who reacted to events more powerfully than he responded to ideas.

Camden's worldly-wise advice helped Robert Stewart to remember that Irish politics were but a part of a much wider political scene, but his own experiences in France heightened what he had already learned from his undergraduate years in England – that the fixed and immovable passions of Ulster politics were defective in themselves, and that they were small-minded and irrelevant when contrasted with British and European developments. Breadth of vision, a wholly realistic far-sightedness and a vigorous and unflinching independence of mind characterized his attitudes from the beginning. He fretted against the restrictions of his immediate political circle, but if his friends were puzzled by his conduct they were wrong in thinking that he was simply accepting the values of the establishment. He cherished the British connexion for reasons which reflected his European outlook and his capacity to think on the grand scale. He was not primarily concerned with personal advancement, and although he was sceptical about the benefits of revolution he never lost a cool awareness of the unhappy deficiencies of the contemporary political system in Ireland. He knew that many of the difficulties experienced by the administration in Ireland sprang from supporting 'the present ruinous system' and he was profoundly anxious about the consequences that this short-sightedness would have. It was depressing to speculate what the outcome would be if the people brooded over their wrongs. The climate was unfavourable for reform, but reform alone could prevent an Irish catastrophe.

The war with France, which broke out in February 1793, added a new complication to Irish politics. Anyone with a glimmer of historical awareness knew that England's difficulty had always been Ireland's opportunity, but the ideals of the French Revolution meant that Irish rebels would do more than seek French assistance. The more daring of the Irish radicals began to hope that the ideals of 1789 would cure the ills of Ireland as well as throw off the British yoke. Fired with enthusiasm for an Irish Republic they dreamed of a rediscovery of Irish nationhood in which old quarrels between Catholics and Protestants would be forgotten. A fondness for French ideas differentiated some of the younger Catholic parish priests from their more conservative colleagues. The Irish Catholic bishops were always fearful lest rebellion and violence would make the plight of the Irish Catholics worse rather than better, and they therefore consistently urged obedience to George III. They believed that the way forward lay in cooperation with the British government, not in civil strife. They were appalled by the republican and egalitarian ideals of the French Republic, and they could not forget that the Revolution had been associated first with the civil constitution of the clergy, which was repugnant to all good Catholics, and then with a more direct onslaught upon the Catholic Church in France and even the Christian faith itself. But younger priests, many of whom had been trained in France, were sympathetic to the political ideals of 1789. Similarly, on the Protestant side, those who found Grattan's brand of Whiggism too traditional in character and too modest in its aims had visions of an Irish Republic which would establish itself as wholly independent of Britain. The American example, which had always been potent in Ireland, was given a new urgency by the French experience.

For the majority of the Irish peasants these dreams were remote and artificial. They were preoccupied with grievances such as high rents, insecure tenure, the deplorable consequences of absenteeism among landlords, and the age-old struggle against grinding poverty. Ideas of uniting with the Protestants in a republican crusade against Britain were dim and shadowy: for most peasants the Protestant was the landlord and the rack-renter, as well as a heretic. Beneath the superficial humanitarian zeal which excited republican leaders there smouldered older hatreds and a corroding sense of burning wrongs. When the rebellion came it was neither the united outburst of Irish idealism, which Fitzgerald and Wolfe Tone had envisaged, nor the secular political movement which Presbyterian nationalists had hoped for. Furthermore, French help came too late and in too slight a manner decisively to assist the Irish cause.

Robert Stewart was anxious about the dangers of a French invasion. Unlike many politicians he did not underrate the military resources of the French Republic. He saw the difference in character between the new type of military organization built up by the French and the traditional armies of Europe. The struggle was reminiscent of 'a battle between a fair honest gentleman and a sharper with loaded dice'. The mode of carrying on war which the Jacobins had initiated was new and alarming, and there was no means of measuring the strength of the French Republic. 'It is the first time', he wrote to Camden on 25 September 1793, 'that *all* the population and *all* the wealth of a great kingdom has been concentrated in the field: what may be the result is beyond my perception.'[9]

He did not hesitate to support the establishment of a militia in Ireland, which replaced the old Volunteers, and he was especially gratified that the leadership of the part-time soldiers would rest with men of property. He knew only too well how easy it was for an Irish volunteer force which was not properly scrutinized by the government to become an agency of terror and blackmail, rather than a security for the maintenance of law and order and the defence of the realm. Jacobinism was more dangerous in Ireland than in England because social conflict, class resentment, religious antagonism and a frustrated national sentiment were more common in Ireland than in Britain. Nor did his support of the militia remain a mere form of words. He accepted a commission in a militia regiment which an

Irish M.P., Thomas Conolly, was raising, and in April 1793 he became a lieutenant-colonel in the Londonderry militia.

But military precautions were in themselves not enough. He was convinced that in addition to preparing to meet any French invasion the government should press on with the task of attempting reconciliation with Ireland. In April 1793 he reminded Camden that the war did not mean that the problems of Ireland had been solved, and it was especially important for the government to remember that reforms were needed, perhaps more than ever, if the relationship between Britain and Ireland was to be preserved. 'Let us, for God's sake, have a liberal settlement. It will, I am persuaded, unite more cordially the two countries, will deprive a vindictive Opposition of their ground of attack, and attach to Government many men who now wish them well, but cannot act with them as a party, on constitutional points.'[10]

He remained as dissatisfied as ever with certain aspects of government policy in Ireland. Nothing shook his conviction that Ireland needed protection from French invasion and that Irishmen should play their full part in the defence of their country: in all this the British navy remained the decisive factor. But the government was signally failing in explaining its policy to Irish opinion. Too many Irishmen believed that Britain and Ireland were fighting to restore absolutism in France: they had not been persuaded that France had been the aggressor in the war. Robert Stewart believed that the government would have to be more open in its dealings with the Irish Parliament if allegations that Britain was engaged in a monarchical crusade were not to be widely believed. The only people to benefit from the neglect of taking Irishmen fully into the government's confidence would be the Jacobin extremists, who were only too eager to link Irish grievances with French principles. The Irish government thought too much could be settled merely by the management and manipulation of Parliament. But they had to realize that they were fighting Jacobinical principles just as much as French armies. In fully informed and frank public debate the government's cause would prosper, not suffer. It was as important to challenge Jacobin writers and publicists as it was to strengthen the armed forces of the Crown. It is striking that he should see the significance of winning public confidence in Ireland in what was a war of opinions as much as a struggle for power. Nor was he blindly following the administration. He was showing that he could advocate a firm patriotic policy while still criticizing the government whenever it failed to take the steps that were necessary for the defence of Ireland from invasion as well as for the security of property and the prevention of civil unrest.[11]

While his public experience was being enlarged and his political attitudes were maturing he had taken the plunge into matrimony. On 9 June 1794 he married Lady Emily Hobart, a sister of Lord Buckinghamshire, the wedding taking place at St George's, Hanover Square. His bride was twenty-two years of age, and was described by Dr Haliday as 'a fine, comely, good-humoured, playful (not to say romping) piece of flesh as any Illyrian'.[12] There can be little doubt about the depth of affection which bound the young couple together. Emily's intellect was no match for that of her husband, but she gave him unfailing loyalty, compassionate understanding and boundless trust. More than anyone else she knew the intense feelings which his habitual self-control shielded from the world. On his part there was a profound and loving commitment to his wife. His letters to her abounded in exclamations of affection, flashes of humour, and constant evidence of a sincere respect and care. He found separation from her hard to bear, especially when his political and military duties compelled him to leave his wife for lengthy periods of time. Even when exhausted by the trials of eighteenth-century travelling he usually found time to write to his wife. A typical example of the sort of letter he wrote was that which he penned at Boroughbridge on 19 November 1794:

I cannot retire to rest, Dearest Dr Wife, though a good deal fatigued, without sending you my blessing. Every stage that moves me further from you adds to my regret and makes the time which is to elapse before I again cross the Channel seem of intolerable duration. Perhaps the noise and bustle of London may dissipate the anxiety of separation which reflection uninterrupted dwells on with real pain. My day now passes without an event. I roll on from daybreak till long after the light is gone and, except the relief of reading, I have nothing to divert my thoughts from the loss I have sustained. Tomorrow I shall endeavour to sleep at Newark. I shall then be 126 miles from London: the night after, probably at Biggleswade, – the remainder of the journey will be disposed of easily on Saturday. God Almighty protect you, Dearest of friends.
    Ever your most devoted
        Robert[13]

He always tried to catch the first post and he yearned for his wife's letters as much as she longed for his. He watched for any sign of illness or indisposition in her letters and regularly asked after her health. He was constantly telling her to take care of herself, and he made no secret of the fact that only when they were reunited would his anxieties end. His travels made him all the more devoted to his wife and all the more fond of his home. The companionship of Emily and the refreshing Mount Stewart air were his cures for colds and fevers and most minor aches and pains.

He was also taking the first cautious steps towards a career in the British, as distinct from the purely Irish, political context. In May 1794 he was returned to the British House of Commons for the Cornish borough of Tregony. He sat for this constituency for two years. In 1796 he was returned for Orford, which was one of the Hertford family's boroughs. In July 1797 he resigned this seat when he was appointed Keeper of the Irish Privy Seal. After the Union of 1801 he represented County Down in the United Kingdom Parliament, but when in August 1805 he stood for re-election on his appointment as Secretary for War and the Colonies he was defeated, being returned for Boroughbridge the following January, a vacancy having occurred there because of the death of Lord Eldon's eldest son. At the 1806 general election he transferred to the borough of Plympton, which he represented until 1812, when he was once more returned for County Down. He held this seat until 1821, when he became ineligible for an Irish constituency on succeeding his father as Marquess of Londonderry. He was once more returned for Orford, and he sat for this seat until his death in August 1822.[14]

In October 1795 he made his maiden speech in the British House of Commons. It was significant that he seconded the address of thanks to the King's Speech. His support for Pitt had now become fundamental. He spoke of the contrast between the theory and the practice of the French revolutionaries. Robespierre's system had been founded on cruelty and terror, but the behaviour of the Directory was often in conflict with the principles they were so fond of enunciating. Liberty, equality and justice were preached more than they were practised. The condemnation of men by military and revolutionary tribunals violated every principle of equality before the law. He defended Pitt against the opposition charge that he was prepared to negotiate with one form of government in France and one only. This was not so: indeed, if it had been true Castlereagh stated that he would not have been able to give Pitt his confidence. But Pitt could not act precipitately. A desire for peace, and a willingness to negotiate when it was practicable to do so, ought not to delude the country into relaxing its military efforts. He hoped that in the future it would be possible to look back with pride on the exertions Britain had made, not only in preserving the safety and independence of the country but in contributing to the general security of Europe.

It was not a speech distinguished by dazzling rhetoric or fanciful

literary allusions. But it appealed to the House because of its sound
sense. It showed how closely Castlereagh was aligned to Pitt, not
merely in his political conduct but also in the whole cast of his
thinking. There was the same caution about ideology, whether as a
guide to making constitutions or as a means of conducting international relations. There was the same conviction that peace with
France could not be made unless essential conditions for the security
of Britain were met. There was the same insistence that the safety of
Britain and the stability of Europe were inextricably bound together.
In some ways Castlereagh's speech enunciated principles which
guided him throughout his career. Just as he approached the Irish
problem with an appreciation of the British dimension, so he saw
British foreign policy within a European context. He was now
marked out, not merely as an Irishman who valued the British
connexion while pleading for improvements in Irish administration,
but as a man of ability and promise who looked to Pitt for political
leadership.

But Castlereagh's full commitment to British political life was
delayed by the deteriorating situation in Ireland. He was torn
between his parliamentary duties in London and his responsibilities
in the Dublin Parliament. A further complication was the need to
maintain peace and order on his father's Ulster estates. Castlereagh
supported the policy of trying to prevent violence by the suppression
of the United Irishmen and the disarming of all who were reasonably
suspected of disaffection. He was deeply distressed by the way in
which families had been divided by the activities of conspirators,
whose appeal was often directed to the youngest and most inexperienced. But though he believed that firm measures were necessary if
bloodshed was to be averted he was repelled by the relish with which
some of the yeomanry and gentry went about the task of disarming
the peasantry and rooting out potential revolutionaries.

Old tales about his behaviour during this period are not borne out
by the facts. When in October 1796 he was called north to help in
dealing with the dangerous situation which existed on his father's
estates he acted with discretion and restraint as well as firmness. In
September he had been active in the arrest of a number of men
suspected of plotting against the government. One famous case
involved the arrest of Charles Teeling, a young Lisburn man of only
eighteen years of age. Throughout Castlereagh conducted himself
with courtesy and self-control. He gained no satisfaction from seeing
at first hand the heartbreak caused by the activities of the United
Irishmen. Despite Mrs Teeling's hysterical attack upon him – 'I was

wrong to appeal to a heart that never knew the tie of parental affection – your lordship is not a father!' – Castlereagh went out of his way to ease the burden of imprisonment for the young man. He shared a meal with him, made sure that clothes and other comforts were taken to him, and later procured his release on parole (for which he was thanked by the boy's father). He acted throughout as a man performing a necessary, but unpleasant, duty. He showed no spirit of vengeance and no sign of vindictiveness. He did what he believed had to be done with as much humanity as the dismal task allowed. It was all very different from the legend of a ferocious and bloodthirsty turncoat, savagely crushing men whose opinions he had once shared.

On 17 October 1796 Castlereagh wrote to Pitt stating that he would be unable to be present at the opening of the Westminster Parliament. The critical situation on his father's estates, as well as his public duties, made his presence in Ulster a necessity. But though the situation was serious he saw no cause for panic. A crisis would be created only if the French were able to land troops in the country and give the republicans aid. But it was far from easy to know exactly where the chief danger lay. As in England, so in Ireland: the radicals had used the cloak of legitimate reform agitation to disguise their more questionable activities. Like the English radicals the United Irishmen took care to commit very little of their plans to paper. Everything was done by word of mouth, and the swearing of secret oaths bound men together in a plot against the state. Intimidation and blackmail were used to keep those who had been foolish enough to become involved in treasonable intrigue faithful to a cause they yearned to abandon.

It was important to bring those who had been charged with sedition and with planning an insurrection to trial. If guilt could be established through due process of law the authorities would be strengthened by a rallying of public opinion to their side. If the leaders who had been apprehended were punished the example would deter lesser men. Castlereagh believed that, as yet, the majority of Irishmen were untainted with Jacobinism. But they needed confidence to stand forth as defenders of the constitution. The most difficult battle of all was that which had to be waged for the confidence of ordinary people. Too many believed that most of their countrymen were actively engaged in planning treason, and that the King's authority was maintained by the army alone. 'Unless we can establish the opposite impression,' Castlereagh assured Pitt, 'this kingdom will always be prey to treasonable excesses.' At the same

time he hoped that the necessity of providing some security against
both foreign invasion and domestic unrest would re-unite the
propertied classes in the defence of their country and the constitution. There was little prospect, in his opinion, of an early end to the
war, but it was possible that a national emergency might call forth
a new spirit in Ireland which would mean that instead of being a
charge upon the strength of the sister country Ireland would be able
to contribute her share to the preparation of offensive measures
against the French as well as her own internal safety.[15]

But his optimism was short-lived. He became dismayed by the
extent to which disaffection had made progress among the peasantry,
and his personal experiences in County Down made him aware of the
immensity of the task which the authorities faced. In November
1796 he informed Pelham, the Irish Secretary, of the deplorable
situation. Sadly he confessed, 'Certainly since I came to the country
I have had evidences of the extent and danger of the conspiracy
beyond what I was prepared to find.' He had come to the conclusion
that it was imperative for the authorities to take the initiative and
disarm the population. The possibility of the rebels receiving French
aid added a sinister dimension to the crisis. All the symptoms of
unrest were widespread: housebreaking, armed robbery, assassination. Castlereagh therefore supported the resort to extraordinary
measures, the proclaiming of disaffected areas, with the magistrates
being authorized to search for arms in order to break up cells of
treasonable activity.[16]

Throughout the months and years when fears of a French invasion
were part of the daily life of Irish landlords Castlereagh was active
in his duties as a serving officer in the militia. In December 1796 he
was in the Cork area; in the summer of 1797 he was with his regiment
in Dundalk. He did not shrink from the difficult and often unpleasant
duties which were expected of him, but his reputation has been sullied
by many lies and false accusations. He was always scrupulous in
observing the letter of the law and he countenanced no indiscipline
among his troops. Yet he was blamed for the execution of William
Orr, a young Presbyterian farmer, who was found guilty at the
Antrim Assizes of administering illegal oaths, and who was sub-
sequently hanged at Carrickfergus. But Castlereagh was not even in
Dublin when the Lord Lieutenant was reviewing Orr's case. Since he
was not a member of the Irish Privy Council at this time he played
no part in the withholding of a reprieve.

But the authorities were coming to realize that a man of Castlereagh's abilities could not be passed over. In July 1797 he was

appointed Keeper of the King's Signet (the Irish equivalent of Lord Privy Seal), and in October he was sworn in as a Privy Councillor. His advance was assisted by the fact that his uncle, the Second Earl Camden, had been Lord Lieutenant since the recall of Fitzwilliam in March 1795. Further promotion came his way because of the poor health of Thomas Pelham, the Irish Secretary. There was a strong prejudice against appointing an Irishman to this office, but Castlereagh's claims could not be overlooked. He had courage, a first-hand knowledge of the situation in Ulster and the ability to carry conviction in debate. He could take decisions and he did not flinch from shouldering responsibility. Camden had taken the opportunity of consulting with Castlereagh on his own appointment as Lord Lieutenant, which was itself a sign of the confidence he had in his political judgement. In March 1798 Castlereagh was appointed Acting Chief Secretary because of Pelham's indisposition. When Pelham finally resigned in November Castlereagh was formally appointed Chief Secretary. He was, therefore, in the thick of the fight when smouldering discontent in Ireland burst into open rebellion in May 1798.

Fitzwilliam's short period as Lord Lieutenant had proved disastrous. He had succeeded in rousing the expectations of the Catholics, only to disappoint them, and because of his ill-considered attempt to change a number of government officials he had made the Protestants all the more suspicious of any attempt to meet Catholic claims. Fitzwilliam undoubtedly exceeded his instructions: Pitt had intended that he should cautiously prepare the way for a measure of Catholic relief. Instead Fitzwilliam offended Irish sensibilities on every side. But the British government had contributed to the fiasco by the ambiguity with which Fitzwilliam's instructions had been drawn up. It was something of an oversimplification to see Fitzwilliam in a flattering light as an enlightened friend of emancipation who had been the victim of British duplicity and the intrigues of the Protestant hardliners in Dublin Castle, but, understandably, this was how many Irish Catholics chose to see the affair. When Pitt recalled Fitzwilliam it became all the more difficult for Grattan and the Irish Whigs to retain whatever hold they had over Irish nationalist opinion. Inevitably Catholics felt drawn to the United Irishmen. Fitzwilliam's viceroyalty had only confirmed that there was nothing to be gained by constitutional methods. Fitzwilliam had been an advocate of Catholic emancipation, but he had been unable to overcome the opposition to such a policy in the highest levels of the Irish administration. The British government had seemed to favour emancipation, only to abandon both the policy and its chief exponent at the first sign of trouble. It was against this background that the appeal of an Irish Republic began to exercise a stronger fascination and a more powerful attraction.

The government sought to forestall a rising by disarming the population. In Ulster General Lake carried out his task with ferocity and efficiency. The military and the yeomanry were ruthless in their methods. Though not all officers were indifferent to the considerations of common humanity it was impossible to prevent excesses, inspired as they were by frenzy, zeal and fear. The very secretiveness with which the United Irishmen had organized themselves made it hard for the authorities to track down the ringleaders or to find evidence which was certain to gain a conviction in a court of law. In Ulster the risings of 1798 were less dangerous than they would have been if Lake had not struck first; even so, they shocked the government and appalled the landowning classes. In Wexford the rebellion took on its most savage form. It became a rising of the Catholic peasants, often led by their parish priests. Republican ideals were soon forgotten: ancient wrongs and religious prejudice meant that every Protestant landowner was in danger. Yet the United Irishmen had hoped to win the support of both Catholics and Protestants for a Republic in which old animosities would be forgotten in a re-discovered and re-animated nationalism.

Part of the difficulty for the rebels was the failure of the leaders of the republican movement to provide effective leadership at the decisive moment. The arrest of Lord Edward Fitzgerald had removed the most glamorous of the leaders of the United Irishmen, and his subsequent death in prison from wounds received while resisting arrest added another martyr to the roll of those Irish patriots who had died for Ireland. But Ireland already had martyrs enough: what was needed was skilful, realistic leadership, in which a shrewd sense of what was militarily possible would be linked to an intelligent assessment of what was politically desirable. It was precisely this combination of qualities which was dramatically lacking. Fitzgerald's death was almost as great an embarrassment to the government as it was a tragedy for his friends. He was related to the Duke of Richmond, Charles James Fox, and Lady Castlereagh. He was personally popular, since whatever the extravagances of his political conduct he was a charming and magnetic personality, capable of inspiring intense affection. The authorities had no wish to hound him to death. They had hoped that he would tactfully leave the country before affairs reached their climax: Castlereagh himself had dropped several hints to this effect. But the death of Fitzgerald and the dispersion of the Protestant leaders of the rebellion meant that those who took up arms were without effective leadership at the highest level and without any coherent long-term strategy. French help was the essential prerequisite for a successful rising, and French help did not come until it was too late.

The rebellion was bloody and violent. Ferocious atrocities were committed on both sides. Far from being a patriotic war against the British it became a bitter civil conflict between the Irish. Instead of healing the divisions within Irish society it embittered them. Protestants who had sympathized, at least in part, with the ideals of the United Irishmen before 1798, became the stern foes of republicanism because of what they had seen and experienced during the rebellion. French Jacobinism divided Irishmen still further. The growing tendency of Protestants, especially in the north, to identify their own interests with the maintenance of the British connexion was given added impetus. Fitzgerald and Wolfe Tone, two of the most famous of the Irish republican leaders, were both Protestants, but this did not prevent the rising of 1798 taking on an essentially Catholic character in the eyes of most Irish Protestants. In so far as Jacobinism was deemed to be interfused with the Irish struggle it seemed only to heighten an innate intransigence and an intense dedication to political violence.

Castlereagh worked hard to avert bloodshed. He had been anxious to forestall insurrection, but once it occurred he knew that it would have to be speedily suppressed. He was desperately conscious of the slender thread by which law and order and a respect for property were sustained. It was imperative to disarm all those suspected of treasonable conspiracy, and it was essential to afford protection to loyalists. The military were empowered to take all steps necessary for pacification, and to do this a wide range of discretion had to be delegated to the commanders on the spot. This discretion was often – but not always – abused. Although Lake and Campbell were ruthless and unyielding, Abercromby and Moore restrained their men from inflicting unnecessary hardships and excessive punishments upon the people. Castlereagh did his best to keep the armed forces of the Crown under effective control. He promised personally to investigate allegations of military ferocity; he offered redress for proved grievances; he stated that courts-martial were to sit only under the direct authority of the Commander-in-Chief; and he attempted to hold back troops from committing offences against property, especially in cases where they were compulsorily quartered on families or in houses that had been requisitioned.

Anything smacking of retrospective legislation was abhorrent to him, and he was opposed to sweeping and indiscriminate acts of mass punishment or reprisal, however much these were urged as effective deterrents. He believed that exceptions to the normal course of the law should be kept to a minimum. It was necessary to punish with the utmost severity the ringleaders and those guilty of offences against person and property, but he believed that it would be wise 'not to close the door of mercy against the deluded inhabitants of Ireland returning to their loyalty, whom the government would be happy to embrace in the arms of paternal affection'.[17] He never forgot that once the rebellion had been crushed the task of reconciliation would be the chief problem claiming the government's wholehearted attention. It was unrealistic to dream of any final and comprehensive extermination of all those involved in the rebellion, and he therefore constantly made a distinction between the leaders and organizers of the rising, whom he held responsible for so much bloodshed and violence, and those who had been swept into the rebellion by poverty, agrarian or religious grievances, unthinking emotion and delusions of liberty.

But he sensed how deeply the religious aspect of the rising was warping Irish political attitudes. Though he believed that it might be to Ireland's ultimate advantage that the British connexion was seen as the means by which total catastrophe had been averted he did not want the British government to become too closely identified with any single section in Irish political life, and he recognized the deep feelings of outrage which had been provoked by the religious persecution endured by the Protestants in Wexford at the hands of the rebels. In that county the rebellion had been 'perfectly a religious phrenzy'. Priests had led the rebels into battle; they had prayed on the march; and in battle they had shown the most desperate resolution in attack. Protestants who were suspected of being Orangemen had been killed. In such a situation it was not surprising that the loyalists had been roused to similar acts of frenzy. But the rising was not just a religious conflict: 'It is a Jacobinical conspiracy throughout the kingdom, pursuing its object chiefly with Popish instruments; the heated bigotry of this sect being better suited to the purpose of the republican leaders than the cold, reasoning disaffection of the Northern Presbyterians.'[18] He anticipated a long and bitter struggle, since the number of men joining the rising in Wexford had been great, and since it would be difficult in any case to penetrate that part of the country there was every indication of a protracted conflict. It was all the more imperative, therefore, not to do anything which could affront or depress loyalist feelings, and for this reason Castlereagh arranged for Lord Edward Fitzgerald to be buried at night. Far from being a wanton insult to the dead rebel, this was an attempt to combine a generosity of spirit towards his family with a respect for the understandable feelings of those who saw Lord Edward, not as a gay, romantic boy, but as one of the instigators of a rebellion which threatened the stability, perhaps even the existence, of Irish society and the safety of every Protestant in the kingdom.

The government unearthed enough evidence to demonstrate that the United Irishmen had planned a comprehensive rising on a national scale, with French intervention as the surety for success. It was something of a relief that the rebellion was so heavily concentrated in Wexford, Wicklow and Carlow. General Lake stormed the rebel camp at Vinegar Hill on 21 June 1798. When the French eventually sent help it came too late and it was in the wrong place. General Humbert inflicted a humiliating reverse on the militia, putting them to flight at a skirmish at Castlebar ('the Castlebar races'), but he was forced to surrender at Ballinamuck in August 1798. In October Wolfe Tone, seeking once again to bring French aid to the Irish rebels, just as he had abortively tried to do two years before when sailing with Hoche's ill-fated expedition to Bantry Bay, was arrested on board a French ship in Lough Swilly. Rather than face the inevitable he cut his throat in jail.

Although outbursts of violence, arson, and murder continued, the rising was, for all significant purposes, over. It had failed to achieve any of the objectives which the United Irishmen had hoped to win, and it left behind it a bitter legacy of hatred, remembered wrongs and frustrated passion. Protestant suspicions of the Catholic peasants had been heightened, and Protestant dependence on Britain emphasized. The Catholics romanticized their defeat in legend and song, immortalizing the memory of the men who had died for Ireland in the year of liberty. But a viable political solution to the ills of Ireland was further away than ever. Any confidence that the British government had had in the Dublin Parliament had been finally eroded.

Things could not remain as they were. There could be no return to the situation on the eve of the rebellion, and Castlereagh did not regard this as desirable, even if it had been practicable. Though some of the Protestants believed that once the rising was crushed life could resume as if it had never occurred, Castlereagh knew this to be an illusion. He had had his own misgivings about the Irish situation

long before the rising and he was convinced that the rebellion had
confirmed the correctness of his diagnosis. The constitutional
relationship between Britain and Ireland would have to change, and
a serious effort would have to be made to meet the legitimate
grievances of the Catholic majority, since if their grievances were
allowed to fester the outcome would be another rebellion, and
should the French succeed in sending aid in time, the consequence
would be even more uncertain.

Castlereagh concentrated all his energies upon constructing something of value from the confusions and hatred which had torn
Ireland apart. Out of chaos he hoped to bring a better order, which
would heal ancient animosities and direct Irish patriotism into
positive channels. But his uncle, Earl Camden, had wilted under the
strain of office. He had neither the toughness of mind for a policy of
repression nor the skill and judgement for a policy of conciliation. In
his heart he yearned for peace, but he could not discern the means by
which it was to be achieved. He gave up the post of Lord Lieutenant
with relief, being succeeded by the experienced soldier and diplomatist, Lord Cornwallis, whose defeat at Yorktown had now been
happily overshadowed by his achievements in India. Castlereagh
soon found that he could cooperate with the new Lord Lieutenant.
They shared a common dislike for pretentious political speculation
and a common dedication to public service, untarnished by selfish
ambition or any reluctance to look facts in the face. Cornwallis was
quick to tell the Duke of Portland how highly he rated Castlereagh's
worth: he spoke appreciatively of his abilities, temper and judgement. On his part, Castlereagh had a deep respect for Cornwallis's
sterling qualities. The two men shared a desire to bring reconciliation
to Ireland and security to Britain. Even more significantly, they did
not hesitate to turn their attention to seeking possible solutions to
the constitutional problems which were responsible for much of the
tragedy of 1798. They saw the need for change, but, unlike Fitzwilliam, they never forgot the need for circumspection.

Even before the fighting had finished Castlereagh had reminded
General Lake of the wisdom of tempering justice with mercy. The
wretched peasants had been instruments exploited by more subtle
men, and it would be wrong to force them once more into the arms of
extremists by driving them to despair. The leaders were fit objects of
punishment, but for the rank and file clemency was the best policy.
To withhold it would compel desperate men into intransigent
resistance. Even after the victory at Vinegar Hill Castlereagh knew
that there was much smouldering disaffection which an unwise

severity might easily fan into flame. He sought – without much success – to detach the Catholic rank and file from the leaders of the rebellion. Whenever he could do so, his own influence was exercised in favour of clemency, especially when there were extenuating circumstances which could be cited in mitigation. Although he was unable to save Michael Byrne, one of the leading rebels in Leinster, from the gallows, he had the satisfaction of seeing another convicted rebel, Oliver Bond, reprieved. Castlereagh saved the lives of a number of other rebels – Arthur O'Connor, Thomas Emmett, and William MacNevin – but his compassion was rewarded only by the enthusiasm with which those who had benefited from his humanity later blackened his name.

It was a difficult task trying to decide cases where mercy was appropriate or severity called for: those who had committed murder, or who had been found guilty of conspiracy to murder, could not be included in any general pardon, and the same held true for men who had deserted from the militia. Other exemptions from a general pardon included those who had had direct communications with the enemy or who had played an active part in the organization of the rebellion. For many rebels Castlereagh favoured banishment, rather than the death penalty. He admitted that it was a stern sentence, but surely it was to be preferred to capital punishment. But even here there were complications. The United States was uneasy at the prospect of receiving large numbers of Irish immigrants who had been involved in the rebellion. Castlereagh thought that American fears were exaggerated:

It is perfectly natural that America should be very jealous of receiving Irish convicts; but, unless she prohibits emigration from this country altogether, she will infallibly receive United Irishmen, and the majority of our prisoners are not more dangerous than the general class of American settlers. Were it not that the loyal would be disgusted and indignant at their being at large in this kingdom, the greater part of them might be discharged on bail without much danger to the State.[19]

He thought it desirable to get rid of as many of these Irish prisoners as quickly as possible. Keeping them in jail was both costly and inefficient. On the other hand, many of the United Irishmen were as averse to taking up residence in the United States as the Americans were reluctant to receive them. They talked of President Adams and William Pitt in much the same terms, and saw little to choose between the British and American governments as agents of tyranny. But those who were weary of political enterprises, and who were

C

longing for the opportunity to begin their lives anew, unhampered by the follies and mistakes of the past, looked to America as the only part of the world where they could settle with any advantage to themselves. Even before the rebellion had been finally suppressed Castlereagh was exploring every opportunity for showing that the government was capable of blending a judicious concern for the security of the state with a humane care for those who could be regarded as the victims of misplaced idealism or the dupes of more sophisticated or more dangerous men.

Nothing is further from the truth than the suggestion that the British government provoked the rising of 1798 in order to facilitate the Union of Great Britain and Ireland. It is true that in September 1798 Castlereagh was hoping that the rising could be turned to good account by making opinion in Ireland more amenable to the possibility of a change in the constitutional relationship between the two kingdoms, but this was a lesson which he drew from the rebellion, not an explanation of the policy of the British or Irish administrations in the years before 1798. Throughout the 1790s the authorities had been anxious to avoid trouble, and they were too aware of all the risks inherent in any Irish rebellion to think of stimulating an outbreak which would jeopardize so much that they held dear. The enfranchisement of the Catholic freeholders and the disarming of the Ulster peasantry stemmed from a fundamental determination to ward off a political confrontation by whatever policies seemed expedient for doing so. The British government had no deep-laid plans for Ireland. Their policy, rightly or wrongly, was primarily one of improvisation, and this, rather than any astonishing sophistication, explained its inconsistency and contradictions. Pitt's own attitude towards Irish questions was coloured by the defeat of his free trade proposals in 1785 and the conduct of the Irish House of Commons during the Regency Crisis of 1788, but it was only after the rising of 1798 – with all that it implied about the régime in Dublin – that he came to contemplate a parliamentary Union as part of what he hoped would be an overall solution.

Castlereagh had also come to favour such a policy, chiefly because he could see no other way of preserving the British connexion and the Protestant establishment while holding out some prospect of dealing with the Catholic problem. The rebellion of 1798 reinforced Castlereagh's conviction that as long as the Irish Catholics were excluded from the political nation they would readily be seduced from their allegiance, but only within a British context would it be practicable to give to the Catholics the civil and political status they desired without endangering the Protestant establishment or the British connexion. After the experience of 1798 Protestants were all the more sensitive to threats of Catholic violence or to dark forecasts of the dangers of a Catholic-dominated Parliament in Dublin. Far from being a fraud perpetrated on his unsuspecting countrymen by a political renegade, the Union became attractive to British and Irish politicians because it seemed to afford an escape from what had become an unbearable and agonizing political dilemma. Realists such as Castlereagh could not understand how Whigs like Grattan clung to their belief that the Dublin Parliament could ever solve the Catholic problem without endangering the Protestant ascendancy.

After 1798 fears of republicanism and dreams of total separation from Britain added new complexities to the already perplexing shifts of opinion. The Catholic peasants lay crushed and quelled, but their bishops were all the more eager after the experience of 1798 to search for a solution which would satisfy Catholic claims without drenching the country in further bloodshed. The savagery of the rebellion had demonstrated how a fusion of Jacobinical ideas with traditional grievances could threaten the basis of society. But a parliamentary Union would not be attained without exhausting negotiation and sustained political campaigning. The more conservative Protestants remained suspicious of any policy which could be interpreted as a prelude to the erosion of their privileged and highly valued political status. Irish Whigs resented the idea of losing all that they had imagined had been gained in 1782. Reactionaries and liberals could make common cause in defence of the Dublin Parliament. Powerless though they had been to prevent the rising of 1798, and impotent as they found themselves in the face of a rebellion, had it not been for British aid, they nevertheless rejected suggestions that their independence might be voluntarily given up for a greater measure of public security. A parliamentary Union amounted to a confession of political failure and dependence on Great Britain, and this confession was something which the Irish political nation found it humiliating to make.

Just as a strange alliance sprang to the defence of the Dublin Parliament so an equally curious alliance came to support the idea of parliamentary Union. The British government courted Catholic opinion, seeking to assure Catholics that only a Union held out any possibility of an improvement in their lot. There were also conservative Protestants who, however much they sensed the dangers of a Union, had come to the conclusion that it was the only constitutional answer to the relationship between Britain and Ireland, and that if the issue of a Union could be detached from Catholic relief it might be possible to carry a Union into effect without necessarily following it up with emancipation. Men such as Lord Clare were therefore prepared to advocate a Union provided that it was discussed separately from the Catholic question. The British government was in the predicament of having to appeal, in a generalized fashion, to Catholics for support, while attempting to reassure Irish Protestants that their own privileges were not in jeopardy. This was the confused situation in which Cornwallis and Castlereagh had to negotiate. They showed remarkable skill in dealing with a wide variety of Irish interest groups, and despite all the pressures of political negotiation they acted honourably throughout. Even so, they were unable to succeed without suffering a rebuff of considerable magnitude.

Clare made his own position clear on 16 October 1798. Writing to Castlereagh from London he stated that he had seen Pitt, Loughborough and the Duke of Portland, and that they were aware of the 'critical situation of our damnable country' and convinced that Union alone could save it. Clare believed that the policy of making concessions to the Irish Catholics had contributed to the rebellion and he could not resist pointing out that the events of 1798 must have opened the eyes of all Englishmen to 'the inanity of their past conduct, with respect to the Papists of Ireland' – a reference to the enfranchisement of the Catholic freeholders in 1793.

Castlereagh must have read this comment with sardonic satisfaction. He did not share Clare's unbending rejection of all concessions to the Catholics, but he had always been dubious about the effects of enfranchisement within the terms of the Irish political system. But unlike Clare, Castlereagh was not concerned with harping on the past in a mood of plaintive self-justification. There was no going back: he was now devoting all his energies to creating a new political framework, in which the enfranchised Catholics would be able to use their political privileges without danger to the state.

Clare complained that the British government was as full of popish projects as ever, which could only mean that Pitt and his colleagues were contemplating some measure of Catholic relief, but he took comfort from the indications that Pitt was preparing to bring forward the Irish Union without 'encumbering' it with emancipation. He also commented on Cornwallis's acquiescence on this point and on Pitt's desire to exercise some control over the Catholic clergy in Ireland. The British government was considering paying moderate stipends to the Catholic parish clergy, insisting in return that every priest should be licensed from the Crown for the performance of his ecclesiastical duties.[20]

The idea of some compromise solution regarding the payment of Catholic clergy was one which Castlereagh himself found attractive, and which he was to canvass in various forms and on a number of occasions over the years. Clare's letter afforded ample grounds for misgiving, however. It was not only its tone which was ominous. Castlereagh believed that a parliamentary Union and Catholic relief were the components of a single policy to soothe Irish discontents. Although, on tactical grounds, he was willing to accept necessary restraints on the way in which the subjects were to be brought forward, he had no desire to see one objective accomplished without the other. It was imperative, above everything else, to avoid repeating Fitzwilliam's mistake of raising Catholic hopes, only to dash them, while simultaneously rousing Protestant antagonism.

The tactics chosen by the British government were confirmed in a letter which William Elliot, the Irish Under-Secretary, wrote to Castlereagh on 24 October. The Union was to be put into effect before Catholic emancipation was to be raised. There were two reasons for this. First, the government had no wish at that stage to provoke a debate involving the discussion of the religious laws in England as well as in Ireland; and secondly, there was no purpose in inflaming the prejudices of Irish Protestants by associating a parliamentary Union with concessions which many of them would find unpalatable in the aftermath of their experiences during the rebellion.[21]

Clare had convinced Pitt of the folly of antagonizing Protestant opinion in Ireland, but Pitt was still disposed to the belief that in the long term justice would have to be done to the Catholic claims. It was reassuring to know that throughout his discussions with Elliot Pitt had spoken of Castlereagh in the most cordial terms, reiterating his appreciation of Castlereagh's political skills and judgement and of the contribution he had made to the conduct of Irish administration. It was Pitt's confidence in Castlereagh which had much to do with his formal appointment as Irish Secretary, and amid all his anxieties Castlereagh had the satisfaction of knowing that he had earned the respect and gratitude, not only of Pitt, Cornwallis and Portland, but, at least for the present, of the King himself.

The struggle for the Union was a protracted one, and initial defeat had to be painfully redeemed before the Dublin Parliament was persuaded to vote away its own life. At one time it was usual to imagine that the Union was carried merely by bribery and corruption, and that its passage was a unique example of eighteenth-century politics at their most devious and most questionable. Phrases such as 'an orgy of corruption' were deemed fully adequate as summaries of what transpired in Irish parliamentary politics between 1798 and 1800. But modern research has significantly qualified this image.[22]

The methods which Castlereagh and Cornwallis adopted were the ones usual in their own time. No eighteenth-century borough owner was prepared to vote away his privilege of nominating members of Parliament without adequate compensation. Essential assumptions concerning property and charter rights were involved, and one has only to cast one's mind back to the India Bill crisis in 1783 to realize how potent such ideas were in eighteenth-century politics. Compensation had been incorporated by Pitt into his abortive reform proposals in 1785, and this in itself was a sign of the tenacity with which charter and property rights were revered and defended. Reform, in both Britain and Ireland, implied disfranchisement and disfranchisement entailed compensation if it were not to be denounced as expropriation. Compensation did not necessarily take monetary forms. There were several methods available: promotions in the peerage, knighthoods, household or sinecure offices, preferment in the Church, advancement in the army or navy. Borough owners were preoccupied with the fortunes and status of the family, as well as their own personal position, so some provision for needy or ambitious relations was often acceptable. The Irish patrons and the Irish M.P.s were neither disinterested nor selfless: they knew their price and they held out for it.

Far from being corrupted by a sinister government, the Dublin Parliament simply set a high value on its own demise. Peers and patrons came to terms with the Union because they were able to negotiate a level of compensation which they thought sufficient for the loss of their independence. Nor did they see the process of political negotiation in the dim and dingy light with which late Victorians invested such proceedings. They accepted the rules of the game, but they exploited every trick in the contemporary repertoire. When the government returned to the attack after its initial defeat Irish boroughmongers came to terms because they believed it to be in their own interests to do so. They acted throughout as realistic political operators. They were preoccupied with defending their own interests; they did not share that romantic dedication to Irish nationalism with which later generations of Irish patriots sought to credit them. Even Grattan and the Irish Whigs shared these self-interested motives. On both sides, Unionist and anti-Unionist, the normal conventions and assumptions of eighteenth-century political life were dominant. No one was more hard-headed than the tough-minded Irish Protestants, who hated the rebellion because it threatened the Anglo-Irish ascendancy, and who yet distrusted the British because they feared that the British government would impose unpalatable reforms upon the country by means of a united Parliament.

Castlereagh knew the men with whom he was dealing. Unlike many of the other participants in the struggle he had a sufficient insight into the feelings of those who were excluded from the establishment to sense the limits within which the Dublin Parliament could be regarded as being representative of the Irish nation. Despite his hatred of the rebellion he was neither a bigoted anti-Papist nor insensitive to the feelings of the Presbyterians of the north. He knew that if politics were the art of the possible this implied recognizing facts even when they were disagreeable. His own efforts to preserve the British connexion and to advance policies of conciliation, in the hope of undermining the nascent disloyalty of both Catholics and Presbyterians, were influenced throughout by his sense of what was politically possible. He was no idealist, seeking to impose some abstract truth or transcendent pattern of behaviour upon the selfish and obscurantist monopolists who clung to power in Ireland. Rather, he was a working politician, seeking a viable solution, however imperfect, to a series of problems, each of which was intertwined with the others and each of which called for a different order of political skills and a different set of political assumptions.

By the end of 1798 Castlereagh and Cornwallis were authorized to sound out opinion in Dublin about a possible merger of Parliaments. Camden, still nursing his own wounded susceptibilities, warned his nephew of the need for tact. The warning was scarcely necessary, but it showed the extent to which British politicians feared any repetition of the Fitzwilliam episode. Camden told Castlereagh to discover what the reaction of influential individuals to the idea of parliamentary Union would be, and to take special note of the objections put forward by various interested parties; he should lose no time in meeting the expectations of favourably disposed individuals and in counteracting the objections of vested interests. He begged him to keep the government in London fully informed of the general tendency manifested in these preliminary soundings of opinion. The Duke of Portland had complained of Cornwallis's neglect in keeping the government in the picture.

Castlereagh wasted no time in sounding out opinion. But since it was necessary to raise the question of a parliamentary Union in such a way as to encourage those who favoured the idea to express their approval there was bound to be a vigorous debate, and it would not be easy for the administration to control the direction or nature of discussion. The government needed the help of all capable journalists: Castlereagh knew the power of language and oratory over the Irish mind. From the start of the controversy he recognized that the Dublin Bar would be hostile. It was feared that Union would prevent men from combining a career at the Irish Bar with membership of the House of Commons. Lawyers were a most significant element in the Irish House of Commons, and Castlereagh was right in forecasting that some of the most vehement opponents of the Union would be Irish attorneys. It was unfortunate that the initial soundings took place before the Irish Parliament was in session. He feared that this would make it easier for the enemies of Union to make preparations before the matter was debated in Parliament. In taking the initiative in courting extra-parliamentary opinion the government had lost the initiative inside Parliament.

Castlereagh showed considerable tact in making approaches about the Union to various leading Irish politicians. John Foster, the Speaker of the Irish House of Commons, who eventually became a fierce opponent of the Union, was initially cultivated with great care. The Speaker was a crucial figure; his conduct in debate might well influence a considerable number of M.P.s. Castlereagh emphasized the importance of the Union in preserving the Protestant establishment. Many Protestants had come to favour the measure as 'the only means of preserving the Protestant state against the Irish Papists and *their English supporters*' – a reminder that the Foxite Whigs, with whom the Irish Whigs had often acted in collusion, were for the most part committed to Catholic emancipation and the repeal of the Test and Corporation Acts. Dublin was likely to be hostile, but Castlereagh believed that Cork and Limerick supported the Union while, so far as he could judge, opinion in the north was 'torpid'. Before the government embarked upon a public controversy the likely response of major interests had to be discreetly explored. If the government gave the impression of being too heavily committed to the measure this might only provoke a negative reaction. Castlereagh feared that too many people were forgetting that they were surrounded by treason and conspiracy. In his heart he despaired of the country if it rejected both timely reform and the British connexion. But one problem was the different meaning which men attached to the notion of securing the Protestant establishment. Castlereagh believed that the Union would remove the threat of Catholic predominance and that this would allow Catholics to be admitted to full citizenship. Since there would be a Protestant majority in the united Parliament there would be no risk of the Church of Ireland being disestablished. Furthermore, if a scheme could be worked out by which the Catholic clergy were paid by the state, then a better relationship between the various denominations might come about. But many of the men with whom Castlereagh was negotiating interpreted the Protestant establishment in a much narrower sense. For them, any concession to the Catholics implied jeopardizing the Protestant ascendancy, and if they were willing to contemplate Union it was as a means of ensuring that no concessions would be made to the Catholics and that Protestant supremacy would be preserved in the most absolute manner. There was throughout the discussions a very real danger of misunderstanding on both sides, and this made it easier for charges of deception to be levied at Castlereagh and Cornwallis. The very discretion with which they went about their task enabled their enemies to accuse them of duplicity.

Meanwhile, in London Pitt had sounded out both Foster and Parnell, the Chancellor of the Irish Exchequer. Their response had been suitably vague; both of them were too experienced to be drawn out too clearly on what was bound to be a highly controversial issue. Elliot immediately realized the danger of their slipping over to the anti-Union side. He hoped that the Catholics would acquiesce in the Union, since it was in their own best interests to do so, but he recognized that they had grounds for complaint. Elliot regretted that Pitt had yielded to prejudice by divorcing the Union from emancipation. Whatever the extenuating circumstances, he feared that this choice of tactics would have dismal consequences.

Castlereagh took every opportunity to convey the impression that the Union would strengthen the British Empire. He was hoping to exploit memories of the rebellion and fears of a French invasion, and he therefore repeatedly stressed that the Union would make Ireland secure from French attack. He assured merchants and manufacturers that the economic prospects for the Union were good: he anticipated that Irish trade would flourish once the Union had been carried. He lamented the baleful influence of religious animosity upon Irish life, but he feared that, without Union, religious bigotry would become more strained and more bitter. The Union was the only means of enabling conciliation to take place. Castlereagh hoped that if the parliamentary Union were achieved the Protestants would feel less exposed to rule by the Catholic majority and that they would behave less like a beleaguered garrison and more like a responsible governing class, while the Catholics in turn would benefit from the liberalization of the laws which only Union would make possible.

But while he was authorized and encouraged informally to take up the subject of the Union with leading Irish Catholics he was told to avoid anything like a specific pledge that emancipation would inevitably follow. He had to raise Catholic hopes, without making them believe that emancipation was imminent. He was free to suggest that the Union would lead to improvements in their status, while steering clear of too precise a commitment as to what such an improvement meant by way of legislation. It was a daunting assignment, and one which would have challenged the most resourceful and experienced of diplomatists. Within the excruciating confines of the political situation Castlereagh performed his duty admirably. He was scrupulous, discreet, respectful even of those opponents who abused and misrepresented him shamelessly. On 5 December 1798 Cornwallis told Portland how things were going:

I am happy to observe that the leading Catholics, notwithstanding the measure is understood by them to be unconnected with any immediate extension of constitutional privileges to their communion, express themselves highly in its favour. Lord Fingall . . . has expressed much satisfaction that it was not meant to complicate the question of Union by attempting, at present, any change in the Test Laws. He considers it would be injurious to the Catholic claims to have them discussed in the present temper of the Irish Parliament, and was satisfied it would hazard the success of the Union, without serving the Catholics; and considers it much more for their interest that the question should rest, till it could be submitted, in quieter times, to the unprejudiced decision of the United Parliament, relying on their receiving hereafter every indulgence which could be extended to them, without endangering the Protestant establishment.
Lord Kenmare joined in this sentiment, and is a warm advocate for the measure; both these noblemen expressed an anxious wish to see the Catholic clergy rendered less dependent on the lower orders, by having a reasonable provision under the State.[23]

Castlereagh had seen Dr Troy, the principal Catholic bishop, and his sentiments were in full agreement with those of Fingall and Kenmare. Cornwallis believed that so far as he could judge there was every reason to expect the Catholics to support the Union, but too active a commitment to the Union by the Catholics would not help the measure to win the confidence of Protestants. The danger was that if the Catholics became too eager or too vocal in promoting the

Union the suspicions of Protestants would be roused and they would then be less inclined to support the proposal.

Towards the end of 1798 Castlereagh's father told him of the way in which opinion in the north was reacting to the idea of Union. There had not been much public awareness of the question, but it seemed that at the very least popular opposition to the measure would not be strong. Londonderry assured his son that many of those who were usually radical in politics had little love for the Dublin Parliament. They despised it as a corrupt and privileged assembly, and they would not be averse to a change which would rid the country of a symbol of the exclusion of the mass of the people from political power. Among merchants and manufacturers, especially in Belfast, the feeling was growing that the Union would bring immeasurable commercial benefits, and that Belfast would benefit most from an influx of wealth and a more extensive and flourishing commerce. But among the lower orders there was little interest in the question.

It must be remembered that those who were most articulate in their opposition to the Irish Union were likely to lose something by it. Opposition was strongest among members of the Anglo-Irish ascendancy, who disliked Catholics and Presbyterians with equal intensity, who expected Britain to protect them from French invasion or domestic rebellion, but who nevertheless distrusted British intervention in Irish affairs. The majority of Catholics were indifferent. They had little cause to love the Dublin Parliament, and especially for those who had been active in the rising the controversy over the Union was no more than a squabble among their oppressors. It was understandable that much of the controversy should centre in Dublin, which had so much to lose. If the Union were carried it would cease to be a governmental capital and the professional classes who valued the Irish Parliament as the agency of their own political advancement resented an innovation which struck so powerfully at their own status. Bitter though the debate over the Union was it was relevant only to a small section of the Irish population, most of whom were bored by the controversy. Only after the frustration of Catholic emancipation and the fall of Pitt did retrospective affection for the Dublin Parliament become part of the standard rhetoric of Irish agitation. It became conventional to speak of the Union as a premeditated betrayal, and this mythology did essential service for those seeking to repeal the Act of Union and the religious laws discriminating against Catholics. One of the chief victims of this mythology was Castlereagh. He was denounced by Protestants for being too sympathetic to Catholic claims, and he was reviled by Catholics as a man who had sold his country and failed to honour his word. These charges were exaggerated, unrelated to the evidence and grossly unfair, but since it was convenient to so many to believe them – and what was worse to disseminate them – Castlereagh became a symbol of treachery and corruption.

The beginning of 1799 saw misgivings about the Union manifesting themselves among Catholics in Dublin, where the general clamour against Union was vociferous. Opinion in the provinces remained neutral, although Cornwallis noted that the merchants of Londonderry supported the Union in the hope that it would bring advantages to the linen trade. Castlereagh warned Portland of the intensity of opposition in Dublin, but he qualified his warnings with the comment that opposition was chiefly confined to the upper and middle classes. If the mob became active he believed that this would be in response to encouragement and direction from above. He was sceptical about the genuineness of spontaneous demonstrations. He understood why the Union was so hated in certain quarters. He appreciated why Irish M.P.s, who were to lose their parliamentary seats without any prospect of a seat in the new united Parliament, saw the Union as tantamount to committing political suicide. Furthermore, it was one thing to follow a parliamentary career in Dublin, but it was another matter to be committed to membership of a Parliament in London, with all that it entailed by way of personal inconvenience and expense and professional difficulty. He understood the impact which the forceful expression of anti-Union sentiment among the respectable and propertied classes in Dublin would have upon many professional men who were peering into an uncertain future with considerable anxiety.

The only hope of success lay in the British government remaining absolutely firm in its advocacy of the Union. Any suggestion that it might be dropped would inflame opposition and erode the confidence of the supporters of the measure. It was essential to convey to men that the Union was not just an attractive idea which was being floated in the aftermath of the rebellion, but that it was a viable political probability and that it represented a fundamental policy on the part of the British government. He went so far as to state his conviction that an initial defeat ought not to be accepted as final. It was imperative for Pitt to indicate by every means in his power that the government would not meekly submit to defeat, and that it was their intention to return to the issue again and again until it was successfully accomplished. It was unfair, Castlereagh thought, to ask

Irish politicians to risk so much by way of commitment to the Union if there was a shadow of doubt about the depth of the British commitment to the measure.

It was ironic that a man who was fighting such a hard battle should be abused by Catholics, when, amid all their other worries, Castlereagh and Cornwallis had succeeded in ensuring that, while the emancipation question was not to be officially linked with the Union, there was no danger of the extreme Protestants persuading the British government that a formal stipulation condemning Catholic emancipation should be incorporated in the Act of Union. It was easy for liberal historians to complain that emancipation was divorced from the carrying of Union in the first place, but they ignored the struggle that was necessary for emancipation to remain as a possibility once the Union had come into effect. The complexities of the Irish political situation compelled caution. The real alternatives were not Union with emancipation, as against Union without it. Rather, when the Irish context is taken fully into account, the choice lay between the survival of the Dublin Parliament – without emancipation, even as a possibility – and an Act of Union which at least left the Catholic question open, or an Act of Union which ruled out the granting of Catholic relief. These were the confines within which Pitt, Cornwallis and Castlereagh had to conduct their complicated negotiations with a diversity of conflicting Irish and British interests. Anti-Catholicism was still a potent force in British politics, as well as in Irish controversies, as the triumph of George III in 1801 eventually made clear and as the defeat of the Ministry of All the Talents in 1807 later confirmed.

On the eve of the first crucial division in the Irish House of Commons Castlereagh's spirits had recovered and he was optimistic. He thought that the government would be able to count on the support of between 160 and 170 M.P.s, the opposition having about 100 committed supporters. Although the violent part played by the Orange Order had had a considerable impact upon Protestant opinion, Castlereagh did not anticipate defeat. Clare was deeply shaken, however, and was unhappy about the prospects in the House, and events justified Clare's gloom, not Castlereagh's confidence. On 23 January 1799 an amendment put forward by Ponsonby after the address from the throne called upon the Commons to maintain an independent Irish Parliament at Dublin as a final settlement of all constitutional differences between Britain and Ireland. In the division this amendment was defeated by only one vote. This made it difficult for the government to proceed. The initiative had passed to the opposition. Castlereagh was disgusted by the vehemence and extravagance with which many of the anti-Unionists had attacked the government. He told Portland that the country gentlemen had behaved as if they had been engaged in a foxhunt instead of a debate on a momentous question. Much of the opposition's rhetoric had been far from constitutional in spirit. Another disgusted colleague thought that the M.P.s had behaved like members of a Polish Diet.

One modern historian[24] has suggested that although the temper of Castlereagh's contribution to the debate was characteristically realistic it was ill-chosen, given the prevailing nationalist disposition of the Irish House of Commons. There is no doubt that Castlereagh outraged his opponents by pointing out the contrast between all the fine talk of Irish independence on the one hand, and the country's dependence on Britain for its defence on the other. He insisted that in practice Ireland was subordinate to Britain in all imperial and military questions. The Union would replace a false and delusory independence with a real partnership, but this suggestion offended many backbenchers. They were too fond of flaunting their independence to enjoy being reminded of the crude realities which the rebellion had all too recently revealed.

One anti-Unionist argument which made a powerful appeal to Irish M.P.s was the claim that the Irish Parliament could not constitutionally vote its own demise, and that it lacked any mandate from the people – by which most members meant the political nation, not the majority of the population – to enter into negotiations for a Union. The precedent of the Scottish Union of 1707 was dismissed as irrelevant and inapplicable. Government assertions that commerce and business would profit from the Union were swept aside by declarations that the constitution mattered far more than the sordid and petty considerations of trade. It was argued that 100 Irish M.P.s at Westminster would be inadequate for the defence of Ireland's interests, and the question of which Irish constituencies would survive and how Irish representation in the new Parliament was to be apportioned added to the embarrassments endured by the government. The narrow escape of 23 January was followed by defeat on the 24th. A motion to delete the paragraph in the address referring to the need to consolidate the British Empire was carried by 109 votes to 104.

But in London Pitt was following Castlereagh's advice for the government to be unflinching in its labours to secure the Union. Despite the defeat for the Unionists in Dublin Pitt committed the

British government to strengthening the connexion between the two countries. In his speech in the British House of Commons on 22 January he had argued that only an impartial legislature, free from local prejudices and above local pressures, could tackle the problems afflicting Ireland. A United Kingdom Parliament would, he hoped, yield 'neither to the haughty pretensions of the few nor open the door to popular inroads'. On 31 January 1799 the British government introduced nine resolutions in the British House of Commons containing the draft proposals for an Irish Union.

The defeat in Dublin had been galling for Castlereagh but he was heartened by the evident determination of the British government to press on with the Union. Defeat meant that even greater care had to be shown in courting significant interests. But there were times when even Castlereagh's self-control cracked. Some of his language in parliamentary debate had betrayed his exasperation with his opponents. To describe the opposition of Dublin lawyers as 'petty-fogging' was accurate enough, but it commended neither him nor the Union to the Dublin Bar. His assurances that the Union would not mean subordination carried little conviction with opponents. But despite frustration and tiredness Castlereagh's spirits rose. Even when explaining the defeat of 24 January to Portland he discerned signs of hope and encouragement. The refusal of the House to commit itself to the prohibition of any future discussions of a scheme of Union showed that all was not lost. Some anti-Unionists might yet be brought over, and he began to think that the response of the country gentlemen might become more sympathetic if the right tactics were adopted. There were many waverers in the Irish Parliament, and it was to this section that Castlereagh looked for reinforcements for the Union cause. He emphasized the importance of cultivating the country gentlemen: 'Were it possible, by adopting the principle of partial compensation, to give a greater proportionate weight to the counties, without provoking an increased resistance from the borough proprietors, the measure would meet with much less resistance, particularly with that class of men who carry most weight with them – the country gentlemen.'[25] The mood of the Irish Parliament made it injudicious to re-agitate the question in the current session, and he had doubts about the chances of success within the lifetime of the current Parliament. But something might be gained from resolutions committing the government to the principle of Union even if these were not immediately taken further.

Castlereagh recognized the danger that the opponents of Union

would seek to exploit the grievances of the Catholics to make it less
convincing for the government to claim that only after a parliamentary Union could the Catholic question be honourably settled. Castlereagh never abandoned his own belief that the Union should be
speedily followed by a liberal measure of Catholic emancipation, but
he saw that if Catholic opinion was to be brought round to supporting, or at least acquiescing in, Union, it was imperative to hammer
home the futility of Catholics hoping for a Dublin Parliament to
grant significant concessions to Catholics in a non-Union situation.
Another question which was one of the most prickly issues in Irish
politics was the controversy over tithes, and Castlereagh argued that
the Union must be put forward as the only means by which this
problem could be constructively handled. He remained unrepentant
in his conviction that the opponents of the Union were motivated by
private interests, rather than public spirit. He had no illusions about
the strength of the political influence which was operating against the
Union. He told Pitt that not less than a million pounds in value
represented the resources which were being exploited against the
government.

Soon Castlereagh was addressing himself to the practical problems
of political negotiation which any renewed attempt to carry the
Union would involve. He classified the nature of opposition under
several heads. There were borough proprietors, whose property
would obviously fall in value; there were those county interests who
felt that they would suffer if only one M.P. was returned from each
Irish county to the United Kingdom Parliament; there were the
barristers in Dublin, who believed that the Union would deprive
them of opportunities for advancement; there were those who had
purchased seats in the Irish Parliament, and who saw the Union as
implicating them in financial loss; there were those who owned
property in the Dublin area, who feared that the end of the Irish
Parliament would mean that their property would depreciate in
value. To challenge these interests would mean substantial financial
compensation, or even outright bribery. Castlereagh summed up the
process as buying out and securing to the Crown forever 'the fee
simple of Irish corruption which has so long enfeebled the powers of
government'. He also regarded the persistence of the Irish Parliament, with all the practices which had grown up round it, as a
standing danger to the security of the British connexion.

Within the limits set by the traditional system and the conventional attitudes shown by those in public life towards anything
which jeopardized their political privileges or private property,

something more subtle than mere bribery was called for. Castlereagh estimated that the total cost of offering adequate compensation to the political interests in the boroughs and the counties, to the barristers of Dublin, and to influential political patrons would come to something in the region of £1,455,000. But he contemplated making the closed boroughs bear the greater burden of the disfranchisement which would be necessary under the Union. He favoured leaving the county representation unaltered, with the open boroughs sending one M.P. each to the new united Parliament. Despite his own cynicism concerning the nature of much of the so-called popular hostility towards the Union, and which was cited by some as a decisive factor in the initial rejection of the measure, he believed that a new assault on public attitudes would have to accompany renewed political negotiation. There was a real public dimension to the controversy, however much this was misrepresented and abused by his opponents. Since the enemies of Union claimed to speak for the Irish nation it was imperative for the government to challenge this claim, and, wherever possible, to demonstrate its fallibility. Pamphlets would have to be distributed; public meetings and addresses organized; interested and influential bodies courted and converted.

The Catholic issue was one which clearly involved the feelings of the majority of the Irish nation. Castlereagh was delighted that in his speech in the British House of Commons on 31 January Pitt had stated that the Catholics would benefit if they were governed by a Parliament which was not dominated by those who were thought to be immediately responsible for many of their wrongs. Pitt had emphasized that when the conduct of the Catholics showed that there was no danger in admitting them to the political nation, and when circumstances favoured such a change, the issue of emancipation would be taken up in a United Kingdom Parliament with greater objectivity and far-sightedness than was possible in any local legislature. It was possible to argue that even in the interim between the carrying of Union and the concession of full citizenship to Catholics they would feel some mitigation of their sense of grievance under the aegis of an imperial Parliament. Castlereagh remained convinced that it was useful to win influential Catholics over to the Unionist camp. But this could best be done by persuading them that their best chance of a fair hearing and liberal treatment lay with an imperial, not an Irish, Parliament. Here the activities of some of the opponents of Union – especially Foster, the Speaker of the Irish House of Commons – were convenient, since they deepened the

certainty among Catholics that they had little to hope for from a
Dublin Parliament. But at no stage did Castlereagh make a firm and
binding promise to Catholics regarding the granting of emancipation
after Union. He was in no position to do so. All he did was judiciously
to indicate where the balance of possibilities lay.

Castlereagh disputed the opposition claim that the settlement
of 1782 was final. It was absurd to invest the 1782 settlement with
finality when the political situation was constantly changing. The
nation was facing new perils, perils which no one could have anticipated in 1782, and new problems called for new solutions, not an
unthinking reverence for a past epoch. Even if it was admitted that
the 1782 settlement had determined the question of the subserviency
of the Irish to the British Parliament, it had not necessarily done so
in quite the fashion that the anti-Unionists supposed. And as well as
the purely constitutional question there were other issues to take
into account, and these remained open – commerce, industry,
foreign policy. In his speeches in the Irish House of Commons
Castlereagh took every opportunity to demonstrate the complexity
of the relationship between the Irish and British Parliaments and
what this meant for the relations between the two countries. In one
speech he posed the question in a most cogent way:

No man . . . could overlook the danger which resulted from two
independent legislatures in the great questions of peace, of war, of
general trade and commerce, and of treaties with foreign nations, not
to mention the difficulties which arose from the Admiralty jurisdic-
tion, and the great subject of our religious establishment which must
be regulated on imperial principles. As to the first of these questions – the question of peace and war – what was not to be apprehended on the subject, under our state of separate legislatures? How
was it possible to conceive that the Empire could continue as at
present, whilst all parts of it were to receive equal protection and
only one part of it to suffer the burdens of that protection? Must we
not of necessity and justice look to some settlement of imperial
contribution? And so soon as a system of contribution should be
established, was there any question of peace or war which would not
agitate every part of the country?

In answer to the claim by the anti-Unionists that they had a
monopoly of patriotism Castlereagh asserted that the Union was the
expression of a more responsible, more far-sighted and more purpose-
ful patriotism. He reminded members of their dependence on British
help, for the defence of their lives and property and the maintenance
of the constitution they so admired, during the late rebellion; and he
went on to stress the importance of the link with Britain:

What then is the security for the connection of the two kingdoms? Is it the discretion of the Irish Parliament? No man had a higher respect than himself for the prudence, the liberality and the loyalty of its members. But had not that discretion already failed in so remarkable an instance as to prove that it was at best a bad security? It was against the principle of human nature that one country should voluntarily or regularly follow the dictates of another; it was against the common principles of pride and independence which must ever grow and increase with the importance of the kingdom. In proportion therefore to our wealth and strength the principle of discretion would be weakened, and the sole security for the continuance of our connection would vanish.[26]

It was surely wiser to recognize how fundamental the British connexion was to the safety and prosperity of Ireland and to give the relationship adequate constitutional form.

Throughout the spring and summer Castlereagh and Cornwallis continued to work for the passing of an Act of Union. The question of Irish representation in the united House of Commons was complex, but, sensitive as he was to the variety of interests intimately involved in the issue, Castlereagh handled it with considerable skill and expertise. In the counties opinion tended to drift over to the government side, although Castlereagh kept a close watch on the conduct of public meetings. Because his earlier confidence had proved ill-founded Castlereagh was cautious when trying to assess what the future would bring. By the middle of April 1799 he was happier about the likelihood of success, but he was careful to warn Portland against making too much of the lessening of raucous hostility to the Union:

I can confidently assure your Grace that the measure of Union is making its way in proportion as it is canvassed and understood. At the same time, I feel it my duty to guard your Grace's mind against an impression which might lead to disappointment, namely as to the degree in which the public sentiment has undergone a change. The clamour has certainly subsided and the measure has more open advocates who were before silent; but I cannot perceive either in or out of Parliament that impression which can lead me to form any opinion of when the measure may be carried. Within the House, some persons who were not decided on a late occasion are now more explicit, but I cannot as yet reckon on many declared converts. I only mention the subject in this point of view, and think it of importance to state that, although the difficulties which stand in our way may yield without any very considerable delay, yet we must neither be dispirited nor disappointed if the resistance should prove obstinate, and the opposition be kept together to a degree which may render the accomplishment of the measure in the next session extremely problematical.[27]

This was the language of a man who had learned from his mistakes, and whose commitment to the principle of the Union was matched only by the patience, skill, and realism with which he conducted protracted negotiations with all interested parties. Conventional influence was the means of bringing pressure to bear upon M.P.s and their patrons, but it had to be exercised with a high degree of political insight and courage.

During the summer of 1799 Castlereagh's spirits rose. In June he felt that the general state of the country was improving. Disaffection and unrest were declining and public order was being restored. But just as the spread of the United Irishmen's conspiracy had affected different areas at different times – first Ulster, then Leinster, then Munster and Connaught – so what Castlereagh called the nation's convalescence followed a similar pattern. There were cross-currents of opinion which made sweeping generalizations difficult and unconvincing. In the early stages of the conspiracy many northern Catholics had remained loyal, since the republican movement in Ulster had been so closely associated with Presbyterian radicals. Now the way in which the rising had been dominated by the Catholic peasantry meant that many Ulster Dissenters deserted republicanism and became Orangemen. Ulster was more tranquil than it had been for years, and another good sign was the prosperity of the linen industry. But the other provinces did not match Ulster's return to loyalty. The organization of the United Irishmen had been smashed, but remnants of republicanism still survived here and there to erupt in sporadic violence. A French landing would almost certainly ignite another rising, but the removal of many state prisoners to English jails and the banishment of many leading rebels had helped to restore law and order and public confidence in the authorities. Summary punishment was stern and severe, but it had counteracted the dominance of terror and the prevalence of victimization. Once again the state could be looked to for the protection of property and the security of the person.

As order was restored so the cause of Union prospered. Castlereagh scrupulously kept Portland informed of the progress made in the winning over of public opinion. On 6 July he told Portland that favourable addresses had been published in the counties of Kerry and Mayo, and what was most significant these had had the support of most men of property in the two counties. A declaration in favour of Union had also gained widespread support in Waterford. One influential convert to the Union was the Archbishop of Cashel, who had assured Cornwallis that the measure would have his decided support. Early in August Castlereagh confided to Portland that it would probably be possible to bring the Union forward in the coming session of the Irish Parliament. Opposition would still be vehement, but it would emanate chiefly from 'private ambition and private interests'. Nevertheless, Castlereagh warned Portland that serious obstacles lay ahead: 'Your Grace must be prepared for a severe struggle, and our strength will ultimately be proportioned to the means we can employ to reconcile the personal interests of individuals.'[28]

The situation in the north was generally encouraging. In Londonderry pro-Union resolutions had been passed without opposition, and there were strong indications of support in County Antrim. It appeared that dominant opinion in Belfast was favourable. But not all attempts at conversion were successful; a number of sharp setbacks were experienced. Castlereagh's old opponent, Lord Downshire, had been courted by both Cornwallis and Pitt. But Pitt came to the conclusion that despite all their efforts Downshire would probably join the opposition, and events proved him right. Downshire became active in opposing the Union, sending an anti-Union petition to the Downshire militia for signature. After the Union had been carried Downshire was punished for his opposition, being dismissed from his posts as Colonel of the Militia, a Privy Councillor, and Governor of County Down. The most bitter blow for Downshire was to see Castlereagh's father, the Earl of Londonderry, fill the post of Governor of County Down.

Castlereagh's judgement about the small number of converts within the Irish Parliament was proved correct. It has been estimated that no more than twelve M.P.s who voted against the Union in 1799 supported it in 1800. Nevertheless, on 5 February 1800, the government had a majority of forty-three in a division over a motion calling for the consideration of the Union. The struggle was not over by any means: Castlereagh had hoped for another twenty votes to swell the majority, and he was disappointed that after the victory in the parliamentary division a greater number of opposition M.P.s did not come over to the government. But it seemed that the tide had turned, and there was growing confidence in the ranks of the administration and a corresponding deterioration in the morale of the opposition after the division of 5 February.

In the debate of 5 February Castlereagh had returned to the theme that the Union represented the fulfilment of Irish nationhood, not its negation. He sought to contrast the failings of the 1782 settlement with the prospect that the Union held out of full Irish participation in a United Parliament. Instead of confining or diminishing Ireland's stature he believed that the Union would enlarge and invigorate it:

It is said . . . that a Union will reduce Ireland to the abject nature of a colony. Is it, Sir, by making her a constituent part of the greatest and first empire in the world? For my part . . . if I were to describe a colony, I would picture a country in a situation somewhat similar to that of Ireland at present. I would describe a country whose Crown was dependent on that of another country, enjoying a local legislature but without any power entrusted to that legislature of regulating the succession to that Crown. I would describe it as having an executive power administered by the orders of a non-resident Minister irresponsible to the colony for his acts and his advice; I would describe it as incapable of passing the most insignificant law without the licence of a minister of another country; I would describe it as a country unknown to foreign nations in the quality of an independent state and as subject to another power with regard to all the questions which concern alliances, the declaration and conduct of war, or the negotiations for peace.[29]

It was therefore all the more urgent that the opportunity should be seized to strengthen the Irish constitution by blending and uniting forever with the great and powerful empire of Great Britain. His appeal to the notion of strengthening the constitution was designed to win support from those who were anxious about the security of the Protestant establishment, but he was also eager to make the most of the argument that Ireland was clinging to a fictional independence, while the Union would ensure that the Irish nation would discover a new confidence and a greater maturity as a component part of the United Kingdom. Historians can now see that the Union played a creative role in the formulation of Irish national consciousness, though not in the way that Castlereagh had hoped, and that through the Union Ireland attained a greater national uniformity than it had previously known. 'There is a real sense', Dr E.R.Norman has written, 'in which it created the modern Irish state.'[30] This represents at least a partial justification of many of the arguments which Castlereagh used to commend the Union to his countrymen as an agency of a greater patriotism.

During the negotiations leading to the parliamentary Union Castlereagh's work was not limited to the struggle for the incorporation of the two Parliaments. He was active in negotiations with the British government over matters such as the level at which duties were to be levied on cotton, muslins, and calicoes. In general he favoured a reduction of duties, but he believed that this process would have to be spread over a long period of time, perhaps as long as twenty years in all. He was sensitive about the impact of free trade upon Irish manufacturers, and throughout the commercial negotiations he was conscious of the need to demonstrate that the Union was not something which was being forced, regardless of opposition or misgivings, upon the Irish. Pitt authorized Castlereagh to make adjustments in the commercial arrangements in the light of his own judgement of the situation. In matters of trade the Union was the result of negotiation, not compulsion, and Castlereagh himself was determined to see that this should be so.

But even while the formal celebrations for the Union were taking place in January 1801 the Catholic question was already causing concern and disquiet among the supporters of a liberal policy. There were signs that the differences of opinion within Pitt's Cabinet were much greater than had once been assumed. At a time when they might justifiably have rested on their laurels Cornwallis and Castlereagh were distressed by indications that Pitt would have to face formidable and sustained opposition to a policy of Catholic relief, not a mere assortment of misgivings among the more conservative members of his administration. There was no respite for Castlereagh. Even when the Union had been finally carried in June 1800 there had been awkward wrangles over promotions in the Irish peerage and the necessary new creations in the peerage of the United Kingdom. It had been both discreet and expedient for Castlereagh and his father to waive Lord Londonderry's claims to a British peerage. But it soon became evident that the creation of the United Kingdom of Great Britain and Ireland, with twenty-eight representative Irish peers and four Irish bishops in the Lords and 100 Irish M.P.s in the Commons, was only the prelude to further exhausting political conflicts.

Castlereagh and Cornwallis had both been anxious for some months about the way in which the British government might choose to handle the Catholic issue. They had already had to exercise considerable pressure to compel the British ministers to honour a number of pledges given to individuals during the Union negotiations regarding the award of peerages. On 18 June 1800 Castlereagh had expressed himself with emphatic force when writing to Camden about the need for the British government to honour its Irish commitments and support its Irish ministers:

If the Irish government is not enabled to keep faith with the various individuals who have acted upon a principle of confidence in their honour, it is morally impossible . . . that either Lord Cornwallis or I can remain in our present situations: the moment it is surmised that we have lost the confidence and support of the English government, we shall have every expectant upon our backs, and it will remain a breach of faith, as injurious to the character of government as to our own, having given an assurance which we were not enabled to fulfil.[31]

How much more these same misgivings applied to the Catholic question. Cornwallis was deeply uneasy. On 8 October 1800 he wrote to General Ross:

I cannot help entertaining considerable apprehensions that our Cabinet will not have the firmness to adopt such measures as will render the Union an efficient advantage to the empire. Those things which, if now liberally granted, might make the Irish a loyal people, will be of little avail when they are extorted on a future day. I do not, however, despair.[32]

It was, nevertheless, thought necessary to send Castlereagh over to London to have direct discussions with the government, and on 17 December 1800 he sailed for England.

Castlereagh and Cornwallis knew that George III was unhappy about concessions to the Catholics, but, like Pitt, they hoped that a sufficiently united Cabinet would enable the government to persuade the King that Catholic relief was politically expedient and constitutionally viable. George III's serious-mindedness was undeniable. The King believed that to admit Catholics to the political nation would be a violation of his coronation oath. It was tragic that the King's conscientious scruples should be exploited by Lord Loughborough, the Lord Chancellor, who used his position as the keeper of the King's conscience to alert George's suspicions of what Pitt was planning, and to stiffen his resistance to his minister's proposals. The King was shocked that the Catholic issue had been so widely discussed within the administration. As men realized the depth of George III's antagonism to Catholic emancipation and his resentment at the way in which Pitt had handled the question, so the more cautious members of the government, such as Addington, began to slip over to the conservative side. If there had seemed some chance of carrying Catholic relief without a prolonged or bitter struggle they would have acquiesced in it, but they were unprepared to stake their political future on such a question, or to risk the consequences of challenging the King and the Lord Chancellor, backed as they were by so many of the backbench members of the House of Commons.

Castlereagh admitted the need for prudence in dealing with the Catholic issue. He neither desired nor expected any hasty or precipitate approach to the question. But it was one thing to accept cautious delay; it was another to face committed and vehement opposition to the principle of granting Catholic relief, when the hopes and expectations of the Irish Catholics had been roused by the Union. Cornwallis and Castlereagh were sensitive to anything which smacked of betrayal or deception on their part. They had been careful not to make any formal promise that the Union would be immediately followed by emancipation. Throughout they had tried to balance a respect for the political difficulties of the British government with a concern for the feelings of the Irish Catholics. But there was no doubt that the impression had been sustained that Union would make Catholic emancipation more likely, and it was therefore ominous to learn that the obstacles to relief were greater than had originally been anticipated.

Castlereagh had told Cornwallis that the British Cabinet was sympathetic to the principle of emancipation, despite the doubts that were entertained about the admission of Catholics to the highest public offices. The likely opposition of the King had also been recognized, though it was hoped that by tactful management the effects of this could be minimized. It had even been thought proper for the British Cabinet's interest in the notion of Catholic relief to be intimated to leading Catholics in Ireland, even when no precise commitment had been given as to the timetable of reform. But what had been true in the autumn of 1800 was ceasing to be so at the turn of the year. Both Cornwallis and Castlereagh recognized that the type of opposition which Loughborough represented, and which was fanning the flames of both royal and popular prejudice against Catholic relief, had transformed the situation. Not only did it expose Pitt to political embarrassment and possible defeat, it jeopardized all hope of emancipation and undermined the confidence of Irish Catholics in the good faith of the British government. The inner conflicts which were putting new stresses and strains on Pitt's Cabinet were too sophisticated for public opinion in Dublin to follow: the simple knowledge that the principle of Catholic emancipation was being attacked by prominent and influential British politicians would shatter whatever trust existed between the Catholics of Ireland and the British government.

On 1 January 1801 Castlereagh composed a long letter to Pitt, in which he told him of his misgivings, as well as going over the controversy to that date. He was careful to say that Cornwallis had expected some disagreement within the British Cabinet on the Catholic issue, and considerable caution about the way in which any change in the Test Laws would be introduced in the British Parliament. What had not been expected was that members of the government would declare themselves opposed to Catholic relief on principle (as distinct from the timing of such a measure) and express their determination to oppose any concession to the Catholics in the future. Castlereagh insisted that he had not misrepresented the views of the British government, as he had been made aware of them on his earlier visits to London for consultations in 1799 and 1800. He could not recall 'any direct objection stated against the principle of the measure by any one of the ministers', and so far from serious hesitations being entertained about the principle of relief there had even been discussions about the advisability of an immediate declaration being made to the Catholics undertaking to grant relief once the Union was carried and a peace with France signed. Despite all the caution which had surrounded the Catholic question during the controversy over the Union there had never been any suggestion that Pitt's Cabinet would be publicly divided, with various ministers standing forth as recalcitrant opponents of emancipation. He recognized the very qualified nature of the government's commitment to relief. Peace with France was a necessary pre-condition of the Catholic issue being taken up, and even a carefully qualified public commitment had been felt to be injudicious before the Union was accomplished. Castlereagh recalled that any idea of a public declaration on the Catholic question, however hesitant, had been set aside because of fears that it would alienate Protestants, both in Britain and Ireland, without bringing any commensurate benefit to Catholics; but though no direct assurance had been given to the Catholics Castlereagh was anxious lest the initiative on the Catholic issue would pass to the Whig opposition, a turn of events which would be disastrous for the good standing of the government in Ireland, and which Cornwallis viewed with particular uneasiness. Even when Loughborough's opposition had become known this had not of itself been taken to mean that there was no prospect of Catholic emancipation being carried.[33]

Castlereagh was therefore distressed at the evidence that the Catholic issue was more divisive than had been anticipated. He told Cornwallis of Loughborough's opposition and of what it meant in heartening the opponents of relief. Both Cornwallis and Castlereagh realized that the situation had worsened to an alarming extent, although they hoped that despite Loughborough's treachery all was not lost. They both believed that emancipation was necessary for the well-being of the country and for the ultimate success of the Union in healing Anglo-Irish hostility and resentment. However informal their commitment during the negotiations with Catholics over the Union they felt bound to honour the expectations they had roused. Castlereagh went out of his way to convey to Pitt the degree to which any abandonment of the Catholic cause would reflect upon Cornwallis's public standing and personal confidence:

You will easily conceive that, in addition to the public regret his Excellency will experience at the abandonment of a measure which he considers to be essential to the future interests of the empire, he will feel a peculiar degree of pain on finding himself placed in those awkward circumstances with respect to the Catholics, to which he foresaw the transaction in itself was so likely to lead, and which he took every possible precaution to avoid.[34]

As the guns in Dublin fired off their salutes on 1 January 1801 and the new Union Flag was hoisted on public buildings, Cornwallis grieved over the prospect that 'the evil genius of Britain' would induce the British Cabinet to continue the proscription of Catholics. The Catholics remained quiet because they still hoped for the repeal of the old laws which barred them from public life, but if they were disappointed Cornwallis expected the worst, and, if Pitt were thwarted and if he were driven to resignation, both Castlereagh and Cornwallis felt themselves bound in honour to follow him.

The King made his own position clear at a levee on 28 January. He approached Dundas in some excitement, and, pointing a finger at Castlereagh, he exclaimed: 'What is it that this young Lord has brought over and which they are going to throw at my head? I shall reckon any man my personal enemy who proposes any such measure. The most Jacobinical thing I ever heard of!' Dundas replied that the King would find among those who were friendly to such a measure some he had never supposed his enemies, but George III was in no mood to discuss the finer distinctions of political morality. He blurted out that he wanted no 'Scotch metaphysics' and made it plain that if his ministers thought they could soothe his ruffled feelings by special pleading they were deceiving themselves. Once the issue became a matter of public controversy the balance of opinion swung emphatically against emancipation. Portland, Chatham, Auckland, Westmorland and Liverpool all moved into the Protestant camp. Addington, the Speaker of the House of Commons, emerged as a possible Prime Minister. The entire strategy on which Pitt had based his plans for Catholic emancipation had foundered disastrously. Pitt no longer believed it right to stay in office if he was incapable of carrying Catholic relief. There was no alternative but resignation. In

March 1801 Pitt left office. Grenville, Dundas, Windham, Spencer and Camden followed him, and the two architects of the Union with Ireland, Cornwallis and Castlereagh, also joined their leader in giving up their offices. Victory over the Union had been followed by humiliation and defeat on an issue which they believed was inextricably bound up with the success of the Union they had worked so hard to achieve.

At one time Pitt's resignation was seen as little more than a ruse, retirement on the Catholic question being merely the pretext to cloak the resignation of a minister who had failed in war and who could not bring himself to make peace with the French. But there is now a much greater appreciation of the pressures and political considerations which made Pitt's decision comprehensible and creditable, however much it was to be regretted. Pitt was not a modern Prime Minister, with a dependable majority in the House of Commons committed to supporting him wherever he led. His personal following in the House was small, being rarely more than about fifty strong, and despite his long years in office he had neglected to build up a party pledged primarily to himself. His traditionalist outlook on constitutional matters, and his belief that he was before everything else a loyal servant of the Crown, made him a poor party leader. He had, after all, come into power as the King's choice as first minister, and the victory of 1784, dramatic though it had been, was as much a triumph for George III as it had been for Pitt. Pitt's respect for the constitutional position of the King led him to defer to the King's will, and he was always dubious about anything which smacked of imposing a policy upon the King in a way which violated the legitimate rights of the Crown.

The Catholic question posed special difficulties for Pitt in his dealings with the King. Pitt knew of George III's religious prejudices: there was nothing surprising about the antagonism shown by the King to Catholic relief, for he had always been a staunch and loyal Anglican, distrustful of Popery and determined to maintain the Protestant establishment as set up by the Revolution Settlement. It was his knowledge of the King's prejudices which made Pitt decide that only when the Catholic question had been thrashed out in the Cabinet would it be expedient to approach the King on the issue. A united Cabinet might have been able to persuade the King that concessions to the Catholics were not a violation of his coronation oath; a divided Cabinet had no chance with George III. Here Loughborough was the crucial figure. If the Lord Chancellor had given the King advice which made it clear that Catholic emancipation was consistent with the maintenance of the Protestant establishment, and that in the context of the United Kingdom concessions to the Catholics were an additional security for the established Church in Ireland, there might have been some hope of George III acquiescing in what his ministers believed was in the national interest.

But when Loughborough presented the King with powerfully argued memoranda taking up an anti-emancipation position Pitt was placed in an intolerable predicament. Loughborough did not create the King's convictions, but he made sure that there was no chance of those convictions being softened in discussion with Pitt and the other ministers of the Crown. Pitt was right in concluding that after the events of 28 January there was no prospect of carrying a measure of Catholic relief. The Protestant susceptibilities of the House of Commons were as raw and as sensitive as those of the King, and without royal support there was little hope of overcoming them. Given Pitt's commitment to the Catholic cause he had no choice but to leave office. Nor was the threat of resignation a useful weapon in Pitt's armoury. Once George III knew that he had an alternative Prime Minister in Addington, and that many members of Pitt's administration were prepared to serve under him, Pitt's resignation was welcome. It no longer contained any terrors for the King. He had his alternative government, and, in his view, the Protestant establishment was saved.

George III parted with Pitt with remarkable indifference, but Pitt was still moved by feelings of affection and respect towards the King. When George III had another bout of serious illness he exploited Pitt's feelings by accusing his former minister of bringing on his breakdown by raising the Catholic issue. Subjected as he was to emotional blackmail by his sovereign Pitt promised never again to raise the Catholic question during the King's lifetime. This pledge has often been criticized as a sentimental gesture made to a stubborn old man, and it has sometimes been cited as evidence that Pitt was contemplating an early return to office. But Pitt neglected to build up his following in opposition. He had little heart for systematic opposition, and he offended George Canning by giving general support to the Addington administration. He approved the peace negotiations with France: unlike Burke he had never regarded negotiations with the French Republic as unthinkable under any circumstances. Pitt believed that a politician had to work within a framework of accepted conventions and that he had to come to terms with political realities. His promise to the King seemed little more than a recognition of the inescapable. The King's opposition to Catholic relief was unshakeable. It was also popular. But since the King was ageing fast there was the consolation that before long the question would be raised again, when George IV had succeeded his father. No one thought that both Pitt and Fox would be dead long before the King, and as George III's health deteriorated many men felt that it was improper to do anything which would distress the King and bring on another attack of his disorder. Nor was it clear that the Catholics would benefit in any way by a refusal to give the King the assurance he sought. Pitt sensed that the conversion of the Lords and the Commons would be a longer and more complex task than he had originally thought. He can be criticized, not for recognizing defeat when it came, but for being too optimistic in the early stages of the crisis.

Castlereagh tried to put his own thoughts on the Catholic controversy in order. Resignation was the inevitable outcome, given the support which had rallied round the King and the erosion of the pro-Catholic party in the Cabinet. Castlereagh believed that Pitt and his friends had no alternative to resignation. They had believed that 'a system of comprehension' was essential for the future stability and prosperity of the United Kingdom and for the Union to bring about the benefits for which they had hoped. For two years, despite all their caution about specific pledges, they had allowed the Catholics to assume that the Union would lead, before very long, to emancipation. But the attitude of the King made it impossible for Pitt to accept temporary frustration on the Catholic issue while carrying on in office until times were more propitious. The government was too divided for its credibility to be unimpaired. Emancipation was clearly impossible in 1801, but the ministers could not be held responsible for a breach of the spirit in which the Union had been negotiated.

It is significant that Castlereagh believed that if Pitt was to work effectively towards the achievement of Catholic emancipation he would have to place himself at the head of a party. Both Canning and Castlereagh agreed on this point, but they chose to implement their beliefs in different ways. When it became evident that Pitt had no intention of becoming a party leader Castlereagh accepted the facts of the situation and agreed to serve under Addington. But he remained a Pittite in conviction and temperament: the service of the state took precedence over the claims of party. Unlike Canning he made no attempt to force Pitt's hand. Nor did Castlereagh regard it as necessary for Pitt to insist on Catholic relief as a condition of his taking office again. He thought that if Pitt insisted on such a pledge being given it would give some credibility to the notion that Pitt had exploited the question merely to get out of office at a difficult moment. His resignation was ample proof of his sincerity, but he would be making a grievous error if he committed himself too narrowly for the future. He would be wiser to continue to argue the case for relief, while recognizing that it would only become a question of current politics when circumstances had changed for the better. Pitt and his friends would gain nothing, either for the Catholics or for themselves, if they tried to make the Catholic issue the primary question of the day. Even when they left office Pitt and his colleagues had been anxious lest the Catholics should play into the hands of their enemies: any resort to violence or insurrection would confirm the assertions made by opponents of emancipation. Good conduct was bound to help the cause in the long run.

Castlereagh tried to convince the Catholics of the extent to which he and his friends were committed to their cause. Whenever it was practicable to reopen the controversy they would be able to rely on the goodwill and support of those who had left office with Pitt. But nothing would be gained by 'a hopeless attempt at this moment to force it on', just as unconstitutional behaviour by the Irish Catholics would help their foes. Yet, even while giving Catholics these assurances, Castlereagh felt compelled to emphasize that a change of mind by the King was unlikely. No 'solid ground of hope' could be held out of any such event taking place in the foreseeable future. The King's death was the only solution to the difficulty, and this was something which all parties to the dispute deprecated. 'The prospect', Castlereagh confessed to Cornwallis in February 1801, 'is, therefore, not very encouraging in itself,' but it was necessary to convince the Catholics that their interests and their public duty alike would be better consulted by 'temperate and loyal conduct' than 'by giving way to the feelings connected with disappointment and despair'.[35] He had no doubt as to the principles which should guide the Catholics in their response to a frustrating situation, but there was considerable uncertainty as to the extent to which they would be generally acted upon.

Castlereagh's commitment to the Catholic cause was sincere and honourable, but throughout the crisis he had acted as a responsible politician, not a rash idealist. He consistently sought to relate his principles to the limits imposed by political realities. He hoped for a particular outcome, but he knew that the means by which it was likely to be accomplished were conditioned by circumstances outside his control. Principle and expediency both influenced his conduct, and both were assessed in the light of a sober analysis of the context in which he was working. He did not believe that principles alone could transform the harsh world of political negotiation. He did not expect that even the most perceptive choice of tactics would of itself resolve the clash of conflicting interests. He experienced both triumph and defeat, and he knew that defeat meant resignation, even humiliation. But he believed that it was necessary. He owed a debt of honour to the Catholics, to Ireland, to the Union, to Pitt and to Cornwallis. He felt especially close to Cornwallis, whose feelings on the issue were so similar to his own, and whose anguish, embarrassment and disappointment he fully shared.

The Catholic question had represented a political problem which Castlereagh had hoped to solve by conventional political means. Just as the Union had involved protracted and sometimes distasteful negotiations, so the Catholic issue implied making concessions which were as much the product of necessity as of choice. Castlereagh's attitude towards the Catholic problem in Ireland sprang from his awareness of the particularities of the political situation in that country. He firmly believed that Ireland's prosperity and future development were intimately bound up with the preservation of the British connexion, and that this would be increasingly apparent as the years went by. But the Scottish Union had proved successful because it had been linked with commercial and religious concessions and a similar approach was necessary if the Irish Union was to work. In England and Scotland the established churches represented the majority of the population, but this was not so in Ireland. Much to the anger of supporters of the Protestant establishment, such as Clare, Castlereagh thought it inevitable that in dealing with a country with a Catholic majority special provisions, however distasteful to Protestants, were necessary. To admit Catholics to civil equality was essential for the security of the constitution. Without it hostility, distrust and bitterness would remain, vitiating every attempt to reconcile the two communities in Ireland. The majority of Irish Catholics would feel betrayed if the Union were to be followed by a rejection of emancipation, whether for the present or for the future. Catholics had been excluded from public office in the seventeenth century in order to preserve the constitution, but Castlereagh argued that changing circumstances had rendered their continued exclusion unnecessary. Exclusion had never been an end in itself; it had been the means whereby the constitution had been saved from the designs of James II. The relaxation of the principle of discrimination against Catholics was legitimate and necessary, as the concessions made in 1793 had demonstrated. Castlereagh believed that with the Union safely accomplished the principle could be totally abandoned, and, far from jeopardizing the constitution, this would place it on firmer foundations. It was, of course, desirable that the constitution should be preserved, but Castlereagh called for the means by which this was to be done to be adjusted to nineteenth-century conditions: the unimaginative repetition of outmoded seventeenth-century expedients would endanger the constitution, not safeguard it. The exclusion of Catholics and Dissenters from the political nation was unwise and unnecessary. In both denominations attachment to the principles of the constitution was evident. If the country was to be secured against French ideas it was essential to show that the constitution was capable of admitting both Catholics and Dissenters within its scope. Castlereagh warned that if the Catholics of Ireland were to continue to be excluded then not only would hopes of future progress be dashed but the almost certain consequence would be renewed violence and persistent disloyalty.

But even when emancipation was ruled out, at least for the immediate future, Castlereagh continued to seek means of eroding the appeal of republicanism and Jacobinism to the Catholics of Ireland. One way of doing so was to tackle the problem of tithes and to provide some means of winning the loyalty and goodwill of the Catholic clergy. Castlereagh believed that there were four major objections to the payment of tithes in Ireland. Firstly, they discouraged improvement, acting as what he called 'a bounty against cultivation'. Secondly, they were difficult to collect and uncertain in value: clergymen often found it expedient to delegate the collection of tithes to agents, and if the agents used harsh methods of collection they brought the established Church into disrepute without improving the financial position of the Anglican clergy. Thirdly, the practice of tenants offering to pay their tithes in kind simply encouraged methods of defrauding the clergy. Fourthly, all these objections were heightened in Ireland where seven eighths of the population were either Catholics or Dissenters, and where it was essential to improve the security of tenure in order to encourage tenants to improve their holdings. Castlereagh believed that the tithe problem would have to be tackled on a long-term basis. He favoured working out an agreement for, say, twenty-one years, with a monetary assessment being calculated for each type of produce liable for tithe. At the end of the stipulated period revisions of the assessment could be applied, in proportion to the value of the tithe over the previous eight years.

D

Castlereagh hoped that both Dissenting and Catholic clergymen could be paid out of state funds. But he also knew that both Dissenters and Catholics were suspicious of any system which seemed to be an unwarranted interference with the independence of their Church. The Presbyterians already received a subsidy from the Crown, the *Regium Donum*, which had been paid regularly to the Synod since 1690. By 1800 about £5,000 were paid to the Presbyterians in this way. But Castlereagh thought that it would be better if an annual grant were paid to each clergyman by name, not to the collective body of ministers or priests. This would make it clear that the appointment of ministers and priests rested with the Churches concerned, according to their own rules of Church order and discipline. Upon a minister or priest being appointed to a charge or parish it would be fitting for the authorities to be given a certificate of character and good standing by the Presbytery, in the case of the Presbyterians, and, should such a scheme be adopted for the Catholics, by the relevant bishop, the Lord Lieutenant being asked to pay the royal bounty to the clergyman who had been named. Each clergyman would receive the bounty for as long as he remained in a particular charge or parish – that is, until the Church authorities themselves arranged for his induction into another charge or deprived him of his pastoral responsibilities for disciplinary reasons of their own. Castlereagh believed that this system was particularly suitable for application to the Catholic Church in Ireland, and in his view there was the additional advantage that the Roman Church was used to arranging various systems of oversight with secular rulers in various countries. Castlereagh was convinced that Catholics had, in general, a greater respect for the principle of authority than Presbyterians, whose Church he described as republican in its forms of government, and even – at times – in its sentiments, occasionally too much so for the good temper of the authorities. He sounded out the Catholic bishops on his plans, and in a letter which he wrote to Addington on 21 July 1802, he assured him that the Catholic bishops were agreeable to the sort of financial settlement he had suggested.[36] Castlereagh guessed that the majority of Irish Catholics, both clergy and laity, were sympathetic to his scheme, but he thought it preferable that they should take the initiative in formally opening the question. But the Catholics were understandably cautious about raising the hopes of their people in the aftermath of the Union and the fall of Pitt's government: the bishops were acutely conscious of the dangers should Catholic opinion once again be disappointed. They were deeply embarrassed at the prospect of a further rebuff or failure, and Castlereagh recognized the reasons for their reserve about expressing their feelings. He appreciated that it would be essential to ensure that a measure of the type he had outlined could be enacted without trouble and without controversy before the matter was officially raised in dealings with the Catholic clergy. It would also be wrong, in his opinion, for something extra to be done for the Presbyterians without coming to some agreement with the Catholics.

Events showed that Castlereagh over-estimated the backing which the Catholic laity in Ireland were prepared to give their bishops on some compromise with the state. He was also able to achieve very little on the tithe issue, since he was too advanced on this question for most of his colleagues in the British government. Only in the 1820s was a cautious attempt made to tackle the tithes question along the lines he had suggested, and it was 1838 before a Tithe Act passed by Lord Melbourne's Whig government soothed the inflamed passions of the Irish on the issue. The Irish Catholics were suspicious of a system of state grants to their priests because they resented anything which smacked of subordinating their Church to the British Crown. Payment by the British state was also distrusted because it appeared to confirm and strengthen the ties between Britain and Ireland and the apparently final nature of the Union of 1801. The tragedy was that the Union was not only not accompanied with Catholic emancipation, decisive as that was to prove, but also that the Union was not followed up with a satisfactory solution to the tithes dispute and the problem of the payment of Catholic clergy. What must be emphasized is that Castlereagh was far-sighted and imaginative in his approach to the problems of emancipation, the tithe and the relations of Catholic and Presbyterian clergymen with the state. His perception and intelligence, his compassionate insight into the deep emotions which these questions roused, and his judicious recognition of the complexity of the decisions which the Catholic bishops, as well as British ministers, would have to make, are abundant proof that he was far from the icy reactionary of legend, shackled to a past he could not comprehend because he lacked the boldness to understand the present or the imagination to envisage the future.

He reached his conclusions by the application of a controlled and searching intelligence to political and religious problems of great complexity. He was unmoved by generalized appeals to vague feelings of benevolence or progress. The very subtlety of his approach baffled both friends and foes. He was no rhetorician, seeking by a phrase to provoke passion or devotion. He fastidiously refrained from striking public postures. But there was wisdom and charity, a breadth of vision, and a profound humanity in what he wrote and said and urged on the British government on the Catholic question, in all its aspects. Because he confined himself to the usual channels of political negotiation and discussion few had any idea of the extent to which he had involved himself in the attempt to achieve, not merely the Union of the British and Irish Parliaments, but the comprehensive reconciliation of the Catholic and Protestant communities in Ireland. He was eager to demonstrate that it was possible to meet the legitimate aspirations of the interests whose antagonisms and conflicts had so mystified British governments in the 1790s. Castlereagh did not expect either the Presbyterians of Ulster or the Catholics of Ireland to be contented with what he knew was a position of frustrating subordination. He sought to make it possible for their hopes of progress to take forms consistent with public order and political harmony. Justice was more to him than a reverence for noble ideals or appeals to woolly sentiment: it implied the judicious satisfaction of explicit political expectations. In accepting this Castlereagh believed that he was doing no more than recognizing the facts of life, but his reputation has suffered at the hands of those who glibly assume that politics consist chiefly in exhortation or the naïve enunciation of generalized moralizings, and history in the exposition of alternative developments that the past obstinately refused to take.

Castlereagh shared the dominant belief of his age and class that the British constitution was unequalled and that to it the country owed its stability, harmony and prosperity over a century of progress. It is difficult to recapture the warmth and exhilaration with which eighteenth-century Englishmen sang the glories of 1688 and the splendours of the Revolution Settlement. There was much that was fanciful and even absurd about the praises heaped on the Glorious Revolution and all that it was taken to mean for the preservation of English liberties, and the constitution was conveniently deemed responsible for everything which Englishmen thought admirable about their country. Nevertheless, it remains true that the constitution had succeeded in combining liberty and stability to an extent unequalled in any state of comparable power or prestige, and continental liberals were envious of the way in which Britain had overcome the problems of reconciling efficient government with free speech, a large measure of religious toleration, and representative institutions. Castlereagh's view of the constitution was an organic one, but he accepted the inevitability – indeed, the naturalness – of development. 'Nothing in our system is absolutely unchangeable,' he wrote in his paper on the expediency of making further concessions to the Catholics.[37] It was unfortunate that the Irish Catholics had risen in arms against legitimate authority, for this roused all the inherited distrust of Catholicism which most Britons shared, but he did not feel convinced that the majority of British Protestants wished indefinitely to uphold the principle of excluding Catholics from public life. The constitution was threatened by more potent and more recent dangers than those traditionally associated with the Church of Rome.

As in so many matters Castlereagh placed his consideration of the claims of Catholics to relief within a European context. He was never parochial in his approach to Irish problems, although this did not endear him to those Irishmen, whether Catholic or Protestant, who insisted on regarding Irish problems in a narrow and insular spirit. He deeply wanted to unify the Irish nation by getting rid of sectarian struggles. An Ireland which was freed from religious strife would be a stronger and more reliable partner within the United Kingdom. Reverence for the constitution was all very well, but at all times the constitution was subject to the overriding provision for the public good. This implied development, within a given political tradition, but development nonetheless. Castlereagh never forgot that the men of 1689 had been practising politicians, dealing as best they could with a particular series of problems. He therefore reiterated that the exclusion of Catholics from public life at the time of the Glorious Revolution had merely been the means, necessary in the circumstances of the age, by which the constitution had been secured. But by 1801 exclusion was no longer necessary for the safety of English liberties and the stability of the state. In itself, exclusion was a misfortune: it was absurd and unrealistic to view the problems facing the country as if the situation was the same as it had been during the reigns of the last two Stuart kings. Once Union had been accomplished it was folly to perpetuate the principle of exclusion as it applied to the Catholics of Ireland. Even so, Castlereagh recognized that in some respects the Catholics of Ireland had been given concessions which had not been extended to their co-religionists in Britain. But it was impossible to stand still: either the government moved forward, in a spirit of conciliation and in an effort to make the Union transmit the benefits of the constitution to the whole of the United Kingdom, or, in practical terms, it moved back.

Castlereagh believed that he had only to state the intention of thrusting Catholics back into the suppressed condition they had endured at the beginning of the eighteenth century for the absurdity of such a policy to be evident. The continued exclusion of the Catholics from the political nation – without hope of amelioration of their lot or of acceptance as equal citizens – would bring about a state of affairs which the Ultra-Protestants claimed to deplore, the increasingly close identification of Irish Catholicism with French Jacobinism. Jacobinism was the real danger to the constitution – 'the enemy of the present day', as Castlereagh put it – and the comprehension of the Catholics within the political establishment was the only way of sapping the appeal of Jacobinism and republic-anism in Ireland. Even within the narrower field of security for the established Church, both in England and Ireland, Castlereagh saw little risk in a generous measure of Catholic relief. 'So long as the King, who chooses the Ministers, is Protestant, as the great mass of the population is Protestant, I see little, if any, probability of a Catholic being called to his Majesty's counsels; or, if it should occur, I see much less probability of his being enabled to exert any influence which could be prejudicial to the Establishment.' Ideas of the British Parliament being swamped by a mass of Catholic M.P.s were fantasies, as outmoded and as futile as fears of the temporal authority of the Pope.

Castlereagh was convinced that it was imperative for the British government to take the initiative. Many of the advantages of relief would be lost if emancipation came only as a concession apparently extorted from the government by agitation and the threat of violence. 'Should the measure of concession be decided on, the advantages of it proceeding from Government will naturally suggest themselves . . . It would make Catholics in Ireland feel that their exclusion had been the necessary consequence of a separate Constitution, and that their advantages have arisen out of an incorporation with Great Britain.' The Union had removed an impediment to a better system, but it would do little by itself. It had to be followed up. Reform was not synonymous with weakness.

In addition to the steady application of authority in support of the laws, I look to the measure which is the subject of the above observations, to an arrangement of tithes, and to a provision for the Catholic and Dissenting Clergy, calculated in its regulations to bring them under the influence of the State, as essentially necessary to mitigate, if it cannot extinguish faction; to place the Established Church on its most secure foundation; and to give the necessary authority, as well as stability, to the Government itself.[38]

It may be objected that Castlereagh was attempting the impossible, the conciliation of the Irish with consequential security for the establishment. But to assume that such an aim was foredoomed to failure in 1801 is to indulge in superficial historical hindsight. In the circumstances of the time it was unthinkable for any British politician to contemplate the disestablishment of the Church of Ireland. Because Gladstone finally disestablished the Church of Ireland it is unwarranted to assert that this was either necessary or expedient seventy years earlier. Despite the obsession with inevitability and doom which afflicts so many of those who impose their own mythologies upon Irish history the options were not always as closed or as limited as retrospection suggests. It is hard to evaluate Castlereagh's policy because it was never tried: however attractive Castlereagh's approach to the problems of Ireland was it is impossible to be wholly confident about what might have happened had he been able to persuade a sufficient number of British politicians – and most of all, King George III – of the wisdom and practicability of his schemes. But Castlereagh was almost alone in his commitment to Ireland within British governing circles. No one else was as willing as he was to take the initiative. Because he accepted the political conventions of the day, placing the service of the state above privately preferred policies, his name has been blackened by those who ignored the depth of his devotion to Ireland and the sophistication with which he probed the complexities of Irish politics. Because others failed to share his insight, and because he lacked the political support to bring governments round to his way of thinking, his dedication and integrity have been impugned and abused. Unlike the Whigs Castlereagh could not content himself with a self-righteous detachment in futile and aloof opposition. He was too convinced of the urgency of the various problems facing British governments to opt out of the responsibilities of public life.

The failure to carry Catholic emancipation, and the depressing spectacle of Pitt's departure into uneasy opposition, reflected the constraints which the political system imposed upon reformers at the close of the eighteenth century. It is easy to assert that certain reforms ought to have been carried, that in some fashion an alternative strategy existed by which liberal policies could have been successfully implemented. But this suggestion suffers from the same failing that characterizes the parallel claim that peace with France was possible in the 1790s. Pitt and Castlereagh had no substantial and organized party to sustain them in the Commons. Opinion within the Cabinet was divided, and Pitt was acutely aware of the restrictions this imposed upon his choice of tactics. Pitt and Castlereagh were dependent on persuasion, not the resources of party discipline, for the implementation of policies which they were convinced were in the national interest. Although over the Catholic question they demonstrated a sensitivity towards extra-parliamentary opinion in so far as they had courted the goodwill of Irish Catholics over the Union they knew that British public opinion was deeply suspicious of anything which smacked of concessions to the Catholics.

The sad truth was that George III and the opponents of emancipation spoke and acted for the majority of the nation. Pitt knew only too well from his own experience that the King was by no means lacking in perception when it came to guessing what the dominant opinion was in the country at large. There was no overwhelming or irresistible reformist lobby outside Parliament. The impact of the French Revolution and the tribulations of war had made conservative M.P.s all the more sensitive towards anything that implied disturbing the balance of the constitution as it had been generally understood in the years since 1689. Castlereagh's argument, that exclusion had been the means by which the constitution had been preserved from a particular threat at a precise time rather than being a fundamental principle which was valid for all time, was historically sound and politically judicious. It was fair to both the anti-Catholic and pro-Catholic sides of the controversy. But its very impartiality meant that backbench M.P.s regarded it as a dubious type of special pleading. The only hope for success therefore lay – as Pitt had hoped – in convincing a majority within the Cabinet that emancipation was the logical and expedient sequel to the Irish Union. When he failed to carry his colleagues with him, and when waverers, such as Addington, shrank from a conflict in the light of Loughborough's conduct and the obstinacy of the King, Pitt knew that he had no hope of carrying any measure of Catholic relief. Even the famous promise which George III extorted from Pitt – that he would never again raise the Catholic issue during the King's lifetime – was little more than a sober recognition of the inescapable and distasteful facts of the situation. As long as George III lived the Catholic cause would face the opposition of the King, and as the King's health became more precarious – breakdowns occurring in 1801 and 1804 – no responsible politician could be expected to take the risk of provoking another royal collapse.

It was, therefore, understandable that Castlereagh should agree to mute the furtherance of Catholic claims, and that he should accept office under Addington in July 1802. There was nothing sinister or dishonourable in so doing. His own loyalty lay to Pitt. He remembered the encouragement he had received from Pitt and he hoped that soon Pitt would return to office. But Pitt made things difficult for his friends, especially for younger men such as Castlereagh and Canning, in the years 1801 to 1804. Pitt held aloof from active opposition. Like his father he distrusted a formed opposition, and he had no wish to stand forth in sustained opposition to the Addington ministry. Here he conformed to the political conventions of the age. He could hardly expect young men, who shared his own sense of devotion to public service, to allow a personal political loyalty to himself to prevent them taking every legitimate opportunity of furthering their own careers and widening their administrative experience. In serving under Addington Castlereagh was not abandoning Pitt. He saw Addington as a caretaker Prime Minister, but, oppressed as he was by the signs of French aggression, he believed it to be his duty to give all reasonable assistance to the government in coming to grips with the problems of war, defence and foreign policy. Even a temporary government deserved patriotic support: it was consistent both to hope for Pitt's return to Downing Street and to serve Addington in the meantime. The judicious support which Pitt gave to the Addington administration gave further sustenance to this viewpoint, and enabled Castlereagh to feel that he had not acted improperly or disloyally.

But the mere fact of Castlereagh's acceptance of office under Addington gave circumstantial support to those who alleged that he had never been wholeheartedly committed to the Catholic cause. In Ireland the subtleties of British politics and the complexities of political alignments were not appreciated. There was little patience with the turns and twists of political manoeuvre in London. Regrettably, Castlereagh's conduct enabled opponents to smear his reputation, arguing that the Union and the denial of emancipation were part of a systematic conspiracy, first to divide and then to cheat the Irish nation. Those who had seen the Dublin Parliament as a security for their own political pre-eminence resented its disappearance, and they were only too eager to cast Castlereagh in the role of arch-traitor. His reluctance to indulge in public self-justification, his controlled self-confidence in the integrity of his conduct, and his hope that in the not too distant future there might be some possibility of carrying a significant measure of Catholic relief, intensified the hatred which his embittered fellow-countrymen felt towards him. Protestants loathed him as the man who had destroyed the

Dublin Parliament and who still yearned to implement Catholic emancipation. Catholics questioned the sincerity with which he had urged their cause, and suspected that perhaps he had not tried as hard as he might have done to honour the informal undertakings he had given them during the passing of the Union.

Castlereagh was not surprised when Irish crowds bawled out songs calling for a high gallows and a windy day for Billy Pitt and Castlereagh. He had no illusions about the crudity and volatility of public opinion, and the ease with which it could be inflamed and exploited by interested and unscrupulous persons. He had never expected the Protestant hard-liners to love him, and he had always known how fickle any gratitude on the part of the Catholics was likely to prove, even if he had been successful in the struggle for Catholic relief. He had recognized that the King's triumph would automatically call in question both his own integrity and that of Pitt. Yet he was unmoved by the prospect of unpopularity. He scorned both the cheers and the jeers of the crowd. The service of the state still beckoned. He had known both success and failure, and neither could distract him from the tasks in hand. His own reputation mattered less than the public good, and he had shown that he could surmount the frustrations of defeat as well as bearing with due modesty the plaudits of victory. Undeterred by abuse and misrepresentation he calmly faced new problems in a new range of responsibilities. He had confirmed that he had the right temperament for the trials and tribulations of politics. At the moment of testing he had demonstrated his courage, his judgement, his fidelity, his determination to press on with what needed to be done. Disappointment had not deterred him; success had neither flattered nor deceived him.

But the Irish experience remained fundamental to his understanding of the nature of politics and to his sober recognition of the faults and flaws of human nature. The bitterness of sectarian strife, the rebellion of 1798, the controversy over the Union, and the defeat of Catholic emancipation ensured that he had no illusions about what a politician was likely to achieve and what he had to endure both in triumph and disaster. A sense of the fragility of political achievement and the vulnerability of good intentions became a permanent part of his public consciousness and coloured the whole of his later outlook. He retained an intense conviction of the complexity of human motivation and the consequent folly of expecting gratitude from those he sought to serve. He had a cool disdain for those who blithely talked of putting the world to rights without counting the cost in conflict and suffering. His Irish experience ensured that

Castlereagh defied the usual categories of political description. He was a reformer who prided himself upon his realism, a conservative who accepted change as the price of preserving the constitution, a Protestant who favoured Catholic emancipation, a Pittite who was prepared to serve under Addington, an Irishman who saw Ireland's destiny as inextricably bound up with the British connexion, a British statesman who appreciated the demands of British policy against a European background. In every aspect of his public career Castlereagh manifested a subtlety of perception which few politicians equalled and few contemporaries were capable of understanding. The maturity of his judgement and the sophistication of his grasp of the essentials of the statesman's craft made it all too easy for men to forget that when he accepted responsibility for the administration of Indian affairs in July 1802 he had just turned thirty-three years of age.

3

THE LEGACY OF PITT

When Castlereagh accepted the Presidency of the Board of Control he had had no experience of colonial affairs, unless it is thought appropriate to classify his Irish secretaryship under such a heading. The relationship between the British government and the East India Company was an uneasy one, and even when relations between the government and the directors of the Company were good there was always the problem of effectively controlling the Governor-General in India. In many ways Castlereagh's years at the Board of Control were frustrating ones. Although he knew greater disappointments and incurred more savage criticism later in his career, especially over the Walcheren expedition in 1809, he had considerable achievements to his credit as Secretary for War and the Colonies, but his India years were dominated by an uneasy and perplexing relationship with Lord Wellesley, the brilliant but erratic Governor-General.

On the face of things they ought to have got on well. Both were Irishmen, and Wellesley was the elder brother of Arthur Wellesley, whose career was to be so closely interwoven with that of Castlereagh. Wellesley was committed to a forward policy in India. He challenged the power of the Mahrattas and he won more territory and a greater influence for Britain and the East India Company in the Indian sub-continent. But Castlereagh was unhappy about a policy of expansion. His own interests were concentrated on the struggle with Napoleon and the problem of French expansion in Europe. There seemed to be no end to Wellesley's ambitious schemes. Though his wars against the Mahrattas were crowned with success the British government was always uncertain about what Wellesley's policies implied. Wellesley acted first and explained afterwards and the difficulties of communication and distance made it easy for him to behave with a strong and incisive awareness of his own independence. He was eager for fame and fortune. He believed that his talents were seriously undervalued at home, and he resented the efforts made to moderate his policies as futile interference by men who lacked wisdom, insight and imagination, and who were too far from the problems of India to have any conception of the immensity of his task and the tremendous opportunities which lay before him for the extension of British power in India. There were powerful arguments on both sides. The British were already heavily committed in India, and when the French sought to recover their own prestige and influence there Britain could do little other than continue to extend her own power and stabilize her own areas of supremacy. On the other hand, men such as Castlereagh, who were preoccupied with the situation in Europe and who were sceptical about the permanence of the Amiens peace settlement, were reluctant to embark on far-reaching projects of imperial expansion in India when the military and financial resources of the country were stretched to the limit by events nearer home.

Castlereagh was no imperialist: although he sought to defend British influence and prestige wherever they were threatened, he had no overall concept of empire, and he was not committed to expansion as a self-evident principle of policy. His cool mind was oblivious to any notion of empire as a transcendent ideology. Commercial advantages, the security of British nationals and the maintenance of definable British interests were the primary considerations which determined his thinking on colonial affairs. It was inevitable that he should regard Wellesley with some suspicion as an irresponsible colonial adventurer, who resented and evaded control from London, and that Wellesley, in his turn, should distrust Castlereagh as a tepid compromiser, seeking to win colonial benefits on the cheap while ignoring the dramatic gains that a policy of vigorous expansion would bring. Wellesley saw in India a great opportunity for the expansion of British power and prestige; Castlereagh was oppressed by the size of the sub-continent and the dangers of becoming too involved in the complex and apparently interminable conflicts between various Indian princes and embattled Indian peoples.

But even Wellesley came to recognize that Castlereagh had done well in a situation of immense difficulty. They had differed about the Mahratta War: nothing could disguise a significant divergence of view on that question. But Castlereagh had consistently defended Wellesley against the more irresponsible and damaging attacks made upon him by opposition M.P.s at Westminster. Castlereagh believed that whatever misgivings he entertained about policy it was his duty to defend the conduct of the Governor-General whenever it was being unfairly impugned. His Irish experience made him sensitive to the pressures bearing so heavily upon the man on the spot. The government had every right to endeavour to restrain the more extravagant of Wellesley's policies, but it was inevitable that he should be empowered to act, since no one in England could presume to control events thousands of miles away. Wellesley was sensitive and neurotic, and his great gifts were vitiated by a volatile and unpredictable temperament. But towards the end of his life he conceded the consistency which had guided Castlereagh's performance of his duties at the Board of Control, and he singled out for special commendation the way in which Castlereagh had scrupulously refrained from dabbling in Indian patronage for dubious political or personal ends. Wellesley always remembered Castlereagh's support for his scheme for the establishment of a college at Fort William for the education and training of boys sent out to India. The project was intelligent and far-sighted, but the directors of the East India Company thought it wasteful and unnecessary and ordered the college to be closed. An opportunity to improve the quality of British administration was lost, but Wellesley appreciated Castlereagh's quick insight into the benefits of the scheme and the toughness with which he had fought for the idea in his dealings with the directors of the Company.

Castlereagh was eager to improve the administration of the East

India Company's affairs, but he never lost sight of the main sphere of political conflict – Europe. He was worried about the prospects of a renewed war with France. With every day that passed he became more sceptical about the possibility of the Peace of Amiens lasting for more than a brief period of time. He reviewed the balance of power in Europe and compared the resources of Britain and France. He believed that it was necessary to contemplate the possibility of a renewal of hostilities even while hoping that peace might endure. He thought it impossible to predict the course and duration of a war. If war broke out he anticipated that it would bring about a change of government, but a long war would threaten the country's financial stability, no matter who was in office. If public opinion supported a resumption of war with France, and if the country threw itself boldly and wholeheartedly into such a conflict, he thought that war could be successfully waged for three, four, five or even ten years. But the chances of a decisive victory being won by a purely maritime strategy were remote. British sea power could strip France of her colonies, but it would not, of itself, free Europe from French domination. As long as any hope for peace remained then Castlereagh thought it right to continue with negotiations, but he thought it essential for Britain to be firm: 'Perhaps it is difficult to distinguish between the language of decision, which I think we cannot but hold, and the precise pledge which I wish to avoid. What I desire is, that France should feel that Great Britain cannot be trifled with.' But it was still important to recognize that British policy should be sufficiently flexible to respond to changing circumstances, and diplomacy would be best carried on through discreet private negotiations with the French and the other European Powers. Even at this stage of his career Castlereagh distrusted broad public commitments and dramatic parliamentary pledges: the subtlety which he believed essential to the effective practice of diplomacy was not to be lightly exposed to the crudities of passion or the vulgarizing impact of prejudice.[1]

But a suspicion of public diplomacy did not mean that Castlereagh was insensitive to the necessity for the government to justify its policies to the public. At the beginning of the war against the French Republic he had warned against the disastrous consequences in Ireland of a failure adequately to explain the reasons for British entry into the conflict: now, as the Amiens settlement was exposed as defective in its securities for peace, he affirmed that if war were resumed the causes of a resumption of hostilities would have to be fully explained to Parliament and to the British people. This was an inescapable condition for the popular support which he believed essential for the successful conduct of the war. A renewal of the war did not mean that the Peace of Amiens had been foolish or ill-advised. In making peace Britain had sought to divert the energies of France from military aggression to necessary domestic improvements. The peace had been necessary because it had proved impossible to defeat the French in war, but this did not imply that vital British interests had been ignored. Unfortunately, the British government had looked in vain for an adequate French response to the moderation with which Britain had sought to win the confidence of the French in the prospects for a better understanding between the two countries. British restrictions upon commerce with France had been removed: there had been no similar relaxation of French prohibitions upon the import of British products into France. If French policy threatened British interests war might well be the only means of securing the well-being of the United Kingdom. Any nation which showed 'a systematic spirit of interference, destructive of the independence of other States' had to be resisted. There were strong grounds for such resistance in the general law of nations, but the case for standing up to aggression was all the stronger when there had been specific violations of precise treaty obligations. It was right to use every means short of war to confine French aggression, but when Bonaparte insisted that the alternatives were the British evacuation of Malta or war, and when he further demanded that the traditional freedoms of the British press should be restricted because the British newspapers had been critical of French policy, then Bonaparte's conduct intensified the chances of a renewal of armed conflict. The humiliation of Lord Whitworth, the British ambassador in Paris, was the final provocation. In May 1803 Britain and France were once again at war.[2]

Castlereagh was concerned that Malta should not be regarded as the sole cause of the war. The dispute over Malta was merely the symptom of a more fundamental clash of interests. On 19 August 1803 Castlereagh wrote to Lord Hawkesbury saying that it would be difficult to persuade the world that Britain was not fighting for Malta alone, unless some clear general statement was made of the principles which were guiding British actions. The war was being fought for reasons of general European security, and it was imperative that the other Powers should be made aware of this fact. Castlereagh favoured making confidential approaches to Russia. He suggested that the Russians might be offered the chance of garrisoning Malta in return for accepting a British naval base in Corfu. If Britain showed that she was willing to work out the possibilities of a negotiated solution she would win the confidence of other countries which were anxious over the implications of French aggression. Britain had much to gain by demonstrating the moderation of her standpoint: 'I cannot but feel it of some importance that we should indicate a disposition to yield a portion of our own claims, with a view not only of relieving the immediate sufferings of the Continent, but, as far as means can be found, of providing for their future security.' The long-term interests of Europe should not be forgotten, but the doubt in Castlereagh's mind turned, not so much on the degree of concession which such schemes might entail, but on the misgivings which existed throughout Europe about Britain's capacity to resist Bonaparte. Offers of agreed spheres of interest would come to nothing if there were deeply felt doubts about Britain's will to resist and ability to stand up to the French. The decisive defeat of Bonaparte's invasion plans was the necessary preliminary to the creation of an effective European coalition against France.[3]

It is evident that long before he became Foreign Secretary Castlereagh saw the conduct of the war against the background of the general European situation. There was nothing confined or small-minded about his outlook. He had no illusions about the scale of the conflict or the likely duration of the war. He recognized that in order to defeat the French Britain needed continental allies, and he wanted a positive foreign policy to be exploited to the full for this purpose. He was not content simply with thwarting French invasion schemes. Just as he had placed the Irish problem within the larger framework of the United Kingdom, so he envisaged a truly European policy as the only method of winning the war, and more significantly, of providing for European security in the future. Within a few months of the breakdown of the Amiens settlement Castlereagh demonstrated his insight into the problems of European security, and even before the war was won he was anxious that British policy should take into account the best means of preventing another outbreak of armed conflict in the future.

There was nothing unrealistic about this preoccupation. Castlereagh knew that clashes of interest were inevitable in international relations. He did not dream of universal peace flowing from a general upsurge of benevolence and altruism. Peace would come into being when a satisfactory balance of interests had been struck. Diplomacy and military operations were both needed to contribute to this process, and this meant that the war would have to be fought in a particular way. Castlereagh had learned from the frustrations of the

1790s. Maritime success, however satisfying and flattering in itself, was not enough. A victorious alliance with the Powers of Europe meant entering into a new relationship with Austria and Russia, and possibly Prussia too, a relationship which would be more than a purely military alliance. Whatever bargains might be struck in order to defeat Bonaparte it was essential not to lose sight of the situation which would come into being once the war ended: victory would not solve all problems; it would almost certainly create new ones of its own. The conduct of war was subordinate to the practice of diplomacy. No matter how testing the struggle against France was, Britain could not afford to forget the constant and fundamental elements which moulded the pattern of relationships between the Powers of Europe.

Castlereagh's attitude thoughtfully combined traditional eighteenth-century notions of limited war and the primacy of diplomatic considerations over the conduct of military operations with the conclusions which he had drawn from his own experiences during the war against the French Republic. Basic to his outlook was Pitt's own primary emphasis upon British security, but Castlereagh grasped that British security had a European dimension, and this implied changes in familiar methods of warfare and a stronger commitment on Britain's part to her continental allies. Much of the vision and insight which Castlereagh showed in his conduct of foreign policy after 1812 was already evident in his reflections on the nature and practice of war as early as 1803. There was imagination in his concept of waging war, as well as a capacity for integrating diverse aspects of policy into a coherent whole. Just as he showed perception and a high level of competence as a war minister, so he related the immediate demands of the war effort to long-term issues of diplomacy and foreign policy. He was sound in principle and flexible in method, combining a profound grasp of essentials with the ability to respond to events.

Even while Britain was still threatened with invasion Castlereagh kept the need for offensive action in mind. He had no wish to stand passively on the defensive. When he became responsible for the administration of the War Department in the summer of 1805 he insisted, not only that troops should be stationed at decisive points for the defence of the country against a French invasion, but that they should also be prepared for swift transportation to other theatres of war, should the need and the opportunity arise. Some 30,000 infantry and 8,000 cavalry were stationed at Cork, Portsmouth and East Kent, and although this information was speedily communicated to Napoleon it reflected Castlereagh's eagerness to bring a more aggressive spirit to the conduct of the war.[4] He believed that allies were necessary if the war was to be won, and he knew that Pitt was seeking, painfully and laboriously, to build up a Third Coalition against France. Despite the inefficiency of early nineteenth-century military administration Castlereagh tried to improve both the numbers and the quality of troops available for active service and to ensure that they would be used in a bold and active strategy.

He also took an interest in the development of new weapons. He hoped that the French flotillas at Boulogne might be destroyed by launching rockets from small craft. He took a keen personal interest in experiments with rockets and primitive torpedoes, and he was sufficiently impressed with the results to write to Nelson with some enthusiasm about them. On 27 October 1805, writing before the news of Trafalgar and Nelson's death had reached England, he reported on the performance of the new weapons: 'By the application of a sufficiency of cork, to correct the weight of the carcass, and to render it liable to the influence of the tide, it was, in the late experiment, so balanced as to be at once swept under the vessel, and consequently was placed in immediate contact with and under her bottom. The explosion taking place at the moment to which the lock was adjusted, it blew the ship into fragments, as your lordship will see from the enclosed official report.'[5] The technical limitations of such weapons in the age of sail were too great to allow any decisive breakthrough in the technology of war, but since Castlereagh is still frequently despised as an unimaginative defender of the *status quo*, a man incapable of venturing beyond the familiar and the conventional, it is worth emphasizing that he had a shrewd appreciation of what might be achieved by the application of technology to the invention and manufacture of the weapons of war.

Like Pitt Castlereagh was deeply distressed by Nelson's death, but he did not allow his grief to blind him to the possibilities of taking the offensive which the victory of Trafalgar opened up. In November he told Collingwood that although the urgency of an operation against the Spanish ports had been lessened by Nelson's victory there were still good reasons for examining such a plan in all its details, providing that it did not interfere with projects of a greater magnitude.[6] He was also interested in dispatching expeditions to the Cape of Good Hope, and, once Austria had entered the war, to the Elbe, in the hope of making a decisive contribution to the German theatre of operations. He hoped to form a British expeditionary force under the command of the Duke of York, and that, by the beginning of 1806, 60,000 men would be available for service in Europe. He was constantly on the alert for any chance of seizing the initiative from Napoleon.[7]

Castlereagh recognized the all-important principle of the concentration of effort in war. On 23 December he emphasized the point in unmistakable style in a letter to Lord Cathcart: 'The wisdom of making a great effort against the French, in the first instance, in Germany, does not admit of a question; and, as a general proposition, it is certainly better policy to be exposed, for a time, in certain quarters, than, by attempting to defend all points, to be powerful and successful in none.'[8] But purely military considerations were not the only factors in Castlereagh's mind. British intervention in Germany might well influence Prussia and bring her into the war on the side of the allies. Since the French were concentrating their forces in southern Germany, British intervention in northern Germany would have an impact out of all proportion to the size of the forces engaged. Unhappily, the means for carrying out these ambitious and imaginative plans did not exist in sufficient strength. George III was anxious about the fate of Hanover, but he was cautious about the over-commitment of British and Hanoverian troops, and British military opinion was apprehensive about the possible loss of an expeditionary force. Small as such an army was, by continental standards, it was nevertheless irreplaceable. Castlereagh himself confessed that British operations on the continent were dependent on keeping an army in being and on extricating it from any catastrophe which Britain's allies might suffer. The defence of the United Kingdom and the successful resumption of offensive operations when the time was ripe were both conditional upon an expeditionary force being recalled to Britain whenever circumstances justified such a step.

In addition to the problems of fighting the French Castlereagh had had to grapple with the complexities of a confused political situation. The Addington ministry finally collapsed in April 1804, but Pitt found it difficult to form an administration. He had hoped for an all-party coalition, but his pleas to the King to accept Fox as Foreign Secretary failed to move George III, who remained obstinately opposed to the admission of Fox to the ministry. Fox was willing to stand down, suggesting to his friends that they take office without him, but this they refused to do. Consequently, instead of being a broadly based national government, suitable for the crisis of war, Pitt's second administration looked more like a caretaker government. Although Addington himself came back into the government in January 1805 as Lord President, he resigned at the end of June. There was considerable tension between the friends of Pitt and those who had been happy to support Addington as Prime Minister in 1801. Confidence in the government was further shaken by the vote in the House of Commons to impeach Pitt's close friend and faithful colleague, Lord Melville, on charges of corruption. The victory of Trafalgar raised public morale, though even here Nelson's death meant that the celebrations of his greatest victory were muted by grief at the loss of Britain's greatest admiral. Pitt's health was shattered. Too much depended upon him, and Napoleon's victory over the Austrians and Russians at Austerlitz confirmed the premonitions of doom which Mack's capitulation at Ulm had inspired. When Pitt died in the early hours of 23 January 1806 his ministry broke up. George III submitted to the Ministry of All the Talents, a strange alliance of Foxites and Grenvillites, hopeful of negotiating a peace with France and thus demonstrating that the war was as unnecessary as it had been unfortunate.

Pitt's death meant that Castlereagh left office. Private grief was compounded by political disaster. Like most of the younger men who had served under Pitt Castlereagh looked to Pitt as his political mentor and leader. It was to Pitt that he owed his rise to eminence. He had earned the older man's confidence and esteem by his conduct in Ireland, and no one could ever replace Pitt in Castlereagh's affections. But Pitt's legacy to his disciples was a mixed and ambivalent inheritance. There had never been a well-organized Pittite party. The confusions over the resignation of Pitt and the appointment of Addington had revealed many differences of opinion among men who had all regarded Pitt as the embodiment of a patriotic independence in politics. During Addington's ministry Pitt had neglected to build up his supporters in the House of Commons, for which he was vehemently criticized by Canning. Like his father Pitt relied on the force of his own personality to carry him through, but this was no longer enough. After 1801 the Pittites were divided amongst themselves. Some, like Castlereagh, were willing to serve under Addington and to recognize that for as long as the King lived there was little prospect of carrying any significant measure of Catholic relief. Others, such as Canning, held ostentatiously aloof from Addington, whom they resented as the cause of Pitt's discomfiture and the chief obstacle to his return to office. The fall of Addington had failed fully to reunite the Pittites. Pitt could not make up his quarrel with his cousin, Grenville, and when Pitt died all the dissensions among his followers were once again exposed. There was no recognized successor to Pitt. Men such as Liverpool and Castlereagh were not regarded as possible first ministers, and there was no obvious leader in opposition. No one could guess that the Talents would prove one of the most uniformly futile ministries in English history. Only the failure of their opponents allowed the Pittites to return to power sooner than they had expected, and perhaps earlier than some of them desired.

A number of men could claim to represent those attitudes which had been so closely associated with Pitt. A patriotic dedication to winning the war, a commitment to administrative competence and prudent reform, a scepticism concerning formed opposition and organized party, could all be cited as proof of a politician's Pittite credentials, although not all who staked a claim to wear Pitt's mantle were identified with all the assumptions which had governed his political conduct. The divisions among the Pittites reflected his own reluctance to establish his following on a party basis and the traditional suspicions he had entertained towards formed opposition and party politics. Pitt was a man of government: it was in office, not out of it, that he hoped to infuse his disciples with a distinctive political style and a recognizable political allegiance. Castlereagh had no doubt that to go into a factious opposition to Fox and Grenville was 'unpolitic and unbecoming'. It would have been a denial of all that Pitt had stood for. But this did not exempt Pittites from asking whether in certain circumstances it might be proper to take office with Grenville or, alternatively, whether they would be right to take the initiative in bringing the government down. Castlereagh was apprehensive about the effect upon his fellow Pittites of going into opposition. By temperament and experience they were attuned to office, to the practice of administration and to the exercise of the arts of political management. Although committed to the prosecution of the war against France they were not motivated by ideological convictions. Many of the most promising of the Pittites – Castlereagh and Canning among them – were sympathetic to Catholic emancipation, but this was not a powerful bond, differentiating them from their political opponents and uniting them with each other. The Pittites lacked anything really equivalent to the powerful mythology which was so characteristic of the Foxite Whigs. Fox's friends invoked his advocacy of peace, his defence of civil and religious liberties, and (rather more ambiguously) his support for parliamentary reform as the hallmarks of their party. The experience of office was depressing for the Whigs but they had the convenient alibi that once again they had fallen foul of the anti-Catholic prejudices of

George III, and though the notion of an alternative foreign policy was no more than wishful escapist thinking after 1807 the cry of peace and reform allowed the Whigs to retain their identity. Even Grenville, whose misgivings about the war were largely financial and the expression of a growing pessimism about politics generally, felt under no obligation to address himself to the real needs of policy-making after the Talents fell from power. But in so far as the Pittites had a mythology at all it was associated with fighting the war to a finish. Canning was responsible for popularizing the legend that Pitt was the pilot who weathered the storm, and although many historians have been sceptical about Pitt's credibility as a great war leader there is no doubt that after his death he became the symbol of the national will to resist, of the confidence that ultimately every trial would be surmounted and victory crown all the sacrifices which had been made in the cause of defending the constitution and the liberties of Europe against the aggressions of republican and imperial France.

While the Talents struggled on towards final dissolution Pitt's followers showed that while they were united by a common sentiment they were divided by the exigencies of politics. Canning never hesitated to cast himself as the political heir of Pitt, and he was impatient about the hesitancy shown by many other Pittites. Others sought to find a patriotic compromise between the pull of opposition and a respect for Pitt's Chathamite assumptions about party loyalty and the service of the state: Canning staked out his own claims to pre-eminence. He was admired but distrusted. Men were impressed by his energy, moved by his rhetoric, and dazzled by his ability to exploit the passions of the House of Commons and fire the enthusiasm of the people. But they remained dubious about his integrity, suspicious of his motives, distressed by his apparent duplicity, and disdainful about his antecedents. He had a touch of genius, but he was not what most M.P.s considered a gentleman. Despite the legend of the liberal, far-sighted Canning, there were sounder grounds for contemporary distrust than there were for Victorian respect. Canning escaped much of the odium which came to be associated – however unjustly – with the Liverpool administration, but he was in reality hardly more liberal than Castlereagh was. Canning supported Catholic emancipation, but no more loyally than Castlereagh. He was not a parliamentary reformer and he had no illusions about the need to deal firmly with domestic disorder or civil strife. Canning sympathized with nationalist movements in a way which Castlereagh did not, but he allowed this sympathy to influence policy only when he could advance or secure the interests of Britain by doing so. The contrast between Canning and Castlereagh has often been overplayed. Castlereagh wished to establish an effective Concert of Europe as a guarantee for peace, but he was not opposed to judicious liberalization if this could be accomplished without jeopardizing international stability. But legend could not discriminate between Canning's bolder pursuit of policies which were not too far removed from those of Castlereagh, and Castlereagh's own more cautious acceptance of continental involvement. The popular version of the Canning and Castlereagh rivalry merely confirmed Sir Herbert Butterfield's assertion that trenchant history deals in half-truths. The whole truth is more favourable to Castlereagh than legend, without being unfair to Canning.

At no other time might Castlereagh's reputation have been advanced more easily by a willingness to indulge in sentimental rhetoric than in the fifteen months after the death of Pitt. But he could not bring himself to exploit the political situation in such a fashion. Sceptical as he was about the credibility of the Talents, and the likelihood of the ministry achieving the objectives on which it had set its heart, he was nevertheless bound by principle, training and a sense of public honour to refrain from indulging in the excesses of opposition. He might have exaggerated his disagreements with the ministry, but he believed it wrong to do so. The Talents had to run their course. Once they were tested by events he was convinced that the falsity of their presuppositions would be exposed for all to see. But he could not take the lead in trying to force himself and his colleagues back into office. He could only hold himself in readiness to serve, should he once again be called upon to do so. He was determined to do nothing that could be interpreted as condoning a factious and irresponsible opposition.

The rivalry between Castlereagh and Canning owed much to these years, when they were both out of office as disciples of Pitt and when, if the Whigs had proved their competence in government, they might have ended their careers as men of promise who failed to find a path to fulfilment. The contrast in personality was obvious: Canning brilliant and effervescent, a man of agility and opportunism, Castlereagh a dull though effective speaker, a man of tenacity and controlled self-discipline. But there was also a contrast in outlook. However much he revered the spirit of Pitt Canning was impatient to go beyond the conventions which had determined Pitt's attitude towards the management of Parliament and the cultivation of opinion. Castlereagh more truly reflected the administrative strain in the Pittite legacy. He was at his best in office, in the patient and undemonstrative reduction of a complexity of detail to the semblance of a policy, and he was at his most convincing, not in public debate or controversy, but in Cabinet deliberations. Men saw Canning as a man of ready words, but they did not altogether trust him. They saw Castlereagh as a man who was less scintillating in debate, but whose word they could instinctively depend upon. It was a contrast between a man who saw politics as a contest for public favour as well as political place, and a man who still distrusted the popular element in political controversy and whose primary aim was neither the gratification of ambition nor the cheers of the crowd, but the sober service of the state.

Castlereagh watched the collapse of the Talents with the calm resignation of a man who saw his expectations justified by events. He had never believed that a negotiated peace would be speedily achieved, and when the negotiations spluttered out in recrimination and disgust, with the British deeply resentful of what they considered to be the duplicity of the French, Castlereagh could only hope that men would draw the inescapable conclusion that there was no immediate prospect of an early end to the war. The death of Charles James Fox on 13 September 1806 removed the ministry's most magnetic and attractive figure. But it was another attempt to carry a measure of Catholic relief which destroyed the Whigs. Grenville urged that Catholics should be permitted to hold commissioned rank in the British army, but the ministry could not reach agreement as to whether or not this implied appointment only up to the rank of colonel or to the higher ranks as well. The squabble that followed was made more complex by the King's insistence that, once the abortive measure was withdrawn, his ministers should promise never to re-introduce any measure of Catholic relief. Grenville was no more willing to give such a pledge than he had been in 1801, and in March 1807, rather than yield what they believed to be a point of principle, the Whigs resigned. Fox had warned about the dangers of prematurely raising the Catholic question when they had taken office: his misgivings were amply confirmed. But it would be misleading to suggest that only George III's prejudices destroyed the ministry. There is some evidence that the King hoped to keep his ministry together, despite his determination to stand firm on the Catholic issue, and the ministers had only themselves to blame when Grey and Sidmouth took different sides in public controversy over the precise degree of relief which the government measure implied.

The fall of the Talents created a situation of extreme difficulty which was finally resolved by the formation of a ministry under the Duke of Portland. The Pittites returned to power as a consequence of the foolishness of their rivals. Canning gained the glamorous post of Foreign Secretary, but Castlereagh's return as Secretary for War and the Colonies was generally welcomed. He had already established a reputation as a capable military administrator during Pitt's second ministry. During the Portland administration he achieved great things in the organization of the British war effort and the improvement of army recruitment. It was unfortunate that the tragedy of the Walcheren expedition should cast doubts on the magnitude of his achievement, and that the smouldering rivalry with Canning should finally flare up into open hostility, political treachery, and the public climax of the duel between the two men. The years 1807 to 1809 were more than a prelude to Castlereagh's foreign secretaryship. They were the years in which he demonstrated that he was one of the greatest of British war ministers. Legend has obscured these years with misrepresentation and misunderstanding, but modern research has firmly revealed the scope and comprehensiveness of Castlereagh's greatness as a military administrator. He combined a thorough insight into the nature of the war and a broad conception of the principles of grand strategy with a command of the minutiae of administration. He never lost sight of the importance of the German theatre of operations but he grasped earlier than most men the potentialities of the Iberian Peninsula as an area in which Napoleon could be effectively challenged and successfully resisted. The achievements of his years at the Foreign Office owed much to the lessons he took to heart at the War Department.

The war was going badly when Castlereagh resumed ministerial responsibilities. Not only had the attempt to negotiate a peace with France failed ignominiously; throughout Europe Napoleon's armies were supreme. Prussia was defeated at Jena in October 1806: the myth of Prussian military glory was brutally destroyed. Austria had been smashed at Austerlitz, and though the Russians fought stubbornly at Eylau in February and at Friedland in June, 1807, the meeting of Napoleon and the Russian Emperor Alexander I at Tilsit in July confirmed the hegemony of the French Empire in central and western Europe. Britain stood alone, yet she could only fight on. Victory was remote, but surrender was unthinkable.

The chief problem for the British government was the recruitment of a sufficient number of men to ensure that the country was adequately defended while allowing sufficient provision for the formation of an expeditionary force, should some opportunity of intervening on the mainland of Europe present itself. Everyone knows the Duke of Wellington's famous comment to the effect that his army was composed of 'the scum of the earth' who had 'enlisted for drink'. In all essentials Wellington's statement was a bald recognition of the unpalatable facts. In all ranks of society there was considerable hostility towards the regular army. Enlisting as a soldier was all too often the last resort of the ne'er-do-well, of young men evading the consequences of fathering bastards, or of petty criminals seeking to avoid detection and punishment. What was surprising was not the brutality of army discipline, but what it achieved in creating effective military units out of the scrapings of society. The army also suffered from the habitual stinginess of British governments in all matters of military expenditure. The notion of conscription was abhorrent to traditional ideas of freedom, and, at a time when the French were conquering Europe with conscript armies, the British remained opposed to the principle of compulsory military service. They preferred the chances of the press-gang to the certainties of conscription. The army had to make do with what it could get, whether the sweepings of the jails, or the providential successes of able recruiting sergeants and the happy patriotism of those who chose – despite everything – to volunteer. The most the public could be brought to accept was the ballot for service in the militia, and Castlereagh exploited this to good effect, especially when he strengthened the regular army by transfers of volunteers from the militia.

When Castlereagh took office the situation was chaotic. Windham had confused an already bewildering situation by carrying an ineffective Act to impose a period of twenty-four days compulsory military training upon the male population (though he had been unable to explain how this would work). He had suspended the ballot for the militia, and he had allowed the volunteers to run down, so no one knew what resources of manpower were available. Castlereagh acted quickly to restore the morale of the army and the spirit of the militia. By improving the quality of the militia he hoped to increase the number of regulars capable of being used for active service overseas. In December 1807 he outlined his plans. He envisaged a regular army of 220,000 men, which would be maintained by a combination of conventional recruitment and a sufficient scale of induced volunteering from the militia. The militia was composed of two classes: first, the regular militia, which would provide 80,000 men for Britain and 40,000 for Ireland, and which would be used for general domestic service, and secondly, the local or sedentary militia, which was to provide 200,000 men for purely local defence. The local militia was to be recruited by ballot if necessary, and those who were drawn in the ballot and failed to serve were to be fined or imprisoned. They were to train for twenty-eight days a year, serving in their own counties, except in cases of invasion or rebellion. Men would serve in the local militia for four years, and during this period they would be exempt from service in the regular militia. Castlereagh sought to assimilate the often inefficient volunteer battalions into the new, and he hoped more impressive, local militia units. Men who had completed their service in the local militia would have a further two-year exemption from liability for service in the regular militia. Castlereagh also resumed the practice, which had been abandoned by Windham, of sending Inspecting Field Officers round the country to test the preparedness and efficiency of the volunteer battalions. Volunteer formations which were found to be defective or incompetent were to be disbanded, and in 1808 Castlereagh offered a bounty of two guineas to members of volunteer units transferring to the local militia.

In 1809 Castlereagh tried further to improve the efficiency of the local militia. Local militia units could use either voluntary recruitment or the ballot to bring themselves up to strength at any time. Once they had completed their initial training local militiamen could volunteer for the army. Castlereagh's schemes, amended by Palmerston during his years at the War Office, saw the country through to victory. There was still some confusion and uncertainty, and inevitably there was tension between those who used the local militia merely as a means of evading more arduous service and those who were genuinely concerned with the improvement of all-round military efficiency, but Castlereagh's plans were the best possible, so long as conscription to the army remained unthinkable and the resources of military administration were so limited. The combination of the Duke of York as Commander-in-Chief (until he was compelled to resign because of the allegations of corruption made by his former mistress, Mary Anne Clarke) and Castlereagh as War Secretary was the most successful partnership in British military administration during the Revolutionary and Napoleonic Wars. But Castlereagh had no illusions. He knew only too well that there were grievous flaws in military organization: judged by abstract standards the defects in the various militia and volunteer schemes were obvious. He attempted to bring the army and the militia up to the highest peak of effectiveness while working within the restraints imposed by public opinion and the policies of previous administrations. The mood of the country was unsympathetic to far-reaching innovations. It is significant that Professor Richard Glover has praised Castlereagh's contribution to the British war effort, stating that he did 'more than any other man . . . to enable Britain to fulfil the role of a great power in continental war'. Nor does Professor Glover confine his tribute to the narrow bounds of military administration. He rightly links the achievements of 1807–9 with the years of acclaim in 1814 and 1815, arguing that Castlereagh's policies at the War Department as well as the Foreign Office 'contributed to securing that balance of power through which the Treaty of Vienna was to preserve international peace among its signatories for longer than any other great treaty before or since'.[9]

Castlereagh never overlooked the purpose for which armies are created: the defeat of the enemy in the field. He was never indifferent to the way in which the army was employed in striking against the French. In the dismal aftermath of the defeat of Austria, the humiliation of Prussia, and the agreement at Tilsit which transformed the Russian Emperor into Napoleon's accomplice in the division of Europe, Castlereagh remained sensitive to the demands of grand strategy. He supported the coercion of Denmark in order to prevent the Danish fleet from falling into Napoleon's hands, but he agreed with the naval and military commanders in rejecting Canning's plans to retain the island of Zealand as a base for future operations. As the war assumed the character of an economic conflict Castlereagh believed it essential to use British naval strength to reply to the Continental System. As Napoleon sought to close the ports of Europe to British trade Castlereagh urged the tightening of the British blockade and the assertion of the British claim to the right of search at sea. He recognized the significance of the Baltic for both strategic and commercial purposes, but he always saw the war as a whole: no theatre of operations monopolized his attention to the exclusion of all other considerations.

It was not, therefore, surprising that Castlereagh should be one of the first British statesmen to see the potential significance of Spain and Portugal in the struggle against Napoleon. The French invasion of Spain and Napoleon's designs on Portugal opened up new possibilities of resisting the French, but few men anticipated that the much-despised British army would make its decisive contribution to the defeat of Napoleon by its operations in the Iberian Peninsula. Only as Spanish resistance to French aggression stiffened, and as the Portuguese demonstrated that they would not accept a dictated peace at Napoleon's hands, did the opportunity of sustained and effective military action emerge. But from the beginning Castlereagh perceived the possibilities which were latent in the Spanish and Portuguese situations. Others wavered, but he remained convinced that real opportunities existed for making a resolute stand against the latest example of Napoleonic arrogance. Britain acted, in his view, as the defender of the rights of the Spanish and Portuguese to determine their own destinies, and to decide their own affairs without French interference and the imposition of a foreign dynasty. The offer of help to the Spaniards and Portuguese combined the advantages of supporting truly national resistance and defending the legitimate rulers of both countries. Perhaps Castlereagh recalled Pitt's conviction that Napoleon's overweening power would receive its first decisive check in Spain. There can be no doubting the insight, consistency and imagination with which Castlereagh advocated the campaign in the Peninsula, and the tireless energy he showed in supporting the British commanders with men and materials. The war in the Peninsula enabled one of his own protégés, Arthur Wellesley, to prove that British troops could meet and defeat the French, and to demonstrate that with good training, firm discipline and accurate marksmanship, soldiers in line could repulse the famous French columns.

In June 1808 Castlereagh told Wellesley of his responsibilities as commander of the initial British force being sent to Portugal:

> You are authorised to give the most distinct assurances to the Spanish and Portuguese people that His Majesty, in sending a force to their assistance, has no other object in view than to afford them the most unqualified and disinterested support; and . . . you will act . . . upon the principle that His Majesty's endeavours are to be directed to aid the people of Spain and Portugal in restoring and maintaining against France the independence and integrity of their respective monarchies . . . The entire and absolute evacuation of the Peninsula, by the troops of France, being the only security for Spanish independence, and the only basis upon which the Spanish nation should be prevailed upon to treat or to lay down their arms.[10]

Castlereagh had no doubt that the moment of decision had arrived: at last there was a real prospect of breaking the deadlock. The British government recognized this truth in a spirit of ecstatic desperation. Britain had stood alone for so long, her allies defeated almost before they had taken the field. Despite the satisfaction of thwarting Napoleon's invasion plans the war could not be won by British defiance and naval power alone. The courage of the Portland and Liverpool administrations should not be discounted here. The opposition Whigs were as defeatist about the Peninsular campaign as they were about the war in general. Their lingering if not always coherent admiration for Napoleon blinded them to the facts of the Spanish situation. Their own failure to negotiate a peace in 1806 had only made them more gloomy about the final outcome of the war. They had neither a policy for winning the war nor a means of securing peace. They had no wish to accept the responsibilities of office, but they lost no opportunity of criticizing the King's ministers. The expedition to Denmark had been roundly denounced by the Whigs as an outrageous affront to the susceptibilities of neutral nations. When the early promise of Wellesley's victory at Vimeiro was blighted by the Convention of Cintra, and when the future of operations in Spain was thrown into uncertainty by Moore's dramatic retreat to Corunna, the pessimists were quick to assert that they had been right all along. Moore had thwarted Napoleon's plans and he had saved the British army, but though Corunna was a victory it was the prelude to withdrawal and Moore's death was as depressing as the death of Nelson at Trafalgar. Moore was the man who had trained the British army for victory, and his death and the subsequent evacuation of the British expeditionary force might well have tempted men of lesser nerve than Castlereagh to pull out of the Iberian conflict, and to hope that in the fullness of time the Austrians or Russians might once again challenge the domination of Napoleon. Furthermore, the extent to which the Convention of Cintra – by which the French were allowed to retire from Portugal, and indeed were evacuated in British ships – shattered British morale at home should not be underestimated. Historians have been kinder to the generals who negotiated the agreement than were contemporaries. Whatever may be said in its defence it provoked bitter criticism of the generals in Portugal and it added to the clamour stirred up by those who questioned the commitment to the Peninsular campaign on principle. Castlereagh stood loyally by Wellesley; he knew that Wellesley disapproved of the decision to transport Junot's army home in British ships. But Castlereagh was deeply distressed by the outcome, and it was not easy for him to weather the storm.

He was sustained by his profound conviction that developments in Spain and Portugal represented a crucial change in the fortunes of the war. His preoccupation with Spanish affairs had begun before Spanish resistance to Napoleon became effective and he was concerned from an early stage to ensure the safety of the Spanish colonies in America. Whatever the consequences of the French invasion of Spain might be Castlereagh believed that it was the clear duty of the British government to prevent the Spanish American colonies from falling into French hands. There was little doubt about the abhorrence which the Spaniards felt towards Napoleon's deposition of their King and the imposition of Joseph Bonaparte in his place, and when reports confirmed that in various places the Spanish people had risen against the usurper Castlereagh affirmed that it was necessary for the British to convince the Spaniards that Britain was the only Power capable of restoring the independence of Spain, maintaining the rights of the Spanish royal family and preserving the Spanish colonies from becoming 'the plunder of the French armies'. Despite her anxiety to secure the independence of the Spanish colonies from the influence of the French Britain had no wish to encourage them to declare their independence from Spain. Rather she hoped that they would be instrumental in re-establishing Spanish power independently of France. But Castlereagh recognized that if this should prove impossible there were only two lines of conduct open to Britain. The first was to declare the independence of the Spanish colonies under a prince of the royal house who was opposed to the French; the second was for the Spanish colonies to declare themselves independent republics, erecting governments of their own choice. In either case, the independence of the ex-colonial governments would be recognized by Britain.[11]

It is evident that long before Canning called a new world into existence to redress the balance of the old Castlereagh was prepared to contemplate the partial and perhaps even the entire independence of the Spanish-American colonies as consistent with the defence of British interests. In desperate circumstances desperate measures were fitting. Castlereagh's anxiety about the Spanish colonies was in some ways parallel to similar British anxieties about French North Africa in 1940. His advocacy of Spanish-American independence was conditional. He hoped that it would be possible to combine a respect for legitimacy with the security of the Spanish colonies, but if this proved inexpedient then the colonies would be free to frame governments for themselves. Circumstances altered cases. Castlereagh recognized that there were times when legitimacy was superseded by events, and although he never elevated either the principle of nationality or the doctrine of self-determination to the status of transcendent truth he was by no means as immune to their existence or as unalterably opposed to their practice as legend suggests. Principles were tested by their practicability, by the degree to which they facilitated rather than hindered the formulation and the application of workable policies. His attitude towards the Spanish colonies showed that in his approach to the waging of war he had a far-sightedness and a breadth of vision which few of his contemporaries could challenge, let alone equal. But he was eager that the Cabinet should have a clear conception of what they hoped to achieve by intervention in Spanish affairs. He knew how dangerous and how futile it was to become involved in Spanish politics without a sure grasp of the strategic principles behind British intervention and a sober recognition of the way in which British policy was limited by events outside the control of the British government. He remembered the cautious nature of the instructions which had been given to the British commanders in Portugal, and he was anxious lest opportunities were allowed to slip away, unexploited and lost for ever. He was always realistic in his approach to the Peninsular campaign, but instead of another timid and frustrated continental expedition he looked for a creative and decisive intervention which would have a vital impact on the course of the European war. It was not enough to occupy Lisbon, secure Cadiz or defeat a single French army in battle: the objective of the Portuguese expedition had to be integrated in a grand strategy, capable of surpassing Napoleon's own strategic concepts in grandeur of conception and efficacy of execution.

It was all the more depressing, then, for Castlereagh to receive news of the Convention of Cintra. Wellesley had been superseded in command, first by Sir Harry Burrard, and then by Sir Hew Dalrymple. Both of these generals were incapable of adjusting themselves to the unusual experience of military victory. Rather than grasping at the opportunities which victory held out to them they regarded it with weary and almost incredulous relief. Wellesley himself was disturbed by the turn of events. He had been pleased with the performance of the British army at Vimeiro: had he possessed a few hundred more cavalry he believed that he could have turned a victory into the complete rout of Junot's forces. But he could not challenge Dalrymple's decision to treat with the French, and he was compelled to sign the Convention, despite his reluctance to do so. He begged Castlereagh not to believe that he had negotiated the Convention or that he had approved of it, or that he had had any part in wording it. But even Wellesley admitted that some negotiation was viable in the circumstances. He was agreeable to a suspension of hostilities for forty-eight hours and no more, but, although he thought it wise to agree to a French evacuation of Portugal because there was little chance of cutting off the French retreat, he deplored the extent to which the Convention assisted the French. The mistake was in the generosity with which the French were treated.

E

When he first heard of the Convention of Cintra Castlereagh was reluctant to believe the news. He even suspected forgery: he could not believe that Wellesley had been a party, however indirectly, to such an agreement. With the rest of the Cabinet he tried hard to reconcile himself to what had happened, but 'without effect' as he later told Wellesley. The public was angry, believing that the French had been allowed to escape from the worst consequences of their defeat. Castlereagh believed that the generals responsible would have to be recalled, but he was anxious about Wellesley's future. He wished to defend his reputation and to secure his future services for the nation. But it was understandable that until the matter of the Convention was cleared up Wellesley would have to accept subordinate command. Castlereagh hoped that Wellesley would be able to collaborate with Sir John Moore, who had, in fact, spoken well of him in his reports, but he told Wellesley of his distress:

I need not say how much my public and private feelings have suffered on the subject of the Convention. I hope the anxious solicitude which I feel for your fame and interest is not incompatible with what in justice I owe others. Dalrymple's misfortune I cannot but feel, as having been the person to bring him from a situation in which he was respected and happy, to plunge him in his present embarrassment. But it is vain to dwell longer on this distressing subject.[12]

But however much he disapproved of the Convention Castlereagh sternly set his face against those who argued that the simplest way out of embarrassment was to denounce the agreement completely. He believed that this would be to act irresponsibly and unfairly. It was permissible, in his view, only to invalidate those parts of the treaty which went beyond what any general in the field had the authority to negotiate; otherwise, whatever misgivings were felt, it was incumbent upon the British to honour their obligations. Castlereagh argued that the interests of the British Crown lay in carrying out the agreement, while bringing to account those who had been responsible for its negotiation. He was eager to clear Wellesley's name, for he still wanted to bring him forward in command, but he was determined to do justice to Burrard and Dalrymple, however much he disapproved of their actions. The principle of a negotiated French evacuation from Portugal was defensible, but the terms conceded to Junot had been too generous, especially the provision of British transports to take the French home, the permission given for the French to take much of their plunder with them, and the failure to stipulate that the evacuated French troops should not again be employed in Spain and Portugal.

Sir John Moore had succeeded in drawing off sufficient French troops to save the Spaniards and Portuguese from decisive defeat, but his death and the fact of withdrawal burned deep into British consciousness. It needed considerable courage and determination for the Cabinet to resume the British commitment to the defence of Portugal. Castlereagh had never been content to rely on the defensive. His instructions to Wellesley had spoken of driving the French out of both Portugal and Spain. But in the aftermath of Corunna Castlereagh recognized that the immediate aim of British operations in Portugal had to be carefully defined. Fortunately Wellesley was able to return to take command of the British expeditionary force, his name cleared by the inquiry into the Cintra affair. In March 1809 Castlereagh made his own position clear. Whatever the result of the conflict in Spain he believed that Portugal could be successfully defended. A British presence in Portugal, and a stouthearted resistance there, would invigorate the Spaniards in their struggle against the French. A Portuguese army of 30,000 regulars and 40,000 militia would supplement the British army in that country, and he estimated that even if the French succeeded in conquering Spain they would need 100,000 men to subjugate Portugal. The cost of fighting the war in the Peninsula would run to something like a million pounds, but it was worth it. A British commitment of 30,000 troops could pay immense dividends in the final reckoning. But he thought it necessary that the allied troops in Portugal, both British and Portuguese, should be under British command.

Castlereagh told Wellesley that his first task on resuming command was to equip the British army to take the field; his second objective would be the improvement of the Portuguese army until it was capable of effective cooperation with the British forces. Although the primary concern was the defence of Portugal Castlereagh authorized Wellesley to use his own judgement in deciding how far he should cooperate with the Spaniards, but before he embarked on any campaign in Spain he needed the express permission of the British government: joint action with the Spaniards should have a limited and definite objective in view. But by the end of May 1809 Castlereagh wrote to Wellesley authorizing him to extend his operations in Spain beyond the provinces adjacent to the Portuguese frontier, providing that such operations did not jeopardize the security of Portugal. The military successes which the British achieved under Wellesley's command were especially satisfying for Castlereagh, who saw his judgement vindicated by events.

Wellesley had warned Castlereagh of the problems he faced in disciplining his army. 'We are an excellent army on parade,' he wrote on 17 June 1809, 'an excellent one to fight: we are bad in quarters when campaigning.'[13] But nothing could daunt Castlereagh's confidence in the British expeditionary force, and he felt thoroughly justified in feeling that the British army was second to none in quality and military skill. After the long years of defeat and frustration Wellesley's early Peninsular victories were a welcome inspiration, but Castlereagh confessed that nothing that had happened fell short of what might have been expected 'from the talents of the General and the gallantry of the troops'. As the man who had done so much to overhaul military administration and improve recruitment Castlereagh could take pardonable pride in the achievements of the Peninsular army, especially since it was commanded by the man he had always believed to be a general of outstanding gifts. His confidence in Wellesley had often been written off by the opposition as little more than the patronage extended to one Irishman by another. But victories in the field – victories as yet unparalleled by the armies of Austria, Prussia or Russia – dispelled the uncertainties and suspicions engendered by political rivalry and the strife of party.

If the war in the Peninsula had been all that Castlereagh had to worry about he would not have experienced the distress and humiliation which were his during the final months of the Portland administration. But he knew that however important the Peninsular theatre was it was not the only area in which the power of France had to be challenged. As early as October 1807 he had told Spencer Perceval that the war could not be brought to a successful conclusion until the means had been found of 'making France feel that her new anti-social and anti-commercial system will not avail her against a power that can, for its own preservation, and consequently legitimately, counteract at sea what she lawlessly inflicts and enforces on others'.[14] Castlereagh was quick to see the threat posed to Britain by Napoleon's Berlin and Milan decrees, and if the French extended the scope of the war by interfering with the legitimate trade of continental nations then it was right that Britain should retaliate. Castlereagh hoped that the matter might be handled in such a way that the resentment of neutrals would be directed against France rather than Britain, but this hope proved vain. The Orders in Council and the rights of search claimed by Britain at sea antagonized the United States of America, and did much to bring about the war of 1812, which Castlereagh regretted and which as Foreign Secretary he was eager to bring to a speedy conclusion on the basis of a generous peace.

Castlereagh believed that any peace which failed to restore the principle of free commerce would be as futile and as short-lived as the Peace of Amiens had been: he never forgot that the Amiens settlement had not been followed by the resumption of normal commercial intercourse between Britain and France. British naval power and Britain's existence as a trading nation were at stake, and no negotiation was tolerable which did not terminate what he called 'the social and commercial warfare between the two states, as well as the contest in arms'. He was never under any illusions about what this meant for the duration of the war, but he was confident that the British people were convinced that a tough response would have to be made to Napoleon's disruption of trade. The war would be long, but if the commercial aspect of the struggle was recognized as being as significant as the clash of arms then it might lead to a lasting, rather than a nominal, peace. It is noteworthy that a man who has so often been decried as cold and unimaginative should appreciate the scope and nature of the war and that he should hold firmly to his essential insight throughout the conflict. Just as Castlereagh's grasp of grand strategy was impressive, so his understanding of what it meant to fight a total war, in nineteenth-century terms, was perceptive and far-sighted. He combined a comprehension of the ultimate aims of the war with a mastery of detail and a command of administration, together with a willingness to trust the commanders in the field with the responsibilities of deciding how best the war was to be fought in the light of local circumstances. This combination of qualities made Castlereagh a great War Secretary. Even so, he was not exempt from the perils of war, from experiencing the way in which the fortunes of war brought ambitious plans to nothing and involved members of the government in bitter personal rivalry and intense political enmity.

The Walcheren expedition was, in some ways, the Gallipoli campaign of the Napoleonic War. Like the Gallipoli expedition it was an attempt to break out of deadlock and bring effective aid to an ally, the final outcome being a reminder of how expansive military inspirations can end in frustration, confusion and disaster. There was nothing intrinsically wrong in seeking to intervene in the Low Countries in the hope of putting pressure upon the French as a means of helping the Austrians, who had, in March 1809, once again taken up arms against the French. There was nothing new in trying to exploit British sea power to influence the course of the war in Europe: sometimes there had been dreams of a dramatic intervention in the Baltic, possibly involving Sweden in the war and reviving Prussian resistance to Napoleon, while at other times there had been plans for a campaign in Holland in order to threaten the French lines of communication with their armies in Germany and central Europe. After the event many reasons were advanced for the failure of the Walcheren expedition, among them the climate and topography of the island, but there were good reasons for striking at the port of Antwerp. Not only would the military impact have been considerable, there would have been immense commercial benefits from the destruction of French restrictions on trade. There was a familiar logic about British eyes being drawn towards the Scheldt.

What finally brought about disaster was not the choice of the theatre of operations but the incompetence of the men in command. Nothing can exempt the government, and Castlereagh in particular, from the dire responsibility of choosing as dilatory a commander for the expedition as Lord Chatham. Had they shown as much insight in selecting a commander for the Walcheren expedition as for the Peninsular armies the outcome might have been very different. Sir John Moore had originally been considered for the command, so perhaps the ministers were merely unlucky. On the other hand it is possible that Canning, for example, favoured Chatham's appointment for political reasons. Canning was already looking ahead to what would happen when the ailing Portland gave up the premiership and if Chatham made his mark in high command he might possibly have been acceptable as a Prime Minister. As Pitt's brother he could hardly have been objected to by Pittites, and Canning felt confident that his own influence would be predominant in any Chatham administration. From the beginning of the Walcheren expedition military and political considerations were intermingled.

Castlereagh was never inclined to ignore the inherent difficulties in an expedition to Walcheren. The climate was one of the gravest complications. 'It appears', he wrote in a Cabinet memorandum, 'that the troops stationed in the island of Walcheren, more especially those not habituated to such a climate, are liable, particularly in the months of November and December, before the frost sets in, to suffer in point of health.'[15] For this reason he hesitated before committing the government to a landing in the region of the Scheldt, rather than attempting an expedition to the Elbe. He warned his colleagues that because of the health hazards on Walcheren not too large a force should be stationed there, and he urged that whatever happened the army should not allow itself to become bogged down in Walcheren. The island was to be regarded as a jumping-off ground, not a final objective in itself. Amphibious operations in the age of sail were fraught with danger, and both Castlereagh and the King recognized the immense difficulties involved. Castlereagh's colleagues shared his apprehensions about the projected landing, but they believed that the risk had to be taken. The instructions given to Chatham made it clear that the expedition's objectives went far beyond Walcheren. He was informed that his objectives were the capture or destruction of enemy ships, whether afloat in the Scheldt or building at Antwerp or Flushing, the demolition of the arsenals and dockyards at Antwerp, Terneuse and Flushing, and the reduction of the island of Walcheren, all with the intention of rendering the Scheldt 'no longer navigable for ships of war'. These aims were ambitious – perhaps, in the light of the final outcome, over-ambitious – but they were not intrinsically unattainable. However, to achieve such a set of object-ives called for outstanding powers of leadership, an aptitude for intelligent improvisation, and the ability quickly to exploit the opportunities of the hour. Chatham – stolid, unimaginative and over-cautious – lacked all these qualities. But there was no doubt about the Cabinet's desire not to see the British army immobilized in Walcheren. Chatham was told that if his objectives proved beyond his grasp he was to do what he could to inflict damage upon the enemy's installations and shipping in the Scheldt, and then to re-embark the army and return to England. The confusion arose because he was told to leave a sufficient force 'to maintain possession of the island of Walcheren, till our further pleasure shall be signi-fied'.[16]

Castlereagh worked hard in preparing the expeditionary force for the Scheldt and he urged the commanders of the naval and military forces to act energetically and forcefully. He knew that haste was necessary if the operation was to be of any assistance to the Austrians. But by the time the Walcheren expedition was launched the battle of Wagram had virtually settled Austria's fate. The British govern-ment pushed ahead with its plans, hoping desperately that a dazzling success would compensate for other disappointments. Castlereagh attempted to convince Chatham of the need for speed, describing the expedition to him as a '*coup de main*'. The British took Walcheren and Flushing, and for a short time expectations were high, but Antwerp did not fall, and soon disputes between Chatham and the naval commander, Strachan, added further confusion and bewilderment to a situation that was deteriorating with every day that passed. The hope that the Austrians would be materially helped by the expedition to the Scheldt proved false, and even the prospect of inflicting a decisive blow upon French shipping in the Scheldt faded. But because large forces had been committed to the project the government was reluctant to abandon the expedition without some compensating degree of success. Castlereagh hoped that if Walcheren could be retained it might prove valuable as a base for future operations. In September he confessed that the major objectives of expedition were no longer practicable, and he gave Chatham permission to bring most of his command back to England. But he added the proviso that effective steps were to be taken for the security of Walcheren, and he failed to recognize that this represented a significant change from his own assumptions about the campaign at its commencement.

It was not that he had forgotten about the health hazards about which he had warned Chatham previously. He did all in his power to increase and improve the provision of medical staff and supplies to the army in Walcheren. He suffered the anguish of learning that the precautions he had insisted upon had been languidly implemented or, worse still, ignored. The reports of widespread sickness among the soldiers were depressing and disturbing. Castlereagh's unease was heightened by his knowledge that the Assistant-Surgeon to the Army's own report had outlined methods of combating the effects of the climate and the spread of disease among the men. Dr Robert Renny had stated, in unambiguous terms, that Walcheren and the neighbouring islands were unhealthy, but he had been equally emphatic that if fresh meat, bread, vegetables and water were provided for the troops, if they were prevented from eating unripe fruit and drinking undiluted spirits, if their quarters were dry and well ventilated and if they were properly clothed with flannel jackets and trousers, then very little sickness should occur. Unhealthy though Walcheren was he thought it no worse than Jamaica or Martinique, and if the proper precautions were taken the island could be secured with as little loss of men as the garrisons of the West Indian islands suffered annually.

But though this medical report stiffened the government's determination to win some tangible benefit from the ruin of their hopes it could not surmount the problems of provisioning and supply. The sad truth was that the expedition had failed to ensure that Austria stayed in the war as an effective ally against Napoleon, and it proved impossible either to take Antwerp or to establish a permanent British base in the mouth of the Scheldt. The attempt to retain Walcheren as a springboard for further operations was foiled by the ruinous ravages of typhus among the troops. There was growing criticism of the government, and Castlereagh as War Secretary bore the brunt of rising discontent. His devoted hard work, his efforts to invigorate the high command and to provide the army with sufficient medical supplies, his determination to wrest some compensation from frustration and despair, counted for nothing against the appalling casualty lists: 20,000 men fell victim to disease. Just when Castlereagh faced the most virulent attacks on his record as a war minister he discovered that he had also been the victim of intrigue within the government itself.

It was in this grim situation, with news of a retreat in the Peninsula to add to his woes, that Castlereagh learned that Canning had been urging his dismissal as War Secretary. Coming as it did on top of opposition attempts to claim that Castlereagh had been involved in corruption during his term of office as President of the Board of Control it seemed like the ultimate betrayal. Castlereagh saw himself as the victim of deception by his colleagues, and he probably feared that he would be made the scapegoat for a government which had seen its hopes of victory vanish, and whose enemies were exploiting the grim horrors of Walcheren and the disappointments of the Peninsula to assert that there was no prospect other than humiliation or defeat. Castlereagh had grieved to see the Duke of York forced into resignation as Commander-in-Chief by accusations of corruption, and he now saw the sinister shadows of intrigue falling upon his own reputation.

Canning had been anxious for some months to secure a reshaping of the ministry. He thought Portland too weak as Prime Minister, and he regarded several members of the government – especially Westmorland and Camden – as ineffective. He believed that Castlereagh's removal from the War Secretaryship was the essential prerequisite for his own continuation in office and for the strengthening of the administration generally. Castlereagh was unpopular with the opposition, especially in the immediate aftermath of the Walcheren episode, and it was convenient for Canning to exploit this to his own advantage and to Castlereagh's discomfiture. Canning had originally supported the Walcheren expedition. Had it been successful he would have sought to push Chatham's claims, but once its failure became obvious Canning was determined to seize the opportunity of altering the balance of the ministry to favour his own fortunes. Possibly he was making a bid for the premiership, although this was perhaps itself a consequence of Chatham's failure. At the very least Canning was trying to win control of the direction of the war effort for himself. He saw foreign policy and the conduct of war as closely linked and he was eager to be responsible for both. He was impatient with his colleagues, resentful of what he despised as their incompetence, and apprehensive lest his own career should fall victim to their mishandling of events. It was essential that the blame for the Walcheren expedition should rest on someone else's shoulders and Castlereagh was the obvious contender for this dubious distinction. Canning's own support of the expedition to the Scheldt made it all the more imperative that he should extricate himself from all responsibility for its failure. Canning was genuinely concerned that the war should be vigorously and effectively waged, but he also had a shrewd sense of the possible consequences of a general withdrawal of confidence from the ministry. If Castlereagh could be discredited, then Canning would have no rivals as the heir of Pitt. He wanted a Prime Minister favourable to his own viewpoint, and, if this should prove impossible, then he was prepared to make a bid for the premiership himself. But this is not to say that he had a consistent plan of action which he pursued throughout the governmental crisis of 1809. He was opportunistic in his methods, and this only heightened the conviction that he was an unprincipled intriguer whose gifts were vitiated by ambition and deceitfulness.

Canning disapproved of Portland's continuation in office, and his own threats of resignation as Foreign Secretary put Portland under intense strain. The Duke was ageing and weary. His health was failing and he was torn between trying to meet Canning's legitimate aspirations and his own sense of loyalty to Castlereagh. It was easy to talk of strengthening the ministry: it was hard to bring it about. Portland shuffled from one suggestion to another. The idea that Castlereagh might give up the War Department, perhaps returning to the Board of Control, was confidentially discussed, although Camden, Castlereagh's uncle, was brought into the secret. George III's confidence in Castlereagh was unshaken. Even Canning conceded that a ministerial reshuffle might be better if it were postponed until after the Walcheren expedition: he had his own hopes for success and what this could mean in terms of a change of ministerial personnel. What was questionable was the way in which Castlereagh was left in the dark about the various schemes which had been mooted. Canning was eager to have a change at the War Department. The atmosphere of intrigue and confusion became more intense and more perplexing. Camden shrank from telling Castlereagh what was being discussed. Canning became impatient with his colleagues' reluctance to tackle the problem of what to do with Castlereagh. He told Portland that he was not in favour of prolonged concealment. He feared that he would be held responsible for everything when the truth at last came out. Camden hoped that the matter would somehow solve itself, and the other members of the government were content to leave the responsibility of breaking the news of what was contemplated to him. They believed that the unpleasant truth would be less painful to Castlereagh if it came from his uncle.

But in August the situation took a turn for the worse. The Duke of Portland had an epileptic fit. Portland's illness meant that the question of Castlereagh's departure from the War Department was involved with the issue of who would head the administration. Portland had finally come to the conclusion that it would be best to tell Castlereagh what had been going on and try to persuade him to give up the War Secretaryship for another office. But the Prime Minister could not act because of his illness and the other ministers shrank from taking the responsibility of breaking up the ministry. The confusion meant that the most sinister explanations of Canning's motives were bound to have greater credibility. A number of names were bandied about as possible successor to Portland, among them Chatham, Harrowby, Wellesley and Bathurst, but most responsible men thought that only two possibilities ought seriously to be considered: Spencer Perceval and George Canning. This was certain to make Castlereagh more resentful of Canning's role in the whole sorry business. When at last he was told of what had been going on he felt that the only possible course open to him was to resign. He came to feel that his honour had been impugned and that it was necessary for him to fight a duel with Canning.

It was a dismal and depressing sequence of events. That a ministry could be so divided at a critical stage of a major war is a comment on the fluidity of early nineteenth-century political alignments. Most of the men serving under Portland thought of themselves as acting in the spirit of Pitt, but their devotion to Pitt's memory, their conviction that whatever the difficulties the war had to be fought to a finish and their deep sense of public obligation did not ensure that they acted with any consistent or substantial degree of collectivity or that they regarded themselves as a party in a formal and organized sense. In a crisis such as that which dominated the final six months of the Portland administration it was impossible to disentangle ambition and public spirit. Canning yearned for the primary responsibility for the direction of the war. The intensity of his feelings on the war issue made him all the more determined to construct a more convincing and durable government than the fallible and vulnerable Portland ministry, but his determination to oust Castlereagh from the War Department went far beyond what the facts of the case justified. Spencer Perceval was just as sensitive to the needs of the hour. He hoped that in a general reshuffle the problem of Castlereagh's future could be handled in such a way as to avert a public split. But Perceval had a keen appreciation of Castlereagh's worth and abilities. At the time of the Convention of Cintra he had paid tribute to Castlereagh's qualities: 'Poor Castlereagh, who has been working night and day to get transports to convey our troops to the scene of the action, will have to plead (and most truly) that all his exertions (and no man ever made greater) were inadequate to enable him to do all that he wished.'[17] Perceval's sensitivity towards Castlereagh only made him more suspect in Canning's eyes. Probably Canning also resented the emergence of the under-estimated Perceval as a credible head of a new ministry. If there were doubts about Castlereagh's popularity there were widespread misgivings about Canning's good faith. Many contemporaries admired him, few respected him. He was distrusted as a man whose restless ambition and feverish rivalry with his colleagues could obscure his judgement. On 6 September 1809 Canning resigned when Portland made it clear that both he and Perceval would resign if Castlereagh's resignation was absolutely demanded. They were prepared to transfer Castlereagh to another post, but they had no desire to humiliate him.

Castlereagh believed that he had been the victim of a sustained piece of treachery. What he found most difficult to accept was that at a time when Canning had appeared to be a loyal and cooperative colleague he had been seeking to procure his own dismissal. He felt in honour bound to resign, and on 21 September he and Canning fought their famous duel on Putney Heath. The first exchange of shots resulted in misses by both men. Castlereagh stated that he was not satisfied and insisted on another exchange of fire. Canning missed again, but Castlereagh wounded Canning in the thigh. Canning was a novice with a pistol; Castlereagh had something of a reputation as a marksman (there were even stories that he had fought a duel in Ireland in his youth). It seemed that there was a touch of austere and calculated malice about Castlereagh's insistence on a second shot. Wilberforce thought that Castlereagh acted in a cold-blooded spirit of deliberate revenge, and Perceval, by no means unsympathetic to Castlereagh's grievances, was horrified by the whole affair. Most men thought that Castlereagh had good grounds for complaint, but they were shocked by the duel. What was known at the time probably put Canning in too discreditable a light, but Castlereagh appeared too eager to push a just cause to the limits of tolerance. Perceval expressed the universal relief when he thanked God that Canning was not seriously hurt and that Castlereagh was untouched, and he put what most men felt into words when he told the Speaker of the House of Commons that the whole affair had made a terrible impression upon the public. Perceval thought that Castlereagh misconceived the case, but he ought to have known how deeply Castlereagh resented a conspiracy to push him out of office when he was devoting all his efforts to the support of Wellesley in Spain and to the attempt to redeem something from the Walcheren fiasco. What also rankled in Castlereagh's mind was the suspicion that while he had been deemed expendable by men he had thought he could trust the same colleagues had been prepared to go to great lengths to prevent Canning's departure from office.

On both sides personal self-esteem as well as public controversies had heightened and inflamed emotions. The duel is a reminder that the notion of Castlereagh as icy and inhuman was always wide of the mark. He habitually controlled his feelings, but this did not mean that he was immune to emotion. His self-control, his dignity of bearing, his reputation for calm assurance were all earned by sacrificial self-discipline. The intensity of his feelings during the duel with Canning makes the tragedy of his suicide more understandable, though not wholly explicable. The affair reflected his preoccupation with his honour. Because he saw Canning as a man who had subjected him to criticisms he could not answer and plots he could not refute he was all the more determined publicly to demonstrate his own rectitude. He had to clear his name, whatever the cost. His own reverence for Pitt made him all the more outraged by Canning's deviousness, his subtle mixture of public service and private advancement, and his ruthlessness in exploiting the weaknesses within the shaky Portland ministry. It was galling that a man capable of such behaviour should assert his unique claim to be the political heir of Pitt.

Castlereagh believed that he was doing more than defending his private honour. He was seeking to establish the integrity of his public conduct, as against the unreliability of Canning. He was anxious that no one should assume that he had been party to the bickering within the Cabinet which Canning had both indulged in and stimulated. Because he was so closely identified with the campaign in Spain and Portugal and with the expedition to the Scheldt he was determined that there should be no suspicions that he had sought, by means of a ministerial reshuffle, to escape from his responsibilities for those operations. Castlereagh was convinced that the shots exchanged on Putney Heath would secure both his private and public character by demonstrating in the most emphatic manner possible that he was not prepared to be 'duped and practised upon' and that he had not been 'privy to my own disgrace'. He knew that for the time being he would have to go to the backbenches, but he had no other choice. Eager though he was to play an active part in the prosecution of the war he could not appear to put place before principle.

He never shrank from defending the Walcheren expedition from the backbenches. He never sought to escape the consequences of actions for which he was responsible and policies with which he was closely identified. He had no desire to shift on to others the responsibility for errors of judgement. He unflinchingly accepted his share of the blame for what had gone wrong. Even so, he maintained that, despite the outcome, the Walcheren expedition had not been without a considerable measure of strategic justification. His contemporaries undervalued his services as War Secretary, but historians have revealed that Castlereagh's record at the War Department was one of which any politician could be proud. Mr Correlli Barnett has gone so far as to call Castlereagh 'the first really able War Secretary'[18], and the tribute confirms Castlereagh's status as a war minister. Castlereagh's own awareness that he had achieved great things – despite Cintra and Walcheren – and that many of his critics were men who had no claim to be either well-informed or particularly percipient on military matters made his sense of insult when the intrigue against him was revealed all the more bitter.

There was no question of his going into opposition on giving up office. He had nothing in common with the opposition Whigs. On most important public issues he gave independent support to Perceval's administration. On occasions his intervention in debate caught the attention of the House of Commons. His defence of his own record during debates on the Walcheren campaign was highly regarded, some M.P.s even comparing his speech with some of the great speeches of Pitt during the darkest days of the war. Another speech defending the continued suspension of cash payments deeply impressed the Commons, and while Mr Denis Gray has dismissed the speech as 'arrant and alarmist nonsense', he concedes that 'as a vote-catching speech it was probably the most successful of the night'.[19] Castlereagh was not at ease with fiscal theories, but the reception given to his speech underlines the fact that while he lacked rhetoric his words usually carried conviction. His speeches represented the triumph of character over eloquence, and the House of Commons has often responded more warmly to the first quality than to the second. The tone of his speech on paper money was well suited to appealing to the prejudices of the Commons. 'An abundant circulation,' Castlereagh assured the House,

by causing an advance of prices, favours speculation and fosters industry, by making the price of produce keep ahead of the cost of production; a restrained circulation, by lowering prices, causes every mercantile speculation to issue in loss, and discourages reproduction, by causing it to terminate in disaster. It is not paper that has depreciated, but gold, which, owing to the excessive demands of the Continent, has appreciated. How could it be otherwise with such a heavy balance of trade against us? Regrettable it may be, but inevitable.[20]

When he claimed that a return to the gold standard would deliver the country economically to the enemy he was indulging in the language of catastrophe, but backbenchers warmed to the notion that the suspension of cash payments protected the value of property and prevented fiscal confusion.

On 23 May 1810 Castlereagh took the opportunity of reaffirming in the House of Commons his support for Catholic emancipation. But he took care to insist that emancipation had to be coupled with adequate securities for the established constitution in Church and state. He viewed the matter as a question of political expediency not of abstract right. Closer links between the state and the Catholic clergy were a necessary security in Ireland: to this end he repeated his belief in the concurrent endowment of the Catholic Church in Ireland. He reminded M.P.s that he had consistently favoured Catholic relief, upon certain conditions, but he was able to establish a reputation for common sense and moderation in a controversy so often inflamed by passion. A judicious approach was necessary if any measure of emancipation was to be carried. Castlereagh knew how deep were the misgivings which many Protestants entertained over any measure of Catholic relief, however modest, and he recognized that while some Protestant fears were exaggerated they were understandable and not to be easily dispersed.

It was this capacity to impress the House in a style which defied the niceties of rhetoric which ensured that Spencer Perceval kept Castlereagh in mind when considering various schemes for broadening and strengthening his ministry. As the fortunes of war in Spain and Portugal justified the support which Castlereagh had given Wellesley, and which had been maintained by Liverpool, so Castlereagh was exonerated from the charges of poor judgement and faulty planning during his tenure of the War Department. What mattered most was that deeds, not words, had cleared Castlereagh's reputation: every victory won by Wellington's army made Castlereagh's judgement appear more sound and more far-sighted.

But Castlereagh was cautious about entering the ministry, especially if this entailed serving with Canning. Nor was Perceval certain that he could broaden his ministry without making some approach to the Whigs. If some agreement could be reached with Lord Grenville's group then the ministry would have a wider base in the Commons. The Prince of Wales was important here. When George III became incapacitated for the last time there had been a possibility that the Prince of Wales would press for an all-party coalition, which would have widespread support and which would be able more effectively to press on with the war. In the past the Prince had been closely associated with the Whigs. In his younger days he had been the intimate friend of Fox, Grey and Sheridan, and though as he grew older he took up political attitudes ever more reminiscent of his father he was moved by sentiment to favour some approach to the Whigs. But there were problems affecting any attempt at reconciliation. Lord Grey and Lord Grenville were both committed to Catholic emancipation – it was virtually the only issue on which they really stood together. They were unsure whether any ministry could merely agree to differ on the Catholic question. Nor were they forgetful that the Catholic question had cost them office in 1807. They were no more inclined to give some undertaking never to raise the Catholic issue than they had been when George III had pushed them out of office. The attitude of the Whigs towards the war was ambivalent. Sometimes it was defeatist, sometimes sympathetic to the resistance of the Portuguese and Spaniards to French aggression. The Whigs criticized the government's conduct of the war, but they had no clear alternative policy. Often they were sunk in pessimism, arguing that the cost of winning the war was more than the country's finances could bear, or that economic weakness would prevent the war from being won. They were divided on parliamentary reform, just as they had been in 1780s. But however cautious the Whigs were about specific proposals for reform they were reluctant wholly to abandon it. Their leaders preferred to leave it as an open question, in the hope that this might prevent the Grenvillites from making their peace with the government. Behind the confused political wrangles between 1810 and 1812 lay the paradox that the Whigs were dependent upon the Prince of Wales for any hope of office at a time when he was moving further away from them. He was more eager to discover some pretext for escaping from old commitments than to bring about a real coalition ministry, but suggestions of some broadly based coalition enabled the Prince to claim that his old friends had abandoned him, not the other way round.

For Spencer Perceval any attempt to strengthen his ministry involved taking a number of contradictory objectives into account. He had to reconcile divisions within the Pittite camp, and while these had been most sensationally revealed by the rivalry between Canning and Castlereagh they were complicated by the wayward and touchy behaviour of Lord Wellesley, Arthur Wellesley's brother and a former Governor-General of India. Perceval could not rule out making some approach to the Whigs, but this was made all the more obscure by the ambivalent attitude of the Prince of Wales and the divisions within the Whig opposition. Probably the Whigs were mistaken in rejecting what may well have been a serious intention on Perceval's part to bring in Grey and Grenville in 1809. By 1811 they had lost any chance of a coalition. The Prince Regent thought that they had behaved with unnecessary arrogance in laying down conditions for the restructuring of the ministry. Whig divisions made it increasingly tempting for the Prince to rely on his father's ministers, once he could assert that the responsibility for his breach with the Whigs lay with the opposition leaders rather than himself. He came to dislike Grey and the antagonism was mutual. Even when Perceval was shot by a madman in 1812 there was no prospect of the Whigs coming in. The ministry was effectively reconstituted under Liverpool on much the same footing as before, and, just at the time when Castlereagh returned to office, Canning ruined his own chances of a political comeback by playing too hard to catch.

When in February 1812 Perceval's administration was jolted by Wellesley's resignation as Foreign Secretary the Prime Minister had turned to Castlereagh with the offer of the Foreign Office. Castlereagh hesitated. Like many Pittites he was unsure of what might happen when the restrictions upon the powers of the Prince Regent terminated, wondering whether some lingering political sentiment might after all persuade the Prince to turn out the Tories and bring in the Whigs. Castlereagh had no wish to act as Foreign Secretary for a few months, only to endure the humiliation of being turned out of office to make way for the Whigs. He did not know how deeply the Prince Regent had come to resent the conduct of his old friends. Castlereagh thought that the ministry should be broadened by bringing in the Sidmouth group. At the same time, if the Prince chose to call upon Lord Wellesley to head a new administration, it was not impossible that Castlereagh, with his links with the Wellesleys, might be offered something. These confusions demonstrated the curiosities of the political alignments of the period. The memory of Pitt and devotion to Fox still influenced men's conduct, but the real issues of the day cut across any conventional Tory and Whig alignment while Pittites and Foxites were sometimes bitterly divided among themselves. There was often as much disagreement and as much personal rivalry within the ranks of both government and opposition as there was antagonism between them. The war, the powers of the Regent, civil liberties, Catholic relief, parliamentary reform and fiscal policy all contributed to this confusion. Even men who were close to agreement on essential issues were rivals. Canning and Castlereagh both supported Catholic relief and the vigorous prosecution of the war, but this did not dissolve the enmity between them, although Castlereagh affirmed that his quarrel with Canning was a thing of the past. On the Whig side there was mounting suspicion between Grey and Grenville and their followers, and the support given to the Peninsular War by Lord Holland, Charles James Fox's nephew, made him unpopular with the more defeatist Whigs.

After careful thought Castlereagh decided at the end of February 1812 that he could not refuse the Foreign Office. Despite all the difficulties of the political situation the Regent had, after all, plumped for a continuation of the ministry, with some broadening of its base. Castlereagh was pleased with Sidmouth's appointment as Lord President of the Council, and with the choice of his relative, the Earl of Buckinghamshire, as President of the Board of Control. The government was now much more likely to appeal to the general mass of the House of Commons. So far as Castlereagh himself was concerned the course of the war in Spain had done much to justify his record as War Secretary from the charges that had been levelled against him in 1809. It seemed that he could not have returned to office under better circumstances.

But on 11 May 1812 Spencer Perceval was assassinated in the House of Commons. There was no political motive for the murder, which was the isolated act of a lunatic called Bellingham, motivated by an imagined private grudge. However, for a few weeks the government's hard-won stability seemed in jeopardy. Wellesley, Canning, Moira, and the Whigs all came into the reckoning again, either as members of a broadened administration or as key figures in a substantially new one. Amind the turmoil one thing emerged clearly: that the Prince Regent had no desire to turn out the men on whom he had come to rely, whatever his desire for a broadly based administration. In June, therefore, Lord Liverpool became Prime

Minister, with Castlereagh continuing as Foreign Secretary and as Leader of the House of Commons. Sidmouth was transferred to the Home Office, with Lord Harrowby taking over as Lord President of the Council. It was this ministry which finally carried the war to a victorious conclusion. It lasted for fifteen years, surviving a number of reshuffles, one of them after Castlereagh's own death in 1822.

Contemporaries were not surprised that Castlereagh took on the responsibilities of Leader of the House of Commons as well as Foreign Secretary. Despite his lack of oratorical brilliance it was a tribute to his common sense and to the general respect accorded to him in the Commons. Like other men who have lacked the gift of easy rhetoric and fluent debating language he impressed more because of the strength of purpose he conveyed than because of the means by which he expressed himself. Liverpool depended on Castlereagh to control the Commons. When he failed to do so – as over the famous backbench rebellion against the income tax – the government was in trouble. The years in which Castlereagh was the government's chief representative and spokesman in the House of Commons are a reminder that M.P.s are not usually as impressed by oratory as so many historians have been. Like Althorp in the 1830s Castlereagh had the measure of the House because M.P.s respected him, trusted him, and regarded him as a man of his word, even when his words lacked wit, brilliance, and fashionable literary and classical allusions. In December 1812 Liverpool told Wellington that the parliamentary session had been most satisfactory: Castlereagh had done admirably and in the Prime Minister's opinion had raised himself 'very considerably' in the eyes of the House of Commons.[21]

But Castlereagh's responsibilities as Leader of the House of Commons had two serious consequences. First, he was more closely identified in the popular mind with policies of domestic repression than would otherwise have been the case, and secondly, his double burden as Foreign Secretary and Leader of the House added greatly to the strains of office.

Castlereagh did not belong to the extreme reactionary wing in British politics. He was no mindless defender of things as they were. His record on Catholic relief was as good as anyone's and better than most, and he regarded the reform of Parliament as an issue which was best judged by a shrewd assessment of the practicalities of politics, not by appeals to high principle. Expediency, in the most responsible and judicious sense, influenced his conduct, not political dogma. He revered the constitution, but although he believed that it was fundamentally sound he did not think it perfect. He was too much of a realist to expect perfection in political institutions or in political behaviour. He recognized that times changed, and that this meant that the means by which the principles of the constitution were to be given effect would also have to change. He believed that property had to be defended, and that if there was a threat to public order then the powers of the law and the discretionary resources of the magistrates would have to be strengthened. But because he was vested with the responsibility of piloting such legislation through the Commons men imagined (often fancifully and usually wrongly) that he was the primary agent in such matters and the principal advocate of extreme and brutal repression. In fact he did little more than act on behalf of the government, and Liverpool and his colleagues were not, in any case, dedicated to repression for its own sake. When their record is compared with contemporary continental governments the moderation and respect for the law and traditional liberties which Liverpool always showed becomes much more apparent. Nor did Liverpool and Castlereagh outrage the feelings of the majority of the political nation. There was more support for, and widespread acquiescence in, the policies of the Liverpool government in curbing disorder after 1815 than radical mythology suggests. But the men in the majority in the House of Commons and in the country did not write the history books, and like other silent majorities they were traduced or ignored by publicists who sought to influence opinion after the event, and who were eager to construct a polemical version of the past, rather than to seek objectively to evaluate a previous epoch.

Looking back from the stable confidence of mid-Victorian England it was hard to recapture the uncertainty and tumult of the Regency years. It was all too easy to assume that there had never been a risk of revolution or of substantial and widespread violence. Probably such a risk never existed to the extent imagined by some alarmists at the time, but given the limits within which the Liverpool ministry had to work there was every justification for the ministers feeling that, whatever else they did, they had to strengthen the powers of the magistrates and loyally support magistrates in their exercise of their powers, whatever private misgivings they might feel over particular instances of strife or unrest. In early nineteenth-century England law and order depended far more upon the local magistrates than upon anything that the central government did. What is striking is not the legislation which was passed in 1819 – the notorious Six Acts – but the restraint shown by the government in doing anything which made innovations in law. Ironically, Liverpool, Castlereagh,

Sidmouth and their critics shared one decisive assumption: the belief that the English constitution was essentially sound and that traditional liberties were the greatest security for national well-being. Where they differed was in assessing where the threat to the constitution came from and how far it constituted a serious threat to law and order.

Some recent historical writing, typified most dramatically by the work of Mr E. P. Thompson, has stressed the revolutionary elements in the English radical tradition which historiography tended to underplay, and has pleaded that the radicals of the Napoleonic period need to be rescued from 'the immense condescension of posterity'. But, as Dr Norman McCord has argued in an important essay, early-nineteenth-century governments need to be defended both from the condescension and the condemnation of posterity and to be judged, above all, by contemporary standards of public behaviour, rather than by the abstract notions of perfection so often invoked.[22] Castlereagh's reputation is closely involved with this process of historical re-interpretation, but there is no doubt that his achievements would have been more generously recognized, and the subtleties of his political outlook more justly appreciated, had he not been Leader of the House of Commons and thereby certain to be at the centre of heated domestic political controversy.

The strain imposed by two of the most important offices of state may well have contributed to Castlereagh's mental collapse and suicide, and both the manner of his death and its timing have led to significant misunderstandings of his role in Regency politics. Fears of blackmail seem to have been the final anxiety which broke his mental balance, but these probably assumed the proportions they did only because they came on top of many years of sustained and exhausting political activity. As early as April 1813 Castlereagh was finding the combination of the pressures of business at the Foreign Office and constant attendance at the House of Commons a heavy strain. But he was not a man to grumble. He accepted the burdens of office as part of the inevitable consequences of political power.

In 1812 he had come back from the political wilderness. He did so because he had remained loyal to the principles of public conduct which he had inherited from Pitt. On the backbenches he had remained scrupulously faithful to the principles which had guided him in office. He had typified a patriotic support for the government, whether in its conduct of the war or its handling of financial affairs. He had made no secret of where he stood on the Catholic question, though he conceded that nothing would be gained by bringing the issue forward prematurely and without adequate preparation. He had engaged in no political intrigues. His response to a number of political approaches had been polite and courteous, respectful both to those with whom he sympathized and those with whom he had little in common. He had made no attempt to force himself back into office. He knew that the initiative lay with others, and that he had to rely upon events to reveal the rightness of his previous conduct.

Probably he had come to admit – at least to himself – that the duel with Canning had been a mistake. But he had believed it necessary at the time to defend his own honour and to demonstrate to the public, in the most dramatic fashion possible, that he had not been a party to the intrigues within the Portland administration. He knew that many of those who regarded him as the victim of a political conspiracy had disapproved of the duel, and had been appalled by his insistence on a second exchange of shots. He had allowed his private sense of outrage to get the better of his political judgement. He could not, therefore, appear in any guise which suggested a relentless or vengeful attitude on his part. Nor could he ever demand that a ban on Canning should be the precondition of his own resumption of public office. The duel belonged to the past: the two men remained suspicious of each other, but neither could afford to perpetuate the memory of 1809. But there was more than good nature to Castlereagh's behaviour here. He knew that Lord Wellesley had affinities with Canning, and that if Wellesley ever became either Prime Minister or a dominant force in any administration this preference would count for a good deal. Once the heat generated by the events of 1809 had been dispelled Castlereagh had also seen that he was not separated from Canning by any major issue of policy. They both supported the Peninsular War; they both advocated a bold and aggressive strategy in the war against Napoleon; they were both committed to Catholic emancipation; they were both hesitant about the premature or untimely resumption of public controversy on either the Catholic question or parliamentary reform. It was essential that Castlereagh did nothing to suggest that he was chiefly or solely to blame for the continued exclusion of Canning from government.

Here Canning was his own worst enemy. His uncertain approaches to the Whigs did him no good, while Wellesley tripped himself up in making a bid for the premiership. Liverpool came to represent patriotic good sense and political integrity. Castlereagh could be seen as acting in a similar spirit. In 1812 most men saw him as the true heir of Pitt, the advocate of both the defence of the constitution and the great patriotic war, who was nevertheless immune from suspicions that he had sought to exploit national crises for private gain or party advantage. In so far as Castlereagh made any contribution, however indirect, to the ways in which men thought of the conventions of politics, he allowed them to think that the familiar Pittite assumptions could still work, and that, while collective responsibility in office was a necessary condition for ministerial stability, there was no need to insist on a similar consistency in the practice of formed opposition. Castlereagh recognized the conventions of party only in so far as these were implied by the conduct of government. This was the Pittite response to those notions of party which maintained that party was the means of securing a more precisely formulated doctrine of opposition. The service of the Crown remained the primary concern of the practice of politics. Conventions affecting the conduct of ministers were determined by this overriding objective. During the war opposition was bound to be suspect, the dubious resource of politicians who were out of favour and out of place.

When Castlereagh accepted the office of Foreign Secretary the first priority of British policy remained the war against France. 1812 was to be the decisive year: Napoleon's invasion of Russia eventually created a situation in which another coalition against France could be brought into being. It was at the Foreign Office that Castlereagh left his greatest mark upon events. But the years between the Catholic crisis of 1801 and Castlereagh's appointment as Foreign Secretary had not been without their achievements. He had proved himself competent in the perennially troublesome administration of Indian affairs. At the War Department he had laid the foundations for future success. He had remained loyal to the Pittite tradition, and despite the Walcheren tragedy and the duel with Canning he had re-established his reputation as a man of sound judgement, devotion to the public service and, not least, an almost infinite capacity for hard work. He had shown that he could win the confidence of the House of Commons by the judicious exercise of the responsibilities of government as much as by debating technique. He had remained faithful to Catholic relief, but he respected those who differed from him on this issue. Canning had seemed over-eager to push himself into the first place: Castlereagh had demonstrated that he was capable of relegating his ambitions to second place. The Peninsular War justified his strategic insight, while Arthur Wellesley's success proved that Castlereagh was a good judge of men. He was soon to show that he was able to hold his own in the world of international diplomacy, in the negotiation of a lasting peace as well as in the prosecution of an arduous war. His political assumptions were traditionalist, but he had confirmed their continued validity by his own political dexterity. The years of achievement were the outcome of the lessons he had learned and the skills he had perfected during the trying years between the death of Pitt and the formation of Lord Liverpool's administration.

4

THE YEARS OF ACHIEVEMENT

The conduct of British foreign policy from 1812 to the end of the war with France was influenced by a number of considerations. The first was the effort to create a new alliance against Napoleon, by which the victories of the British in Spain and the catastrophe of Napoleon's Russian campaign could be exploited to the full. The second was the problem of growing tension between Britain and the United States, stimulated by disputes over British policy at sea, though not exclusively caused by them. These tensions reached their climax in the war of 1812, a war which Castlereagh deeply regretted and which he was eager to bring to a speedy end. The third was the importance of keeping the coalition in being when the confidence of Britain's continental allies was shaken by Napoleon's recovery from the Russian disaster. The fourth was the conflict of interests between the Powers, who had one eye on the eventual peace settlement: Castlereagh had to work hard to prevent disagreements between Austria and Prussia, and clashes of interest between Austria, Prussia and Russia, tearing the alliance apart before the war against Napoleon had been won. The fifth issue was the restoration of a balance of power in Europe, and this involved how best the French problem was to be handled after Napoleon's defeat. Was Napoleon to be left as Emperor of the French, with the boundaries of 1792 for his dominions? Was a Bonapartist Regency viable? Or were the Bourbons to be restored, and if so on what terms? Was France to be punished for disrupting the peace of Europe for over twenty years? How was she to be brought back to the ranks of the legitimate Powers?

The sixth overriding question was how Britain was to settle her own relations with the Powers of Europe, and this called for considerable subtlety on Castlereagh's part. A commitment to Europe was necessary to preserve peace, but it was not always easy to gauge the extent to which the defence of primary British interests might conflict with such a commitment. British policy had a colonial, one might almost say a global, dimension as well as a European one and Castlereagh never forgot this fundamental distinction between Britain and her European allies. Even the primary objective of preserving peace revealed differences of approach between Metternich and Castlereagh. Metternich wished to endow the Holy Alliance with powers of positive intervention for the preservation of international order by the approved exercise of internationally authorized power. His own concern for the security of the Austrian Empire compelled him to take up such a position. Castlereagh was just as anxious to ensure peace and the stability of Europe, but he was more hopeful of doing so by the creation of an effective balance of power, a Concert of Europe, which, while recognizing differences of emphasis and approach, would give due weight to common aims and concerns.

Looking back it is tempting to impose on the sequence of events a greater order than they can actually sustain. The years between 1812 and 1815 were fraught with uncertainty. The final phase of the war was characterized by a bewildering number of changes of fortune, with the allies revising their own hopes, and amending their objectives, in response to the ebb and flow of military endeavour. Castlereagh did not approach the problems of foreign policy in any doctrinaire spirit. He retained several assumptions, most of which could be traced back to the final years of Pitt's political career, but he was thoroughly pragmatic in his diplomatic method. He accepted that both the potency of ideas and the balance of interests moulded the policies and expectations of the Powers, but he saw them as interrelated, each affecting the other, not as predetermined absolutes.

If any single document guided Castlereagh's conduct of foreign policy it was Pitt's famous Memorandum of 19 January 1805, which had been concerned with both the deliverance and future security of Europe. Pitt had been eager to delineate, not only the war aims of the British government, but the principles which he believed essential for a durable peace. He had defined the first objective as 'to rescue from the dominion of France those countries which it has subjugated since the beginning of the Revolution and to reduce France within its former limits, as they stood before that time'. Britain's second aim was 'to make such an arrangement with respect to the territories recovered from France, as may provide for their security and happiness, and may at the same time constitute a more effectual barrier in future against encroachments on the part of France'. The third objective was 'to form, at the restoration of peace, a general agreement and guarantee for the mutual protection and security of different powers, and for re-establishing a general system of public law in Europe'.[1]

Pitt had recognized that there were grave obstacles to carrying such principles into effect. At the time when the memorandum was written he had been sceptical about whether Austria and Prussia would enter the war against France, but, if they did play a part in the defeat of Napoleon, he knew that they would have to be compensated for their exertions by acquisitions of territory. Pitt was emphatic about the need to check French influence in the Netherlands, in the Rhineland and in Italy, and he indicated that consideration would have to be given to the creation, in these areas, of more effective barriers to any renewal of French aggression. He did not rule out making new dispositions of territory, even in a settlement which had as its chief aim the provision of European security. He admitted that it was out of the question to restore the Belgian provinces to Austria: new arrangements would have to be made in that part of Europe. Though a Bourbon restoration in France was probably the most desirable means of settling French domestic affairs with a view to the peace of Europe, Pitt was careful to state that a restoration of the Bourbons was only a 'secondary' objective. If a peace settlement could be achieved which was satisfactory in other respects a Bourbon restoration would not justify the prolongation of the war. Indeed, Pitt had gone so far as to state that the allies ought to take the greatest care in all their public declarations 'to prevent any apprehension in the minds of any part of the French nation, of any design either to dictate to them by force any particular form of government, or to attempt to dismember the ancient territories of France'.[2]

Castlereagh had had several conversations with Pitt on the general subject of the conduct of the war at the period when the memorandum was written, but it would be naïve to argue that he followed the memorandum in any slavish or supine sense. It had defined British war aims in language which was clear, committed and yet conciliatory, but the situation in 1812 was not synonymous with that of 1805, and while accepting the general assumptions of Pitt's paper Castlereagh had to use his own judgement in giving the principles of British policy full effect. Despite the length of the war and the emotions which it had roused, the British government was no more inclined to impose a peace of revenge upon France than Pitt had been. Anxious though they were to establish a lasting peace, Liverpool and his colleagues recognized that if their primary objective was the restoration of the rights of the states of Europe, menaced as they had been by French aggression and disrupted by French domination, such a peace would be defensible only if it acknowledged that despite the excesses of the revolutionary period there were legitimate French interests which any Concert of Europe would be wise to take into account.

Similarly, unlike some of his colleagues, Castlereagh conceded the special difficulties which Metternich faced in handling Austrian foreign policy in the aftermath of Napoleon's Russian campaign. Castlereagh hoped that Austria would come into the war on the side of the allies, and there were times when he became exasperated by the evasive subtleties of Metternich's diplomacy. But he knew that Austrian interests had to be paramount in the formulation of Austrian policy, and until Napoleon had rejected all the approaches made to him by Metternich for a negotiated peace it was unrealistic to expect Austria to enter the war. Despite his exasperation Castlereagh confessed that the key to Metternich's calculations was the possibility that Napoleon could put a new army in the field. The danger was that the Austrian Chancellor would exaggerate the consequences which followed from a French military recovery. On 15 December 1812 Castlereagh's misgivings made him gloomy about the future if Austrian policy proved too apprehensive about Napoleon's powers of recovery:

If we are to implicitly believe Count Metternich's declarations there is no extent of disaster which can befall the French armies beyond the Vistula which would in his conception justify in prudence a change of system on the part of Austria. He represents France as capable of creating and bringing forward another army, were that in the north destroyed, which, united to the troops of the Confederation of the Rhine, would enable her still to hold Germany in subjection against Russia, Austria, and Prussia united. If such is really his opinion, there is no extent of submission to the will of France, whether in peace or war, to which that Minister must not be prepared to counsel his master.[3]

But Castlereagh also remembered that Austria had been the most tenacious of all the European Powers in resisting Napoleon and she had suffered grievously in doing so. In 1809 Austria had challenged Napoleon alone. Despite all Castlereagh's efforts Britain had been unable to give her effective aid and the Austrians had been defeated at Wagram. The marriage of Marie Louise to Napoleon had represented an attempt by the Habsburgs to come to terms with the French Empire. Whatever misgivings the Austrians entertained about their new relationship with France Metternich could not afford to change his policy until it was evident that the tide of war had turned decisively against Napoleon. Austria could not afford to desert Napoleon if there was a risk of facing another Napoleonic peace. Only in 1813 was the full import of Napoleon's failure in Russia appreciated. In February Prussia had signed the Treaty of Kalisch and had thrown in her lot with Russia, but only in August did Metternich take the crucial decision to commit Austria to the grand alliance against Napoleon. As late as June Castlereagh had stated that it was not for Britain to goad other Powers into actions which they deemed inconsistent with their own safety: although he longed for the Austrians to add their armies to those pressing in upon the French Emperor he had the imagination to conceive how powerful were the influences which made Metternich hesitate to do so.

Even before the Austrians joined the coalition Castlereagh had brooded upon the problems of coalition. In April he reaffirmed his conviction that the allies had not only to make war together, they had also to treat together: there could be no separate negotiations with Napoleon. While the Austrians held back Castlereagh recognized that they were needed, not only to win the war, but to hold France in check after the war. The alliance needed what he called 'great masses' both militarily and diplomatically, and this meant that Prussia, Russia and Austria would have to be as great and as powerful as they had ever been. He was active, too, in bringing

Sweden into the war on the allied side. There were problems here, not least the criticism which the proposed transfer of Norway from Denmark to Sweden provoked. But Castlereagh never hesitated to confess that nations would be induced to stand out against Napoleon only when they would earn tangible advantages by doing so. He did not expect them to respond to vague appeals to their sense of international morality. So far as Norway was concerned, the agreement to unite her with Sweden had been made when the situation was adverse. It had helped to save Russia, and in turn Europe, and it had to be honoured. He thought it absurd and dishonourable to allow retrospective wisdom to obscure these facts.

Nor did he overlook the sources of possible conflict between the allied Powers. Although he believed that it was ultimately in the best interests of Austria for her to take up arms against France he knew that rivalry between Austria and Prussia in Germany was likely to complicate any alliance between the two Powers. Rivalry between Prussia and Austria had made it easier for the French to assert their influence in Germany. It was unrealistic to expect either Austria or Prussia to forget their own interests in Germany merely because they happened to be acting together against Napoleon. In theory it was possible to argue that Austrian predominance in Germany might be secured by weakening Prussia, but Castlereagh excluded such a possibility from the practicalities of politics. Prussian help was necessary to enable Russia to carry the war against Napoleon into the centre of Europe. Prussia had to be rewarded for her willingness to stand out against the French. This probably meant that her territories would have to be enlarged and re-integrated. Castlereagh admitted that this created problems in dealing with Austria, but there was no alternative. He hoped that Prussia might be the means of strengthening north Germany against French influence, with Austria performing the same role in the south. This left the issue of their future relations within Germany wide open. But the Powers would be foolish to try to settle all points of controversy in advance. Victory was bound to produce its own crop of problems, but anticipating them would only make it harder to win the war. Castlereagh hoped that the successes of British arms in Spain would convince the European Powers of the efforts Britain was making to defeat Napoleon and heighten the deference likely to be paid to British views on the formation of alliances and the guidelines for a negotiated peace. In addition to her own military exertions Britain was generously subsidizing her allies financially, as she had done at earlier periods of the war.

Nevertheless, Castlereagh recognized that he could not force continental Powers into actions of which they disapproved. Bluster was no substitute for patient advocacy. If the allies lacked the will to fight Napoleon to a finish Britain could not inspire them with such a determination. 'We may animate by our counsels as well as by example,' he wrote to Cathcart, the British minister at St Petersburg, on 6 July 1813, 'but we must avoid the appearance of idly pressing them against the grain.'[4] But there were certain questions on which Britain could not allow her position to be compromised or misunderstood. Apprehensive as Castlereagh was about various attempts which had been made to negotiate with Napoleon he was determined that no concessions should be made or expected concerning British maritime rights. The European Powers had to grasp that Britain would prefer to be driven out of any peace conference than give up her maritime rights. The right of search could not be lightly abandoned. What might appear as a luxury to continental Powers was essential to the preservation of British naval and commercial interests. Britain was willing to recognize the special interests of her allies: she expected from them a similar understanding of her own vital interests.

By September Metternich had broken irrevocably with Napoleon and the grand alliance was in being. For Castlereagh it represented 'the union of nearly the whole of Europe against the unbounded and faithless ambition of an individual'. In some ways the alliance was more of a coalition against Napoleon than a combination against France. Castlereagh believed that the coalition was distinguished not only by its scope, embracing as it did many Powers of the second rank as well as the great states of Europe, but also by its distinctive character. He noted the national character which the war had assumed. He confided his feelings to Cathcart on 18 September 1813: 'On former occasions it was a contest of sovereigns, in some instances, perhaps, against the prevailing sentiment of their subjects; it is now a struggle dictated by the feelings of the people of all ranks as well as by the necessity of the case.'[5] If his powers of eloquence had been equal to his insight he would have escaped much of the odium heaped upon his head as the alleged foe of national feeling. He believed that the grand coalition rested on more durable foundations than the earlier combinations against the French. The sovereigns of Europe had learned that they could not find security by making individual compromises with the enemy. Bitter experience had taught them that submission could win for them neither safety nor repose. They had been compelled, against their better judgement, to become accomplices of France in the conquest and subjugation of other states. But now the Powers were bound together by 'a paramount consideration of an imminent and common danger'.

Castlereagh directed British diplomatists to urge their allies to keep in mind the general interests of the alliance as the first priority in negotiation, both in dealing with the French and trying to settle their own differences among themselves. He was anxious lest Napoleon detached some of the more uncertain members of the coalition by offering to meet their special needs or to satisfy their private ambitions. But the allies had to learn to merge the lesser loyalty in the greater. Only when the primary objective of winning the war was achieved could consideration be given to reconciling the various conflicts of interest between the allies themselves. Castlereagh did not expect victory to solve all diplomatic problems: indeed, he was convinced that the opposite was the case, and that victory would re-open old controversies. But without victory the allies would be able to satisfy neither the longing for stability nor the special preoccupations imposed upon them by their own assessment of their particular interests.

Despite his caution in dealing with Napoleon and the scepticism which he showed towards negotiations with the French Emperor, Castlereagh did not exclude the possibility of a negotiated settlement ending the war. He always saw war as subordinate to diplomacy. The conduct of hostilities was never assumed to be sufficient in itself for the resolution of long-term diplomatic problems. The means necessary for winning the war might complicate the practice of diplomacy, but they were no substitute for it. For the allies nothing could take the place of victory in the field. It was essential if they were to avoid anything which smacked of capitulating to Napoleon's whims. If Napoleon offered to treat, the allies would have to judge his proposals on their merits. Here Castlereagh sought to stiffen the determination of his allies. Too many of them were still dominated by the myth of Napoleonic invincibility. They were too conscious of previous military defeats and former diplomatic humiliations fully to realize the extent of their own success. There was a danger that too much might be yielded to France, because of an excessive anxiety to make peace before the fortunes of war might turn once again in favour of France. But the British were determined to have no part in any settlement which did not confine France within her 'ancient limits'.

Castlereagh doubted Napoleon's good faith. If the French Emperor accepted moderate terms there was always the danger that he would later try to win back what he had lost by resorting to arms. But there was no eagerness on Castlereagh's part to go out of his way to raise the thorny question of a Bourbon restoration. He felt that as long as Napoleon ruled France a risk to peace existed, but he was prepared to acquiesce in the continuation of the Bonapartist régime if other priorities were satisfactorily met. When Napoleon inflicted sharp reverses upon the allies in his brilliant campaign in late 1813 Castlereagh believed that Britain's chief contribution to victory lay in restoring the spirits of her allies. He knew that the Austrians were worried by the unpredictable emotionalism of the Russian Emperor, Alexander I, who was still capable of reverting, if the mood took him, to the spirit of Tilsit, despite the experience of 1812 and the proof that had been given that Napoleon was fallible and failing. Both Metternich and Castlereagh were embarrassed by their dependence on Russian strength, since they regarded Russian diplomacy as wayward and unreliable. They had no wish for a peace to be dictated by the Tsar, and they were uneasy about Russian ambitions in eastern Europe. Nor did they respond to the calls for a peace of retribution which emanated from Prussia. Britain and Austria were drawn together as the advocates of moderation. But this did not mean that they agreed upon all issues and Castlereagh was fully conscious of Metternich's own capacity to deceive or mislead.

Thus, while Castlereagh urged that France be confined within the boundaries of 1790, he was anxious to heal the rifts which opened from time to time between the allies, and he was also sensitive to the interests of those countries with which Britain was especially identified. Like all British statesmen he was closely involved in the problem of the Netherlands. Like Pitt he was drawn to the idea of creating a stronger Holland as the barrier to French expansion to the north. A new kingdom of Holland was to be created by merging the former Austrian Netherlands with the United Provinces. This project was linked with a suggested marriage between the Prince Regent's daughter, the Princess Charlotte, and the Prince of Orange, which the Prince Regent personally favoured. Castlereagh was eager, too, not to overlook the question of Antwerp in any negotiations with France: there could be no agreement to leaving it in French hands. To do so would be 'little short of imposing upon Great Britain the charge of a perpetual war establishment', Castlereagh commented to Aberdeen in November 1813. The destruction of Antwerp as a naval and military base was essential to the safety of Britain.[6]

Castlereagh never lost sight of fundamental British interests, but he came to believe that Britain's influence within the alliance depended upon her reputation for impartiality even more than upon her military resources. Britain had to exercise a reconciling influence, and to be impartial Britain would have to avoid having exclusively intimate relations with any single allied court. Even when Castlereagh found a strong affinity building up between Britain and Austria on the basis of a common desire for a moderate peace he was careful not to give the impression that Britain was committed to taking the Austrian viewpoint in every instance of controversy between the allies. Particular care was needed in dealing with the vexed problems of the future of Poland and the fate of Saxony. Castlereagh sought to achieve a balance of firmness and tact, of principle and flexibility. He attempted throughout to articulate the general interests of the alliance, especially when these were obscured by tension between the allies. British policy had to be applied without either chicanery or excessive dexterity. 'A steady and temperate application of honest principles' was the best way of establishing British prestige and increasing British influence in Europe.

Castlereagh's mission to Basle in the early weeks of 1814 was of immense significance. Although by the time he reached Basle only Metternich, of the allied ministers, was there to welcome him, his decision to indulge in personal diplomacy was of considerable moment. He had to restore the confidence of the allies, to convince them that they were, after all, on the brink of final victory. He had to check the vagaries and wilfulness of the Emperor Alexander. He had to win the personal confidence of Metternich. The morale of the allies was low, but Castlereagh's cool self-discipline and calm resolve impressed his allies and steadied their nerves. Wellington's victories were helpful here, and the Austrians, Prussians and Russians were heartened by the news that the British had invaded southern France. Despite their anxieties about Napoleon they re-affirmed their belief in final victory. Castlereagh had prevented frustration from blighting the alliance and postponing the final onslaught upon Napoleon.

At the end of January 1814 Castlereagh told Liverpool of his misgivings about the Tsar. He confided to the Prime Minister that the greatest danger to the allies' unity of purpose came from Alexander's perverse and arbitrary notions of chivalrous conduct. The Russian Emperor was eager personally to lead his troops into Paris, but his desire for an equivalent of Napoleon's entry into Moscow took a highly personal form. He wanted to enter Paris at the head of his guards in order to display his clemency and forbearance.

This would heighten the contrast between his own magnanimity and the devastation which Napoleon had brought to Moscow. Brooding over his own schemes Alexander became unpredictable in his attitude towards negotiations with the enemy. He veered between urging a policy of noble forgiveness, and seeking to delay a peace settlement until his own triumphant entry into Paris had taken place. There were other intrigues afoot. Russia distrusted Austria over the future of Saxony; Austria feared Russian designs in Poland.

In February 1814 Castlereagh was anxious to secure 'a just equilibrium in Europe'. Because this aim was paramount he was willing to defer to his allies over a Bourbon restoration. But he had not lost his distrust of Napoleon. His own conviction was that as long as Napoleon had anything resembling an army remaining to him he would fight on, seeking to exploit differences between the allies for his own advantage. But there was one suggestion to which Castlereagh was firmly opposed, the idea of a Bonapartist Regency on behalf of the King of Rome. Equally suspect was the substitution of another military leader for Napoleon as ruler of France. Castlereagh knew that Bernadotte was capable of seeing himself as the ruler of France. But while there were some reasons for arguing that as long as Napoleon was acceptable to the French people he should therefore continue as the country's ruler there was no adequate reason for replacing one military adventurer by another, and especially one as unreliable as the Prince Royal of Sweden. If there was to be a change in the rulers of France, the Bourbons were the only possible alternatives to Napoleon. A Regency or another military régime would, in Castlereagh's opinion, be merely transitory. It would be weak and divided and it would be open to the accusation that through it the allied Powers were seeking to exercise too close a scrutiny of France's internal affairs. Stability was the primary quality to be sought in any peace settlement. This implied an arrangement which was as honourable from the French point of view as it was from anyone else's. It was foolish to expect peace by imposing a dubious and arbitrary régime upon the French people. New French convulsions would follow and these would almost certainly lead to another war in Europe. It is interesting that before Talleyrand emerged as the most plausible exponent of a moderate peace, in which France's legitimate interests were as deserving of attention as those of any other Power, Castlereagh was convinced that a just peace implied moderation and that the allies would have to respect the wishes of the French people in making provision for the government of France. Even when his chief preoccupation was stiffening the will of his allies in order to achieve final victory Castlereagh never lost sight of issues which were fundamental in the making of a peace settlement. He was wholly lacking in vindictiveness towards the French. The prosperity of France was the essential prerequisite for the security of Europe.

The Treaty of Chaumont committed the allies to carrying on the war until Napoleon was defeated but it also marked the extension of the alliance beyond the conduct of hostilities against the French Emperor. The allies pledged themselves for the next twenty years to the task of guarding Europe against any French attempt to overthrow the settlement which was to be worked out as the basis for peace. This was less than what the Holy Alliance came to imply, and it fell short of what Castlereagh and Metternich hoped that the Concert of Europe and the Congress system would accomplish towards the pacification of Europe, but the allies did recognize that the maintenance of peace depended just as much upon collective action as victory depended on effective collaboration. Castlereagh welcomed the treaty; he believed that all the essentials of the British point of view had been accepted by his allies. France was to be restrained within her old boundaries. The treaty was an extraordinary display of coordinated diplomacy. Castlereagh believed that British influence had been successfully exercised. This was a hopeful sign. He did not think that there was any prospect of a retreat into isolationism. He had shown that allied cooperation did not mean the neglect of British interests. Both in war and peace British interests could be understood and secured only within the wider context of European stability.

At the end of March 1814 the allied armies entered Paris. Napoleon abdicated, and a provisional French government was established with Talleyrand at its head. The British had the satisfaction of seeing opinion swing towards the Bourbons. Talleyrand had no doubt that despite the vicissitudes of the previous twenty-five years the Bourbons had to be restored. However unromantic a figure Louis XVIII was, he did at least represent legitimacy. He might owe his throne to the fall of Napoleon but he was the rightful King of France, and he came back from exile as the symbol of the nation's historic past. No similar claim could be made for any of the other alternatives, which were, at least in 1814, less popular with the French and more dubious politically. Castlereagh argued that Louis XVIII should make a speedy return to France. Everyone felt released from the oaths they had taken to Bonaparte, but there were dangers in allowing too long a time to elapse between the fall of the

empire and the personal restoration of the monarchy. The sooner
Louis XVIII appeared in Paris the better. Castlereagh was anxious
about the mood of the French army. Although he welcomed the idea
of setting up a constitutional monarchy he criticized some of the
details of the proposals which were being put forward. He singled out
the concession of hereditary rights to existing senators as highly
questionable, and though he thoroughly approved of religious
toleration he regretted that loose language suggested equal endowment for Catholics and Protestants, which, in a country such as
France, was manifestly unrealistic. Like Pitt, Castlereagh believed
that a constitutional monarchy held out the best prospects both for
French domestic stability and for European peace. He thought that
the restoration of the Bourbons was virtually indispensable, but this
did not imply for him the restoration of the *ancien régime*, any more
than it did for Talleyrand.

Similarly Castlereagh hoped that moderation would prevail in
other countries where legitimate rulers were being restored after
varying periods of French domination. He was especially anxious
about the situation in Spain. He doubted the capacity of the Spaniards to devise a sensible and practicable constitution. He was
relieved by the news that King Ferdinand claimed that he was not
seeking to restore the old order of things, but he had little confidence
in the advisers surrounding the Spanish king. He thought that they
lacked the ability and the vigour to sustain any system other than
one supported by the nation as a whole, and yet he suspected that
they secretly yearned for a return to the old style of Spanish
monarchy. He believed that Ferdinand should take the initiative in
winning the confidence and goodwill of the people, but he doubted
his capacity and inclination to do so. Castlereagh told Sir Henry
Wellesley, the British minister in Spain, what he thought the
Spanish king should do: 'To succeed in establishing a permanent
system he must speak to the nation, and not give it the character of
a military resolution; in doing which, the language of Louis XVIII
may afford him some useful hints.' He went on to express the hope
that the Spaniards would not make the mistake of excluding the
ministers of the Crown from the legislature, which had been one of
the most prevalent errors among European constitution-mongers for
a quarter of a century.[7] Castlereagh was well disposed to the establishment of constitutional governments in France, Spain, Holland
and Sicily, but he was cautious about the effects of a widespread
experimentation in forms of government throughout Europe.

On 7 May 1814 he expressed some of his doubts to Lord William

Bentinck, the British minister in Sicily, who was enthusiastic about various schemes by which constitutional governments were to be set up in Italy. Castlereagh was not insensitive to the mood of the time. He knew that the defeat of Napoleon did not mean that the clock could be put back to 1789:

> It is impossible not to perceive a great moral change coming on in Europe, and that the principles of freedom are in full operation. The danger is, that the transition may be too sudden to ripen into anything likely to make the world better or happier. We have new constitutions launched in France, Spain, Holland, and Sicily. Let us see the result before we encourage further attempts. The attempts may be made, and we must abide the consequences; but I am sure it is better to retard than to accelerate the operation of this most hazardous principle which is abroad.[8]

Especial care was needed in Italy. Britain had to act in concert with Austria and Sardinia, and it needed considerable tact in dealing with two states whose Italian interests sometimes brought them into conflict. While the French were being expelled from Italy risks had had to be run, but the situation no longer justified taking great risks. Peace and tranquillity were the principal objectives of British policy. Castlereagh thought it best if the Italians awaited the result of constitutional experiments elsewhere, rather than hazarding their own domestic peace by indulging in romantic schemes of innovation.

What is striking is that Castlereagh did not use the language of High Toryism or extreme reaction. A judicious respect for the facts of the case marked his response to changing patterns of government. He approached the problem, not as the application of some transcendent principle to the practice of politics, but as an exercise in adapting constitutional innovation to the particular needs and historical experience of distinct and diverse peoples. He valued the British constitution; he believed that it represented political wisdom to a unique degree. But he was sceptical about the capacity of other nations, whose political experience and social structure differed from those of Britain, speedily to modify their own institutions in order to match the English model. Imitation was the highest form of flattery, but it was not always politically viable. Castlereagh respected representative government, as it had evolved in Britain, but he was cautious about the universal assertion of the proposition which suggested that all countries ought to be governed on democratic lines. Castlereagh believed that property was fundamental to the stable working of representative institutions. Though he had no fully formulated ideology of prescriptive rights he recognized that allowances had to be made for the needs of each nation. It was possible, therefore, to welcome the extension of free government, especially where it was associated with religious toleration, but he believed that it was foolish to ignore the other considerations which necessarily qualified attempts to establish institutions of government on the representative principle. Stability was the first requirement of any system of government, and only when it had been achieved could parliamentary forms of government flourish. Castlereagh knew that a high degree of social harmony and a common set of political assumptions were the prerequisites for the successful implementation of forms of government on the English model. In many of the countries of the continent these conditions were lacking. In some countries there were racial and religious tensions, in others there were conflicting nationalisms or a high level of tension between the various classes of society. The experience of the twenty-five years since the French Revolution had demonstrated the appalling problems which attempts to legislate on principles of abstract speculation produced. The French had challenged the established order throughout Europe, but the régimes set up by the French had in turn left a legacy of distrust and hate. It was impossible to deal with the situation in general terms. It was surely wiser to accept the limitations of human wisdom and, while trying to avoid the re-imposition of régimes whose incapacity had been amply demonstrated over the years, to be equally circumspect in instituting new types and forms of government.

It was not surprising that the principles of liberalism and nationalism were viewed with scepticism and distaste by the statesmen of 1815. Everything that they had endured since 1789 had indicated the contrast between principles of government linked with nationality and representation, and the way in which these principles had worked out in practice. Liberty, equality and fraternity had inaugurated a quarter of a century of bitter and destructive conflict. In France itself there had been fierce civil strife, even periods of civil war. Metternich also knew that the universal application of the principle of nationality would destroy the empire whose security it was his first duty to maintain. Nationalism had never been untainted by the complexities of power politics. A sense of nationality had been stimulated by Napoleon, but it had also played a part in his overthrow, especially in Spain and Germany. The Confederation of the Rhine had been the instrument by which Napoleon had attempted to establish French dominance in western Germany, exploiting sentiments of nationality against both Austria and Prussia. Napoleon never forgot the realities on which hegemony in Europe had to be built, however unmindful he was of the counsels of moderation which Talleyrand had vainly urged upon him. In the struggle against Napoleon the Prussians had re-discovered their own pride and an awareness of their German destiny, but they did not overlook familiar rivalries with other German states, as their designs upon Saxony showed. Neither Metternich nor Hardenburg could ignore the fact that while in one sense it was both convenient and true to call the war against Napoleon the War of Liberation there had also been much sympathy for the French in parts of western and southern Germany (though there was nothing new about that), while Saxony had remained faithful to Napoleon until the end. There was no obvious sense in which the principle of nationalism could have been given coherent expression in the situation as it existed in the states of Germany in 1815. As for Austria, the Habsburg Empire had been created on the dynastic principle. Nationality posed a threat to the cohesion of the empire in Bohemia, Hungary, Austrian Poland and the Slav territories. Though national feeling had been useful in stimulating resistance to Napoleon it had to be severely confined within definite limits. It was a valuable emotion, but a dangerous and disruptive political principle. Once normality had been restored nationalism would have to be closely restrained, especially in Italy.

Castlereagh ignored neither liberalism nor nationalism, but he was acutely conscious of their ambivalence as guides to political action. His Irish experience made him sensitive to the appeal of nationalism and alert to its dangers. He knew that nationalist ideals challenged existing societies and that they were divisive forces, leaving social conflict as their legacy to future generations. The Spanish experience had demonstrated that liberalism and nationalism were not necessarily allies. Some Spanish liberals had supported the Bonapartist régime, because they hoped that it would mean political and social reform and religious toleration. But this had brought them into conflict with Spanish nationalists, who saw the rule of Joseph Bonaparte as a symbol of national degradation. In Ireland Castlereagh's own conviction of the necessity for reform had led him to challenge both the United Irishmen and the bigoted defenders of the Protestant ascendancy as represented by the Dublin Parliament. He had come to believe that only through the Union with Britain would the religious and civil liberties of the majority of Irishmen be secured. His frustrations over the Catholic question had made him all the more aware of how political hopes and calculations could become distorted by the conflict of interests and the fury of rival prejudices.

Castlereagh was not committed to the *status quo* as a sort of permanent settlement. He knew that change was inevitable, and that each age had to re-interpret for itself what was meant by the contemporary application of fundamental convictions. But he demanded that change should be adapted to the particular needs of each nation, that experience should influence decisions more than abstract ideals and that the inescapable tensions within any political society should be accepted for what they were, without the additional delusion that some abstract principle could conjure them out of existence. He conceded the fragility of social institutions, the vulnerability of public order, the tragic tendency for human passions and wild idealism to plunge countries and peoples into conflict, violence and bloodshed. The politician's first duty was to stave off the worst consequences of human folly and greed. So much of what had been achieved had been won at the cost of suffering and torment. But preservation did not exclude change. His attitude both to domestic and to foreign policy was determined by his desire to ensure that innovation did not jeopardize the stability of any civilized society. Experiments in forms of government were to be tried only when the local situation suggested that they stood a good chance of success, and practicability was a better standard of judgement than abstract principle. In so far as Castlereagh had a set of political attitudes they were the product of his own experience, an experience which made him uniquely capable of sympathizing with some of the problems encountered by continental statesmen in their efforts to impose some pattern of order on the intractable confusion of events. Unlike many Englishmen Castlereagh did not assume that social stability could be taken for granted. As an Irishman who believed that Ireland's best interests would be served in partnership with Britain he knew that convictions could divide as well as unite. His knowledge that peace in Ireland had to be earned, and that it did not remove fundamental tensions which lay beneath the surface of events, gave him a realism, an utter lack of illusions, and a humane recognition of the frailty of men, which influenced all his political dealings. This outlook imposed a certain unity upon his policies at home and abroad, but it was infinitely more complex, and certainly more sophisticated, than the legend of the inarticulate and icy reactionary implies. He was often traduced because he failed to share the naïve optimism of his critics.

In 1814 he was concerned with more than Britain's relations with her allies in Europe and the preparations for the forthcoming Congres: at Vienna. In the summer of 1814 Castlereagh turned his attention to Britain's other war, the war against the United States.

It had been caused by disputes with the Americans over the British blockade of France, claims made of the right to search American ships for both contraband goods and British deserters, and the vexed question of Orders in Council. The Americans resented what they regarded as British interference with the rights of neutrals and British violations of the freedom of the seas. But maritime controversies were not the only causes of the war. Anti-British sentiment was strong among those Americans who wished to expand vigorously to the west or who were casting envious eyes northward to Canada. The blockade of French ports, which had caused hardship to the merchants of New England, actually ended a month before the war between Britain and the United States broke out, and the dispute over the right of search was left unsettled by the Treaty of Ghent. To the more bellicose Americans the war of 1812 was meant to complete what the War of Independence had begun. The war did not lack colourful incidents: the naval fights on the Great Lakes, the American invasion of Canada and the burning of Toronto, the British assault on Washington and the burning of the White House, the battle of New Orleans. But Castlereagh was eager to bring the war to an end. What was even more significant, he was far-sighted in his conduct of negotiations. He was much more prepared than any other British statesman of the front rank fully to accept the fact of American Independence, with all that this implied for the conduct – in the long term – of British policy in North America.

Professor Bradford Perkins has commented on the way in which Castlereagh broke free from old attitudes and accepted American confidence and American power: 'He treated the Americans with consideration, avoided controversy wherever possible, and settled outstanding issues on a basis of parity.'[9] Castlereagh scrapped harsh instructions drafted by the Foreign Office for the British negotiators and composed his own. The main issues involved in the negotiations were maritime rights and the impressment of sailors for the Royal Navy, the treatment of Britain's Indian allies south of the Great Lakes, the boundary between Canada and the United States, and the problem of fishing rights, especially in the waters surrounding Newfoundland. Castlereagh preferred to allow controversial issues to lapse, rather than provoking further disagreement by insisting on raising them, and this explains why the Treaty of Ghent avoided tackling the question of maritime rights in a fundamental way with a long-term solution in mind. Castlereagh was more concerned with bringing about a peace settlement than eager to stick out for the pedantic solution of controversial issues of principle. He felt that the right of search would become contentious again only if a major war broke out in Europe. Since he knew that if such a war did take place Britain would be driven by the force of circumstances to resort to all her familiar techniques of search and blockade, whatever undertaking may have been given to the Americans, he was content to let the matter drop, rather than delay a peace treaty because of disputes over abstract principle. The right of search was a discretionary right, which Britain exercised only in exceptional circumstances; Britain had no interest in propounding some theoretical case divorced from the demands of a particular situation. Since the main objective of Castlereagh's foreign policy was the prevention of another major war in Europe he was under no obligation to raise questions which presumed that he would fail in that purpose. But he never abandoned Britain's maritime rights: he simply had no interest in asserting them as part of a purely theoretical controversy.

Castlereagh was eager to win American goodwill. He soothed American feelings over the impressment of Englishmen working on American ships, and he instructed the Royal Navy to be tactful in such cases. Once the war with France was over the need for such impressment vanished, so he felt that he was not sacrificing anything of real importance. But the consideration which he showed towards American sensibilities won him their respect and gained their confidence. His thoughtfulness and sound judgement extended to incidents likely to provoke American anger or resentment.

In April 1815 five Americans were killed and thirty-four wounded (two of them mortally) in a riot at a prisoner of war camp on Dartmoor. Castlereagh promptly suggested an investigation into the circumstances of the disturbance by one British and one American representative. He communicated the regrets of the Prince Regent for what had happened to President Madison and offered compensation to the dependants of the men who had been killed. These gestures of humanity and goodwill confirmed that Castlereagh had a warm appreciation of the value of amicable Anglo-American relations. He was looking beyond the immediate problems of the moment to the future pattern of Anglo-American understanding. Sir Charles Webster went so far as to claim that Castlereagh recognized the friendship of the United States as 'a major asset', and although one should not ignore the insight into the American question which Shelburne had shown forty years earlier there is no doubt that Castlereagh treated the Americans with the respect due to an independent Power. He neither condescended to them nor did he attempt to browbeat them. In his dealings with American diplomatists he showed that habitual courtesy and respect which marked his political conduct and his bearing in society. He studied the background to the war of 1812 and on 4 October 1814 he confided to Bathurst, 'I trust we shall never again commit the egregious folly of spoiling Americans by acts signally unjust to our own subjects and to all foreign powers.'[10]

But there was nothing sentimental in his attitude. He was moved neither by vague feelings of pro-Americanism nor by inherited distrust of a nation which had been established by a successful rebellion against the British Crown. He believed that essential British interests would be served by a speedy peace with the United States and that a permanent improvement in Anglo-American relations would bring significant benefits to Britain. These convictions – the beliefs of a man who was above all else a realist – made him conciliatory in all negotiations with the Americans. When there was trouble between the crews of American and British ships at Gibraltar Castlereagh told the British minister at Washington not to raise the issue unless Adams mentioned it first. Other Foreign Secretaries might well have responded by making precipitate allegations that the Americans had abused British hospitality. After Castlereagh's death Rush commented, 'If anything unpleasant ever arose . . . he threw around it every mitigation which blandness of manner could impart; whilst to announce or promote what was agreeable seemed always to give him pleasure.'[11]

In 1820 Castlereagh told Stratford Canning of the importance which American considerations had in his order of priorities. He urged him to cultivate American friendship, 'always holding in mind that there are no two States whose friendly relations are of more practical value to each other, or whose hostility so inevitably and so immediately entails upon both the most serious mischiefs'.[12] But he also knew how powerful anti-British sentiments were in the United States: because the Americans had once been ruled by Britain they were all the more determined to establish the reality of their independence, and anything smacking of an over-deferential attitude to the British was immediately suspect. This explained the note of harshness, even of provocation, which crept into American dispatches from time to time. Time alone would heal this tendency, which was itself a sign of political immaturity, but Castlereagh assured Stratford Canning that Britain would gain by avoiding unnecessary exchanges of pique or anger and that this in itself would soothe ruffled American sensibilities. Castlereagh showed great skill in choosing British representatives to the United States: the choice of Charles Bagot was particularly happy in implementing the policy of conciliation.

This did not mean that everything was plain sailing. Sometimes Adams was annoyed by Castlereagh, the most embarrassing incident being when the American arrived for a noon appointment, only to find the British Foreign Secretary still in bed. Castlereagh nevertheless hoped that when Adams became Secretary of State this would help to improve the relations between London and Washington. There were rumbling difficulties over Florida. The Spaniards were unhappy over the loss of their colonies in North America. They hoped that Britain would sympathize with their resentment over the forfeiture of Louisiana and West Florida. Although Castlereagh appreciated Spanish feelings he assured the Americans that Britain had no intention of becoming involved in Florida. Suspicions that the British government envisaged intervention in Florida were unfounded and unjust. Whatever misgivings Castlereagh had about the manner in which the Americans handled their relations with Spain he was determined not to jeopardize a good understanding with America because of Spanish susceptibilities.

His awareness of the American dimension in foreign policy is a reminder that he was not solely concerned with European affairs. Despite his commitment to British involvement in Europe and his eagerness for Britain to take part in the Congress system he never allowed his European preoccupations to blind him to British interests elsewhere. Just as during the Napoleonic War he had seen strategy in global terms, so during the peace he never forgot that Britain was a world Power. All this demonstrates that there was nothing original about Canning's involvement in American affairs. Castlereagh had certainly not neglected them, and in this, as on other issues, Canning's policy in the 1820s was a more dramatic continuation of policies which Castlereagh had already initiated in his own less sensational and less provocative style. Castlereagh had no wish to use foreign policy as part of the process of projecting a particular type of political image. To his ultimate cost, in terms of his popular reputation, he neglected to cultivate the art of public relations. But there can be no doubt of his insight, wisdom and judgement in his handling of British policy towards America. He amply deserves the generous tribute to him penned by Professor Bradford Perkins: 'Castlereagh . . . turned the American policy of Great Britain in a new unprecedented direction. In so far as he played a role in the Ghent negotiations he spoke for moderation.

After the war he laboured without cease to smooth relations almost always tempestuous since the first volley echoed across Lexington green.' Professor Perkins regards Castlereagh as 'an instinctive conservative', but he states that sooner than most Europeans 'he grasped the importance of growing American power, the wisdom of treating the young republic without contempt'.[13] It would be an exaggeration to allow Castlereagh's intelligent conduct of a highly sensitive area of foreign relations to justify talk of any 'special relationship' between Britain and America at this period, nor must American power be over-estimated at any period during the nineteenth century. But Castlereagh's treatment of Anglo-American relations, and his attitude to the problem of the Spanish colonies in America, have too often been ignored or underplayed in understanding his career and evaluating his policy. In both cases he showed a degree of perception beyond that shown by either his contemporaries or many later historians. In these spheres of policy-making – as in many others – the truth was far removed from the persistent allegation that he was obscurantist in his assumptions and harsh and vindictive in his policies. It would be truer to say that he was sophisticated and realistic, but neither of these attributes has been understood by mythmakers obsessed by the delusions of a romantic and revolutionary ideology.

Once the Bourbons had been restored Castlereagh was eager to improve Britain's relations with France. He was fortunate in that Talleyrand was drawn to the notion of cooperation, not only from motives of fellow feeling but also because he saw an understanding with Britain and Austria as the best means of enabling France to recover her status as a major Power. Castlereagh had always made a distinction between fighting against Napoleon and fighting against France. His willingness to leave France her pre-war boundaries reflected his desire to avoid humiliating the French, even when he was concerned to guard against any renewal of French aggression. Castlereagh believed that a vindictive peace would play into the hands of those Frenchmen who dreamed of reversing the verdict of arms by resorting once more to a war of revenge. The Hundred Days made the situation all the more complex. The tenuous grip which Louis XVIII had on the affections of the French was painfully revealed, and those who favoured a generous peace found the evidence of the appeal still exercised by Napoleon acutely embarrassing. Nevertheless, after Waterloo as well as before the battle, Castlereagh set his face firmly against a policy of retribution. He continued to seek out means of cooperating with Talleyrand in a spirit which went beyond the mere sharing of common diplomatic initiatives.

The summer of 1814 saw French affairs uppermost in Castlereagh's mind. He wanted to improve commercial links between Britain and France. The war had disrupted the normal pattern of trade between the two countries and had destroyed the system set up by Pitt's free trade treaty of 1786. On 7 August 1814 Castlereagh told Wellington that no prudent means of opening up Anglo-French commerce should be neglected. He regarded Talleyrand's opinions as 'very sound and liberal' on these subjects.[14] He knew that absolute free trade was unrealistic, but he sought to secure a freer movement of goods between the two countries. At the same time he was anxious to avoid doing anything which suggested that Britain was wresting unfair advantages in trade from her recent adversary. But this did not mean that he was unaware that Talleyrand was capable of exploiting a better understanding with Britain in order to divide her from her European allies. Castlereagh was determined to convey to Talleyrand the impossibility of persuading Britain to sever herself from her old connexions. It was legitimate for Talleyrand to seek British co-operation in checking what Castlereagh described as 'improvident schemes and undue pretensions', but this did not imply that Britain would sacrifice her good relations with those states with whom it had carried the war against Napoleon to a victorious conclusion.[15] Britain recognized that she shared certain common interests and viewpoints with the French, and Castlereagh had no objection to conferring with Talleyrand on the way to Vienna. But just as during the final years of the war it had been important for Britain not to favour one ally to the exclusion of others, so it was essential for good Anglo-French relations to be placed within a context of the Concert of Europe as a whole, the interests of Europe having primacy over the particular interests of individual nations.

Castlereagh was influenced here by advice given to him by Wellington, who assured him that it was likely that Britain and France would be the arbiters of the Congress of Vienna if they properly understood each other. But Wellington had warned of the dangers of too close an alignment with France. 'I think', he wrote, 'your object would be defeated, and England would lose her high character and station, if the line of M. Talleyrand is adopted, which appears to me to be tantamount to the declaration by the two powers that they will be arbitrators of all the differences which may arise.' It ought not to be forgotten, Wellington urged, that only a few months earlier the allies had wished to exclude 'the interference and influence of France from the Congress entirely'. But he went on, 'I conceive that these considerations are nothing, when balanced with the great object of your establishing a perfect understanding with Talleyrand on your measures, and on the mode in which you will carry them into execution, which, in my opinion, nobody can do for you as well as you can for yourself.'[16]

Considerations such as these were kept secret from the public. The Congress inspired little enthusiasm among the majority of Englishmen, except perhaps when the future of Poland and the abolition of the Slave Trade were being discussed. The superficial impression made by the Congress of Vienna was almost wholly misleading. The glamour of ceremonial and the glittering sequence of balls and public entertainments obscured the subtle interplay of diplomatic rivalries, the searching assessment of comparative strengths and weaknesses, and the efforts made by the diplomatists to match a concern for the stability of Europe with the due satisfaction of conflicting national interests.

Despite the hope that the Congress would safeguard the peace of Europe for the foreseeable future Castlereagh never forgot that the Powers were preoccupied with the tangible settlement of specific disputes. Throughout the twists and perplexities of diplomatic fortune he never lost sight of certain fundamental objectives. Britain had to maintain her independence in dealing with matters relating to maritime rights: Castlereagh was sceptical about the capacity of the continental Powers to appreciate the significance of the issue for a naval and commercial Power such as Britain.

He hoped that the overriding sense of a common purpose which had been manifest during the closing years of the war against Napoleon would be sufficiently influential at the Congress to enable policies of balance and moderation to prevail. He was prepared to match precept by example. Britain was willing to surrender some of her colonial acquisitions if by doing so she secured the demilitarization of Antwerp and the security of the Scheldt from French influence. Britain remained committed to a strong and independent Holland. Castlereagh favoured Pitt's old scheme for Holland to be given the Austrian Netherlands to build up her resources against any possible French invasion. The independence of Spain and Portugal was essential for any peace settlement to have any prospect of longevity, and here Castlereagh argued that Britain's commitments in the Peninsular War made it impossible for him to compromise the security of the Spanish and Portuguese kingdoms. In Italy the traditional states were to be restored, although with some modifications. Castlereagh thought it expedient to strengthen the kingdom of Sardinia by the addition of Piedmont, Genoa and Savoy. The best security against French aggression in Germany was a strengthened Prussia: by giving Prussia provinces in the Rhineland she would be more involved with the politics of western Germany. In so far as this implied some compensation for Austria, who was naturally jealous of anything jeopardizing her traditional predominance in Germany, then he believed that Austrian influence in northern Italy should be underlined. Throughout the Congress Castlereagh was distrustful of Russia, partly because he suspected Russian designs in eastern Europe and partly because he had little confidence in the political judgement of Alexander I.

It was, therefore, embarrassing that the Russian Emperor should be so popular in Britain. The Tsar's visit to London revealed his popularity, but it also exposed his woolly-mindedness. Alexander's unpredictable behaviour made Castlereagh all the more willing to work with Talleyrand to procure a moderate peace settlement. This did not mean that he was any the less alert for any renewal of French aggressiveness, but it was the consequence of his desire to save Europe from Russian predominance. Castlereagh's anxieties about Russia ensured that he worked with Metternich, and they explained his initial readiness to contemplate the possibility of giving Prussia Saxony in order to balance Russian gains in Poland. His change of attitude on the Saxon question reflected his admission that Prussia was not to be won so easily.

But despite the transfer of various territories which the statesmen of 1815 regarded as part of the ordinary process of peace-making Castlereagh was not indifferent to the interests of the smaller states of Europe. He believed that the decisions of the major Powers were what counted, and that in practice they had to be accepted by Powers of the second rank, but he knew that there was little to be gained, and perhaps something to be lost, by the arrogant assertion of supremacy by the more powerful states. Castlereagh believed that since the great Powers were acting as trustees for the stability of Europe as a whole they were obliged seriously to take into account the interests of the smaller states. The smaller Powers were vital for the establishment of a true equilibrium in Europe, and he saw himself not only as a mediator between the great Powers, but as a mediator between the first-class Powers and the second-class ones. Here his gifts were suited to the task. Throughout all negotiations he was courteous, imperturbable, prepared quietly to listen as well as to persuade others to come round to his own point of view. He experienced disappointments, as over the Polish and Saxon questions, but he was always capable of recoiling from frustrations in order to make the most even of diplomatic reverses. Furthermore, notwithstanding his legendary reputation as a reactionary, he worked hard and steadily towards procuring real progress in the control of the Slave Trade and in moving towards its ultimate abolition.

Castlereagh had an impressive ability to adapt the details of negotiation to the needs of the case, while remaining firm in his pursuit of his long-term objectives. Far from being insular or narrow-minded he always thought in terms of European perspectives. Nor was he incapable of appreciating objections to his plans: he knew that politics dealt with the imperfect, not the perfect, and that diplomacy's chief function was to ease the tensions of a complex situation by recognizing human ambitions and motives for what they were. He was far-sighted without being arrogant, and principled without being obdurate. Despite his awkward language there was a subtlety about his thinking which his critics missed. He never forgot that in the conduct of foreign affairs a number of considerations had to be kept under review, the demands of first one and then another making the first claim for his attention. It was essential to retain a sense of balance and perspective, while remaining agile enough to respond to changing circumstances.

On 1 October 1814 he told Wellington of some of his misgivings as well as his ultimate objectives. If Prussia and Austria were excluded from Poland they would seek compensation elsewhere, and this would pose problems in dealing with German affairs. Similarly, though he valued bringing Prussia to the Rhine as a security against France he admitted that there were snags. One consideration had to be balanced against another: equilibrium was the primary aim.

I am always led to revert with considerable favour to a policy which Mr Pitt, in the year 1806, had strongly at heart, which was to tempt Prussia to put herself forward on the left bank of the Rhine, more in military contact with France. I know there may be objections to this, as placing a power peculiarly military, and consequently somewhat encroaching, so extensively in contact with Holland and the Low Countries. But, as this is only a secondary danger, we should not sacrifice it to our first object, which is to provide effectually against the systematic views of France to possess herself of the Low Countries and the territories on the left bank of the Rhine – a plan which, however discountenanced by the present French Government, will infallibly revive, whenever circumstances favour its execution.[17]

The Cabinet were uneasy about Castlereagh's willingness to strengthen Prussia by giving her Saxony. They felt that this was going too far. Though it was necessary to provide some balancing factor against Russian predominance in Poland, Prussia had no right to acquire Saxony. The Prince Regent was sympathetic to Saxony: his Hanoverian sensitivities were roused by the prospect of the brutal demise of the kingdom of Saxony. Castlereagh was concerned throughout with the need to weaken Prussia's alignment with Russia. And the Polish question necessitated some security against Russian predominance. If Poland was to be, for all practical purposes, part of the Russian Empire, then something would have to be done to restore the balance in eastern and central Europe. It was far from easy to deal with Prussia. Castlereagh confided his feelings on this point to Wellington, who was, as so often, the recipient of his most intimate confidences:

> I was, from the outset, aware of the extreme difficulty of making Prussia a useful ally in the present discussions, connected closely as she has been with Russia; but it appeared to me that, notwithstanding the King's *liaison* with the Emperor, it ought not to be despaired of . . . more especially as it was difficult to found a satisfactory system of balance in Europe, unless Prussia could be induced to take a part.[18]

He was unhappy about the influence exerted by Talleyrand here: Castlereagh thought that the French minister ignored the significance of the Polish question, concentrating too much on Naples and Saxony. Talleyrand did not always serve the interests upon which he was most intent. Brilliant though his diplomacy was, he was negotiating from a position of weakness, and Castlereagh saw that there were limits to what a diplomatist of Talleyrand's subtlety and force could achieve, given the situation in which he was placed. The crux of the problem was that in eastern Europe Russian power was supreme. There was nothing that Britain could do about this, and while France and Austria shared British misgivings about Russian dominance in eastern Europe they recognized that the overwhelming nature of Russian power allowed her to fulfil most of her ambitions in Poland. The question resolved itself into how best Russian influence could be checked in central Europe, and here Castlereagh saw that if Prussia was strengthened in the Rhineland to prevent any renewal of French designs in Germany this might add still further to the difficulties of the situation if Prussia remained too intimately linked with Russia.

Castlereagh was disturbed by tendencies which weakened the alliance but he knew that wartime unity had been achieved only because of circumstances which had already become part of history. The shock of Napoleon's final bid for power had temporarily re-united the Powers against France, but once the adventure of the Hundred Days had ended the thorny question of who was to be dominant in Germany reasserted itself. Two alternatives had presented themselves to Castlereagh. The first was for a united front comprising Austria and Prussia, supported by Britain and the minor German states, in what he described as 'an intermediary system between Russia and France'. The second was an alliance of Austria, France and the southern states of Germany against the northern Powers, Russia and Prussia. He had hoped that a peace settlement might have been achieved which rendered such combinations unnecessary, and that after a long and exhausting war the Powers might have enjoyed a period of repose without forming alliances which added to the risks of war.

But the policies of the Russian Emperor had disappointed Castlereagh's hopes for a peace without competing alliances, and he was driven to consider fresh possibilities which had not been in his mind until the Russians had revealed the scale of their ambitions in eastern Europe. The wayward nature of Alexander I made the calculation of Russian intentions more difficult and uncertain. It was understandable that the Russians should be concerned with securing their own future security against invasion, but this in itself did not explain or justify the Tsar's attitude towards Poland. Castlereagh never forgot that a balance of power was the primary condition for peace. As he moved towards a closer understanding with Metternich's Austria and Talleyrand's France he was conscious that such an alignment was the product of necessity rather than choice. And like all choices in the world of power politics it brought with it its own constraints and obligations. As so often Castlereagh told Wellington of his misgivings about an alliance with France and Austria:

Necessity might dictate such a system, but not choice. It appeared, in the first instance, difficult to cement, on account of the fundamental jealousy existing between Austria and France, especially upon the point of Italian predominance. If adopted in order to control Russian power, and, with this view, should it be supported by Great Britain, it rendered Holland and the Low Countries dependent on France for their support, instead of having Prussia and the northern states of Germany as their natural protectors. It presented the further inconvenience, in case of war, of exposing all the recent concessions by France to re-occupation by French armies, as the seat of war might happen to present itself.[19]

These considerations led him to believe that it would be inadvisable to depend too much on French connexions. He thought that Louis XVIII was friendly, but it would be wiser to preserve, as far as possible, some notion of German unity against Russia, accepting French goodwill, but not taking it too much for granted. If the Polish question were to be resolved without war it meant bringing Prussia forward, for Prussia could present the best barrier to further encroachments by Russia, while providing effective security for British interests in Flanders and the Low Countries. Castlereagh knew that Talleyrand was averse to Russia, but he was also suspicious of any alliance between Austria and Prussia. Yet such an alliance was the only way in which Prussia could be kept within due bounds. 'If France were a feeble and menaced Power,' Castlereagh wrote, 'she might well feel jealous of such a German alliance; but, as her direct interests are out of all danger, it is unreasonable that she should impede the sole means that remain to Germany of preserving its independence, in order to indulge a sentiment towards the King of Saxony, or to create a French party amongst the minor States.'[20] Castlereagh thought that French fears of a German league or confederation were unrealistic. He did not believe that a good understanding between Austria and Prussia would endanger the liberties of other states.

Throughout the conduct of negotiations Castlereagh was troubled by the possibility that he would be summoned home by Liverpool to deal with the opposition in the House of Commons. Liverpool knew that the Whigs and Radicals were critical of British foreign policy and no one could answer their allegations as authoritatively as Castlereagh. But Castlereagh was reluctant to hand over the conduct of negotiations to anyone else, for he had built up confidence in his personal approach to the tasks of peacemaking. He wanted to carry through to a conclusion negotiations for which he felt a high degree of responsibility. But, putting personal considerations aside, he assured Liverpool that 'the conduct of the negotiation ought not to pass, as things now stand, into other hands, except upon some necessity'.[21] The only possible replacement was the Duke of Wellington, but despite his great respect for Wellington's ability and personal authority, Castlereagh thought that the Duke would be unable to take up the negotiations with that instinctive sense of personality and the advantages which confidential discussion had given Castlereagh during his own stay in Vienna. Time was of the essence: the Polish question had been settled, though not to Castlereagh's liking, and the Saxon issue still proved difficult. At the beginning of 1815 Castlereagh was convinced that the fate of Europe would depend on the outcome of the next month's discussions between the Powers.

There was no denying the profound impression which Castlereagh made upon his fellow diplomatists. They were moved to admiration, even when they regarded the policies which he was advocating as controversial or distasteful. Talleyrand objected to the creation of a powerful Prussia, and he was sometimes deceitful in his dealings with Castlereagh, even when events drove France and Britain closer together. The usually critical Gentz confessed that Castlereagh's qualities were outstanding, not least his capacity for sustained and patient hard work. 'He worked day and night,' Gentz remarked, 'sometimes with the King of Prussia and the Emperor of Russia, sometimes with Prince Metternich and Prince Hardenburg.'[22] The abandonment of the idea of giving Prussia the kingdom of Saxony was a reverse for Castlereagh and something of a triumph for Talleyrand, but Castlereagh quickly recovered from the setback, and, most dramatically of all, entered into an understanding with Austria and France by which the three Powers agreed to act together if any one of them were attacked as a result of disagreements over the peace settlement. Anxiety about Russian policy brought about this alignment: Castlereagh was determined that no 'Calmuck Prince' should impose his own terms on Europe. Talleyrand cleverly exploited the differences between France's former enemies. When the Tsar said that the King of Saxony deserved to pay the price for betraying the common cause Talleyrand had retorted by reminding the Russian Emperor that the common cause was merely a question of dates. Talleyrand invoked the principle of legitimacy to defend the King of Saxony, and although Prussia acquired large slices of Saxon territory to compensate her for yielding some of her Polish possessions to the Tsar's puppet kingdom of Poland, the King of Saxony retained his throne and a severely reduced kingdom. The danger of war over the eastern question was over early in 1815, but Castlereagh admitted that his original aims over Saxony had been frustrated. He had been compelled to act more closely than he had wished with Austria and France, but he still believed that Prussia ought to be brought to the Rhine to guard Germany against any resurgence of French expansion, as well as underpinning the enlarged kingdom of Holland.

Castlereagh's relationships with Talleyrand and Metternich were based on the mutual recognition that their countries had certain interests in common. Nothing is more misleading than the suggestion that Castlereagh was the dupe of one or the other. The three diplomatists knew that they had much to gain by collaborating with each other, but this did not blind them to areas of actual or potential conflict. Each sought to ensure that the Vienna Settlement represented the largest degree of agreement among the Powers, but each also sought to secure the vital interests of his country. They accepted that the peace would be the outcome of a balance of forces, and their cooperation was founded on mutual respect, a concern for European stability, and a desire to safeguard national interests, not on sentiment or the chance compatibility of temperament. As the tide of negotiations ebbed and flowed so their relations changed. In November 1814, for example, Castlereagh had been grateful for the signs of a more cooperative spirit on the part of Talleyrand. But though Talleyrand had been 'personally most obliging and conciliatory' he believed it prudent not to disclose too much to Talleyrand. Castlereagh knew that Talleyrand was not always discreet, and he would lose confidence in other quarters if he was thought too closely involved with the French minister. He treated him with all possible regard, and kept him generally informed of his own efforts to promote common objectives, and as a result Talleyrand had become 'infinitely more accommodating in our general conferences than at the outset'.[23] But there was always a reserve on Castlereagh's part, and the clue to their partnership, such as it was, lay in a recognition of common interests. Similarly, Castlereagh was not deceived by Metternich's charm. He knew that Metternich was vain and often indiscreet, and what drew them together to work in closer collaboration was the simple recognition that Austria and Britain shared a common concern to check Russian pretensions, while keeping a cautious watch on Prussia, however much the latter power was needed to provide additional security against French designs in Germany.

The return of Napoleon and the Waterloo campaign did not disrupt the calculations which Castlereagh had made for the protection of British interests and the preservation of European security. There was never any doubt in Castlereagh's mind that Napoleon would have to be defeated in the field. He was more worried by the complications which an abortive attempt to restore the Empire created for long-term policy than anxious about Napoleon's chances of victory. The renewal of the war jeopardized that moderate settlement which Castlereagh believed essential for future stability. Napoleon's return inflamed Prussian yearnings for a tough peace. Castlereagh did not hesitate to urge the Powers to take prompt and resolute action to defeat Napoleon before he had had time to establish himself in power. The longer the war dragged on the harder would be the task facing the moderates at the conference table. But

Castlereagh had no illusions about the difficulties in the situation. It was depressing to see how quickly loyalty to the Bourbons evaporated: he asked Wellington, somewhat apprehensively, whether there were any signs that the Bourbons would be able to get Frenchmen to fight for them against other Frenchmen. If there were any springs of devotion to the monarchy to be tapped then the royalists might prove worthy partisans, rather than men who, when convenient, would shout '*Vive le Roi*' without doing anything. Nothing could be left to chance. The allies would have to act quickly and on a massive scale. It would be a fatal error to underestimate Napoleon's strength or his potential power. Castlereagh believed that France would pay a high price for the Bonapartist restoration, however brief. He was anxious that the allied armies should not indulge in indiscriminate pillage and plunder. Although Britain was prepared to subsidize the allied war effort she could not pay the whole cost of keeping the allied armies in the field.

Castlereagh saw all the old familiar suspicions of France, which Talleyrand's skill had been able to mute in 1814, break out afresh. This endangered all principles which he believed necessary for a lasting peace. Despite appearances it would be foolish to assume that all Frenchmen were secret or unrepentant Bonapartists. But he was under no illusions about the French character. Talleyrand himself could not be relied upon, yet there was no one else on whom the British government could more safely depend. He was unsure of Talleyrand's influence over those who surrounded him. Just as Napoleon's return from Elba had made many Englishmen reassert their innate prejudices against the French, so Castlereagh knew that, assuming that the Bourbons would be restored a second time, the more extreme royalists would argue that the Hundred Days had revealed the need for more ruthless measures to root out Bonapartists and Republicans. 'The fact is', Castlereagh confessed to Clancarty in a moment of exasperation in April 1815, 'France is a den of thieves and brigands, and they can only be governed by criminals like themselves.'[24] Louis XVIII was too honest to keep the French in order. Nevertheless, unless the King was crippled by the demands made of him by his more fanatical supporters, he still deserved allied support and confidence more than any alternative ruler.

It was impossible to choose who would govern France. Even if the Bourbon dynasty was saved this would not of itself guarantee that the most congenial or intelligent French politicians would come to the fore. Men like Fouché and Talleyrand amply deserved the distrust so frequently shown towards them, but they were the only men with whom it was realistic to deal. They were devious, cunning and opportunist, but in political experience and subtle intelligence they outshone their competitors. Wellington's victory at Waterloo ended the danger of a protracted war, but it did not solve the problem of how to deal with the French situation. Castlereagh reminded his colleagues that they had to make the best of the personnel available: he knew how detested Fouché was in England, but such feelings were not a good guide to policy. Castlereagh warned Liverpool that those who knew how difficult it was to find 'men of character' in French public life should be very cautious about exciting any widespread clamour against men such as Fouché. The brutal truth was that Louis XVIII could not do without them. If all men with a record of Republican or Bonapartist sympathies over the previous twenty years were excluded from public life France would be ungovernable. The way would then be open for the disruptive impact of extreme royalism and Castlereagh had no doubt that this would be disastrous. If Fouché were removed Talleyrand would not be able to carry on. Castlereagh was able more than most men to appreciate that the spectacle of Talleyrand depending on Fouché looked too much like vice leaning on the arm of crime for comfort, but the political experience of France for over a quarter of a century meant that very few men had a clean political record, and those whose reputation was unblemished were usually lacking in experience and political skill. The restored monarchy needed men of proven political judgement – a quality in which Castlereagh knew most of the royalists were wholly defective – and this meant that neither Louis XVIII nor the allies could be too fastidious about the men with whom they worked. Castlereagh never forgot how much he needed Talleyrand if a moderate peace was to be won.

It was all the more important, therefore, for the French King to hold his extremists in check. After Waterloo the danger was that an outburst of frenzied royalist feeling would erupt in France. Castlereagh hoped that policies of reconciliation and moderation would prevail, but he had grave misgivings about the probability of extreme reaction. On 14 September 1815 he wrote to Liverpool from Paris, telling the Prime Minister that if the high-flying royalists had their way nothing but confusion and weakness would ensue. Royalist fanaticism was the chief danger: 'If this could be moderated instead of goaded by the Court, the Ministers would be strong enough for every exertion, and they could hardly venture to fall short of their duty. Thus supported and watched, the Bonapartists and Jacobins would sink into insignificance; but I am afraid the game will be otherwise played.'[25] Even when he could speak well of the personal moderation of the Duc de Richelieu he confessed that he lacked administrative and political experience: when it was remembered that he had not been in France since 1790 the immensity of the difficulties facing the King's minister could be appreciated.

Throughout the summer of 1815 Castlereagh's judgement remained unruffled: his capacity to differentiate between the needs of the moment and the demands of long-term policy was considerable. Whatever doubts he harboured about the Bourbon restoration he accepted its necessity, but everything he said about the domestic régime in France revealed a temperament far removed from that of the bleak reactionary of legend. He had a regard for order and an affection for tradition, but he was emphatic that the experience of the French nation from 1789 to 1815 could not be wished away or dissolved in a haze of royalist emotionalism. He opposed a peace of retribution, though France paid for the Hundred Days by reverting to the frontiers of 1790 instead of those of 1792. Whenever he commented on French domestic politics he vehemently criticized anything which smacked of royalist vengeance or the paying off of old political scores. He knew that the régime would have sufficient problems in winning widespread and lasting public confidence without compounding them by acts of provocation or spite. Talleyrand reminded the Powers of Europe – with the honourable exception of Britain – that opposition to Napoleon had been a matter of dates rather than principles. Castlereagh saw that a similar principle operated in French politics. Castlereagh also knew that a peace which humiliated France would unite royalists and Bonapartists in pressing for an active foreign policy to restore French pride and reaffirm the greatness of France. It was impossible to hold France down forever: to attempt to do so would lead to another war, a war in which there might be some public sympathy in Britain for what might seem to be the just demand for the denunciation of a peace settlement which had denied essential French interests and violated French honour. In his memorandum of 31 August 1815 Castlereagh summed up the matter succinctly:

The more I reflect upon it the more I deprecate this system of scratching such a power. We may hold her down and pare her nails so that many years shall pass away before they can wound us. I hope we may do this effectually and subject to no other hazards of failure than must, more or less, attend all political and military arrangements; but this system of being pledged to a continental war for objects that France may any day reclaim from the particular states that hold them, without pushing her demands beyond what she would contend was due to her own honour is, I am sure, a bad British policy.[26]

Castlereagh never saw politics in terms of absolutes, whether these were ideas of representative government or monarchy, liberalism or nationalism, or whether they were notions of a permanent territorial settlement which would be valid for all time. Sir Harold Nicolson criticized Castlereagh for allegedly seeking to impose static principles upon a dynamic world, arguing that he failed to realize that an alliance based upon 'the maintenance of the existing order' could not preserve its unity in a Europe in which ambitions and interests were 'in a state of constant flux'.[27] But Castlereagh was fully aware of the state of flux which was part of the invariable climate of politics. He did not believe that political arrangements could last for more than a limited time. He was sceptical about the precipitate experimentation with liberal and nationalist principles which was taking place in parts of Europe, but he did not deny the force of such principles or even, in a carefully qualified way, their attractiveness. Nor was he as insensitive towards the needs of the smaller states as Nicolson suggests. Throughout the negotiations of 1814 and 1815 he insisted that the great Powers should use their power responsibly: the feelings of the smaller states were taken into account, even when it was thought necessary to overrule them, as over the transfers of Norway to Sweden and Finland to Russia. In the last resort the decisions made by the great Powers had to carry the day. There was nothing, in Castlereagh's view, inherently absurd or reprehensible about this; it merely recognized the facts of political life. He had no concept of anything like a League of Nations. He would have been outraged by the suggestion that a proliferation of small states should by voting strength alone determine the fate of Europe or influence the outcome of complex diplomatic negotiations. But then the experience of the League of Nations between 1919 and 1939 has demonstrated how fragile any international organization is whose structure ignores the realities of international conflict or the clash of interests between the Powers.

Equilibrium was the word which appealed to Castlereagh. It suggested, not the imposition of some *status quo*, sustained by force and perpetuated by terror, but the recognition that the preservation of peace depended on changing interests. Equilibrium implied a balance of power, but it also embraced the notion that as time went on the interests and ambitions of the Powers would change, and that peace would be preserved only as these changes were accommodated within a diplomatic order. Whether liberalism or nationalism are regarded as principles of progress or expressions of disruption is more a matter of private judgement than of absolute truth. The meaning of such terms is conditioned by the context in which they are applied and the background against which they are understood. Castlereagh believed that the way in which such principles were given practicable political expression altered and defined their nature: liberalism meant something far different in England or Holland than in Spain or Italy. It was as much the consequence of various historical experiences as it was of idealistic conviction. Experience was a safer guide in politics than revelation. It was thoroughly consistent for Castlereagh to be cautious about accepting any general principle of the right of the Powers to intervene in the internal affairs of the states of Europe while believing that, if a threat to peace could be proved as actually existent, a measure of controlled intervention might be necessary in certain circumstances. The danger was posed by tangible threats to peace, not by the abstractions of ideology.

Though Castlereagh had entered into an alliance with Austria and France at the beginning of 1815 he tried to avoid the coalition breaking down. The primary aim of British foreign policy was to act as a conciliator in Europe. He impressed upon the European powers that they had survived the threat represented by Napoleon's empire only because they had eventually stood together. A similar union would be beneficial in time of peace. In December 1815 he explained to Rose what he had in mind:

> The immediate object to be kept in view is to inspire the states of Europe, as long as we can, with a sense of the dangers which they have surmounted by their union, of the hazards they will incur by a relaxation of vigilance, to make them feel that the existing concept is their only perfect security against the revolutionary embers more or less existing in every state of Europe; and that their true wisdom is to keep down the petty contentions of ordinary times, and to stand together in support of the established principles of social order.[28]

But at the same time he had no wish to commit Britain to any policy of regular or habitual intervention in European affairs. 'In general,' he assured Rose, 'it is not my wish to encourage, on the part of this country, an unnecessary interference in the ordinary affairs of the continent. The interposition of Great Britain will always be most authoritative in proportion as it is not compromised by being unduly mixed in the daily concerns of these states.'

It was annoying to learn that the French monarchy was proving less reasonable in dealing with its critics than Castlereagh and the British government had hoped. This was especially galling in view of the moderate peace terms which the victorious Powers imposed upon France, even allowing for the provocation of the Hundred Days and the Waterloo campaign. Castlereagh was convinced that the restored Bourbons would win the confidence of the French people only if they followed a policy of conciliation. He was acutely sensitive to the embarrassments which undue severity by the French king would cause for the British government in answering criticisms made by the Whig opposition in the House of Commons. Liverpool had met Grey and Grenville and had assured them that the British government understood that the French did not intend to carry the punishment of Bonapartists to extreme lengths. Nevertheless, whatever anxieties were felt on this score, it would be improper for the British formally to intervene in what was a matter of French domestic politics. Castlereagh argued that if too much fuss were made in Britain it would be less likely that the ministers of Louis XVIII would favour clemency towards their foes, but, at the same time, he impressed upon the French ambassador that while Britain had no wish to interfere in French domestic quarrels the Prince Regent's ministers believed that it was in the common interest that blood should not be shed, however culpable the behaviour of the accused had been. Far from being eager for a policy of universal repression Castlereagh was the advocate of conciliation, even of forbearance. He did not shrink from accepting the responsibility for severe measures whenever these were justifiable, but he always opposed policies of blind revenge or harsh vindictiveness.

As well as pleading for humanitarian policies in France he sought to persuade the European Powers to act together to outlaw the Slave Trade. During the peace negotiations he pressed France to abolish the Slave Trade throughout her dominions within a period of five years. The cause of abolition in France was helped by Napoleon's return, for during the Hundred Days he was eager to establish a reputation as a liberal, and by abolishing the Slave Trade during his brief tenure of power in 1815 he made it difficult for the Bourbons to undo what he had done, in that respect at least. But Castlereagh did not confine his attention to France: he was eager that other Powers should cooperate in putting an end to the traffic in slaves. But he knew that considerations of humanity were not enough in themselves. He warned the abolitionists in November 1814 that he was not dealing with persons influenced primarily by humane and moral considerations. He was aware that politicians were often hard-headed and flint-hearted when they saw themselves as the guardians of the public interest. It would not be easy to convince some of the other statesmen of Europe, especially the Spanish and the Portuguese, that the abolition of the Slave Trade would be compatible with the prosperity of their own colonies and the interests of their planters.

In his own mind he was convinced of the strength of the abolitionist case. Though he had previously argued that Britain would be unwise unilaterally to abolish the Slave Trade he had acted in 1805 to ban the trade in recently conquered colonies. Even if it was impossible to abolish the traffic he had no wish to see it spread. Once the Whigs had abolished the Slave Trade in 1807 Castlereagh's appreciation of the international aspects of the problem made him anxious to procure the degree of international cooperation to make abolition effective. But he could not risk antagonizing countries over the slave question when he needed their collaboration on other matters. He recognized the desire of the Russian Emperor, for example, to link the slave issue with the problem of the Barbary states, and the European Powers were more closely concerned with the latter question. But he worked hard to persuade the Powers to act together, upon what he described to Cathcart as 'the broad ground of giving repose upon Christian principles to the human race, of whatever colour, and in every part of the globe'. If they did so the diplomatists would do themselves credit and 'render a lasting service to mankind'.[29]

Castlereagh attempted to exploit Alexander's vague devotion to Christian principles in order to enlist the support of the Russian Emperor in abolishing the Slave Trade. If the principles of Christianity were supposed to guide the Powers in dealing with the problems of Europe it would have been unworthy to follow a less benevolent principle in Africa and America. Russia, Prussia, and Austria were reasonably cooperative about the slave question, partly because it did not greatly impinge on their own interests, but it was much more difficult to persuade the Spaniards and Portuguese that abolition was in their own best interests. Both the Spanish and Portuguese were already sufficiently embarrassed in their relations with their American colonies without adding further complications to what was for them a thorny problem. They had no wish to accede to what they regarded as British naïvety and self-righteousness. The attitude of the Spaniards and Portuguese was acutely frustrating for Castlereagh. Because of the Peninsular War Britain had close links with Spain and Portugal, but there was growing concern in London about the trend of Spanish and Portuguese politics, and in their dealings with their colonists the Spaniards and Portuguese were acting in a manner which antagonized British opinion. Castlereagh was worried lest too strict an insistence on abolition by 1819 would merely drive the Spaniards and Portuguese into further intransigence. Rather than seeing Spain and Portugal excluded from the operation of agreements on the slave question he was willing to give them special treatment. In this context, as in others, Anglo-French cooperation was essential. If France collaborated with England Castlereagh thought it possible for some influence to be exerted upon Spain and Portugal; without France this would be impossible. On 31 July 1815 he had written to Wilberforce from Paris, 'I have the pleasure of acquainting you that the long desired object is accomplished . . . the unqualified and total abolition of the Slave Trade throughout the dominions of France.'[30] The Bourbons did not believe that the issue greatly affected French interests one way or the other: it had, therefore, been convenient to show that, in certain fields of policy, they were as capable as Napoleon had been of implementing liberal policies.

Nevertheless, it still proved difficult to win concessions from the Spanish and Portuguese. Efforts to limit the Spanish trade in slaves to areas south of the latitude of 10 degrees North were abortive. Only when Castlereagh exploited hopes of British mediation between Spain and her American colonies was it possible to make further progress in discussions about the Slave Trade. In 1817 the Spaniards agreed to outlaw the traffic in slaves north of the equator, but only in 1820 did they abolish the trade. The Portuguese were more obdurate. Although in 1815 Castlereagh had succeeded in persuading them to abolish the Slave Trade north of the equator, with an undertaking that complete abolition would follow in eight years, the commerce in slaves continued. Despite the right of search claimed by the Royal Navy it was easy to evade control. Governments which had conceded the abolition of the Slave Trade in principle resented anything reminiscent of the right of search asserted by the British during the Napoleonic Wars. The Americans were especially sensitive on this point, and the southern states of the Union had a particular interest in the maintenance of slavery. Castlereagh had never harboured false expectations. He had consistently said that while it was not too difficult to convince foreign countries of the justice of the principle of abolition it was much harder to carry the principle into effect and to practise practicable methods of control. Britain could not force the Powers of Europe to act against what they believed to be their own interests: Castlereagh went out of his way to remind the House of Commons that Britain ought not to make the mistake of antagonizing other countries by 'inconsiderate approaches'. As always he preferred the less dramatic tactics of thoughtful negotiation to general commitments of a sweeping but impracticable nature.

The Spaniards were insensitive and intransigent in dealing with their South American colonies and Castlereagh became weary of the folly of the Spanish government. The combination of stupidity and incompetence which characterized Spanish policy was especially infuriating for Britain. Castlereagh was personally embarrassed by the entangled confusions of Spanish and Portuguese politics. In the autumn of 1816 he even contemplated invoking the Congress system to force upon the Spaniards a more liberal policy in South America. He regarded the conduct of the Portuguese as indefensible, but at least the Portuguese could argue in extenuation of their own attitude that by driving their own colonies into revolt the Spaniards were republicanizing the whole continent and subverting the Portuguese monarchy in Brazil. Castlereagh described the behaviour of the Portuguese as 'odious', nevertheless, and that of the Spaniards was little better. He thought that the two governments were 'well matched in dishonesty and shabbiness'. There was little that he could do to bring the two régimes to see reason, but the tenor of his comments on Portuguese and Spanish policies constitutes further proof that however sceptical he was about doctrinaire liberalism he was just as dubious about the viability of reviving obsolete methods of government, denying the aspirations of colonists whose hopes of independence had been roused, and seeking to defer the implementation of representative government. It was an understanding of the nature of a judicious sense of political expediency which made Castlereagh so critical of King Ferdinand and his advisers, not any ideological assertion of the universal applicability of democracy. As a realist Castlereagh had little patience with the monstrous abstractions and demonstrable exaggerations of either the Right or the Left. He regarded the policies of the Spanish and Portuguese monarchies as being just as disruptive of international peace and stability as the conspiracies of nationalists or the plots of revolutionaries.

Despite the frustrations and disappointments which were inevitably part of the political process Castlereagh could take a justifiable pride in the peace treaties. On the whole, they represented the moderate peace for which he had worked so hard. The main terms of the peace settlement were contained in the first Treaty of Paris (May 1814), the Treaty of Vienna (June 1815) and the second Treaty of Paris (November 1815). In Germany the Powers agreed to set up a Confederation of thirty-nine states, with Austria as President.

Prussia gained territories in Saxony, Swedish Pomerania, and the Rhineland. The former Austrian Netherlands were merged with Holland to form the stronger kingdom of the Netherlands as a barrier to renewed French expansion in the Low Countries. Russia gained Finland and Bessarabia, and with the Tsar as king of Poland Russian control over that country was – for all practical purposes – firmly established. Denmark lost Norway, which was given to Sweden. The old dynasties were restored, not only in France, but also in Spain, Naples, the Italian duchies and the Papal States, while Austria regained Lombardy and Venetia. The kingdom of Piedmont acquired Genoa. Britain's reward comprised a number of new colonies, the Cape of Good Hope, Mauritius, Guiana, Tobago, Trinidad, Heligoland, Malta and Ceylon, most of which she had already occupied during the war. Because of the Hundred Days France was reduced to the frontiers of 1790, instead of those of 1792, and she was punished by having to pay an indemnity of 700 million francs, an army of occupation remaining in France until this sum was paid.

In a powerfully argued speech in the House of Commons on 20 March 1815 Castlereagh defended the integrity and wisdom of the allied Powers and the broad outlines of the peace settlement as it was being hammered out. He was eager to assert that throughout the negotiations British good faith and British interests had been maintained and vindicated. He accepted the responsibility for what had been decided, and he defended himself against the charge of seeking to impose terms that were out of step with the general tendencies of the age. In fact, the allies had deliberately refrained from making dangerous assertions of general principle:

> With regard to the European powers, if the assembled sovereigns had put forward a declaration to the effect that all the ancient governments of Europe, which time had swept away, should be recreated; that those rude and shapeless fabrics which had been thrown down, and had long ceased to exist in any tangible form, should be reconstructed, without any general or fixed principle for the reconstruction; if this was to be done without any regard to the corruptions that had grown up under these antiquated and ruinous institutions, without recollecting that those very Governments had produced the calamities by which Europe had been so long and severely tried, and which might in the end have the effect of recreating the dangers from which we have just escaped; if such a declaration had been issued, I should have felt ashamed that my country had belonged to a confederacy founded upon the principle of imbecility. The true question is, whether the deliberations and decisions of Congress were guided by an ascertained and worthy principle;

G

whether the basis they laid of a solid and lasting pacification was or was not in itself sound; and whether for the attainment of any partial or selfish views any of the parties, but more especially this country, had betrayed the trust reposed in them by the confidence of Europe. It is upon these grounds, and these only, that I will argue the question.[31]

This was the language of judicious realism. He spoke as one who was concerned with providing workable solutions for pressing practical difficulties. He had no interest in constructing a doctrine of reaction with which to challenge the ideology of revolution. He reminded his audience of the need to provide for stability in central Europe, and he defended his record on issues such as the Polish and Saxon questions, the problems of Italy, and the transfer of Norway to Sweden. So cogent were Castlereagh's arguments that the Commons agreed to an address approving the draft treaties without a division. The speech was not a display of verbal brilliance. It did not indulge in the purple passages suitable for anthologies of public eloquence. But its close and reasonable blend of realism and purpose typified the qualities which commended Castlereagh to the majority of members of the House of Commons.

The peace settlement was quickly followed by a new issue: the possibility that the Powers would prolong their cooperation in order to preserve peace and stability in Europe. Two differing approaches became apparent, though both presupposed a continuation of international collaboration on the part of the major states of Europe. One was the Russian Emperor's dream of a Holy Alliance, allegedly the expression of Christian principles of benevolence and charity; the other was represented by the more limited and realistic concept of the Quadruple Alliance. Too often these two aspects of the problem of peacekeeping are confused, but Castlereagh always clearly differentiated between them.

He was dubious about Alexander's Holy Alliance, and in a letter written to Lord Liverpool from Paris on 28 September 1815 he made clear his doubts about the project and his misgivings about its origins:

. . . I have . . . to acquaint you that although the Emperor of Austria is the ostensible organ, the measure has entirely originated with the Emperor of Russia, whose mind has latterly taken a deeply religious tinge. Since he came to Paris he has passed a part of every evening with a Madame de Krudener, an old fanatic, who has a considerable reputation amongst the few highflyers in religion that are to be found in Paris. The first intimation I had of this extraordinary act was from the Emperor himself; and I was rather surprised to find it traced back to a conversation with which I was honoured with the Emperor when leaving Vienna. You may remember my sending home a Project of Declaration with which I proposed the Congress should close, in which the sovereigns were solemnly to pledge themselves in the face of the world to preserve to their people the peace they had conquered, and to treat as a common enemy whatever Power should violate it. The Emperor told me that this idea, with which he seemed much pleased at the time, had never passed from his mind, but that he thought it ought to assume a more formal shape, and one directly personal to the sovereigns; that he had communicated that morning to the Emperor of Austria his sentiments upon this subject, and that he would speak to me further upon it in a few days.

Prince Metternich, the following day, came to me with the project of the treaty since signed. He communicated to me in great confidence the difficulty in which the Emperor of Austria felt himself placed; that he felt great repugnance to be a party to such an act, and yet was more apprehensive of refusing himself to the Emperor's application; that it was quite clear his mind was affected; that peace and goodwill was at present the idea which engrossed his thoughts; that he had found him of late friendly and reasonable on all points; and that he was unwilling to thwart him in a conception which, however wild, might save him and the rest of the world much trouble so long as it should last. In short, seeing no retreat, after making some verbal alterations the Emperor of Austria agreed to sign it. The Emperor of Russia then carried it to the King of Prussia, who felt in the same manner, but came to the same conclusion.

Castlereagh went on to say that the Russian Emperor had then brought his plan for universal peace to him, informing him that he intended to write to the Prince Regent to ask him to accede to the project. Wellington had been with Castlereagh when Alexander had called and they had found it hard to go through the interview 'with becoming gravity'; Castlereagh continued:

Foreseeing the awkwardness of this piece of sublime mysticism and nonsense, especially to a British Sovereign, I examined with Prince Metternich every practical expedient to stop it; but the Emperor of Austria, with all his sobriety of mind, did not venture to risk it. When it reached me, in fact, the deed was done, and no other course remained than to do homage to the sentiment upon which it was founded, and to the advantages Europe might hope to derive from three such powerful sovereigns directing all their influence to the preservation of peace; that I was confident the Prince Regent would unite, *cœur et d'âme*, with his august allies in making this the basis of all his policy, and that I would lose no time in laying before His Royal Highness their solemn pledge of the pacific and moderate spirit which actuated their councils.

Castlereagh was relieved that the Russian Emperor's proposal was a personal, rather than an official, proposition. This would obviate the worst complications which might otherwise have issued from Alexander's initiative. All that could be done was to make the best of a bad job:

Upon the whole this is what may be called a scrape; and yet in the long run it may be attended with more beneficial results than many of the acts which are in progress, and which are of a character better to suit the eye of Parliament. The fact is, that the Emperor's mind is not completely sound. Last year there was but too much reason to fear that its impulse would be to conquest and dominion. The general belief now is, that he is disposed to found his own glory upon a principle of *peace* and *benevolence*. Since the point of Poland was disposed of, there has been nothing in his political conduct in the progress of arrangements which indicates another purpose, and he really appears to be in earnest.

Castlereagh told Liverpool that the Austrian Emperor and Metternich were eager for the Prince Regent to accede to the Holy Alliance, despite the embarrassment which they knew was involved in such a proceeding. They believed that no harm and some good might come out of humouring the Tsar. Castlereagh tended to feel that the Prince Regent could sign 'without the intervention of his Ministers, as an autographic avowal of sentiment between him and the Sovereigns his Allies, tending to preserve the tranquillity of Europe'. He concluded by expressing the hope that the Prince Regent 'may find himself enabled to avoid disturbing the harmony which at present subsists between him and his allies'.[32]

Clearly, Castlereagh did not see the Holy Alliance as more than a tiresome instance of Alexander's habitual waywardness. It was little more than a gesture and, though worthless, it was so lacking in serious content as to be foolish rather than dangerous. At this stage Metternich had no conception of the use to which he was later to put the Holy Alliance. But Liverpool's own reaction was firm. He regretted that the project had ever been put forward, but he knew that it was impossible to undo what had been set in motion. 'The work is done,' he wrote to Castlereagh from Walmer Castle on 3 October 1815, 'and it is one thing to wish it not to have been done, at least in such a manner, and another to refuse being a party to it after it is done.' But it was also impossible for the Cabinet to advise the Prince Regent to accede to the Holy Alliance. 'Such a step would be inconsistent with all the forms and principles of our government and would subject those who advised it to a very serious responsibility.'[33] The Holy Alliance was a treaty and treaties could not be entered into personally by the Prince Regent. The Prince Regent therefore refused to accede to the Holy Alliance, stating that the forms of the British constitution precluded him from doing so, although he affirmed his concurrence in the principles underlying the alliance and his approval of the declaration that the precepts of the Christian religion ought to be the invariable rule of conduct in social and political affairs.

Castlereagh had toyed with the idea that by making a purely personal commitment to the Holy Alliance the Prince Regent might avoid irritating the feelings of the Austrian and Russian Emperors and of the King of Prussia, but he was by temperament deeply uneasy about any association of Powers which was indefinite in its implications and sweeping in its scope. Alexander's intention was that the Holy Alliance should preserve peace and spread benevolent paternalism among the rulers of Europe, but it mattered little to Castlereagh whether Alexander was devoted to the ideals of brotherhood or animated by fears of revolution: the major threat to the peace of Europe came from any commitment which allowed Russian troops to tramp everywhere in Europe to preserve order, restore legitimate or tottering governments and protect Russian interests. The trouble with universal principles – however well-meaning – was that they encouraged and condoned universal meddling. The principle of legitimacy was no more than a convenient tool in procuring a sensible peace. Its utility was not synonymous with universality. Only particular political situations gave political principles real meaning. Despite Castlereagh's own scepticism about ambitious constitutional experiments in Europe he had no wish to permit the great Powers to interfere in the domestic affairs of the various states.

Similarly, because diplomacy by congress had proved its value in the last years of the war against Napoleon and in the settlement of Europe, Castlereagh sympathized with suggestions that conferences between the Powers should be held at regular intervals in the hope of preventing major international problems ripening into war. Such conferences might have a special relevance whenever political upheavals threatened international stability, but Castlereagh saw them as more usually applicable to conventional clashes of interest, conflicts over spheres of influence or disputes over contested territories. It was from familiar quarrels such as these that the gravest threat to peace would come. The Congress system was congenial to Castlereagh, but he came to be relieved that George III's incapacity and constitutional reservations about the correctness of the Prince Regent acceding to the Holy Alliance provided Britain with a convenient excuse for opting out of the Tsar's pet project.

Castlereagh was happiest when dealing with the tangible. Appeals to principle and evocations of remote and mystical ideals made little impression upon him. As Dr Henry Kissinger has emphasized, while Alexander symbolized 'the indeterminacy of a policy of absolute moral claims', and Metternich 'an equilibrium maintained by an agreement on a legitimizing principle', Castlereagh represented 'the conception of an equilibrium maintained by the recognition of the self-evident advantages of peace'.[34] Metternich saw the Holy Alliance as the means by which established institutions could be preserved, by international intervention if necessary. He saw the threat to peace as coming from within the states of Europe, as well as from their conflicts of interest. Castlereagh, on the other hand, while valuing international cooperation, was much more concerned with the relations between the European states than conscious of any general principle sustaining social order throughout the continent. He never forgot the importance of preserving for each country the right of dealing with its own internal affairs. Only if domestic upheavals issued in acts of aggression or the encouragement of sedition in other countries was intervention justified. The misgivings which finally led to England's withdrawal from the Congress system were present from the start, but this does not mean that Castlereagh was wrong to give such a system the chance to prove itself in peace as in war. Some means of preserving peace had to be found, and in the light of the terrible experience of the previous quarter of a century the Congress system was well worth trying.

It was also a recognition that the Vienna Settlement needed flexibility in interpretation if it was to be preserved. Castlereagh never expected that the *status quo* would be indefinitely perpetuated. He knew that to impose such a static concept upon the relations of the European Powers was unrealistic. The interests of the states were subject to change; the choice of friends and the pattern of alliances would alter as each country's judgement of what was in its own best interests altered. The Congress system afforded the best means of coming to terms with the essential nature of diplomatic relations without jeopardizing the peace of Europe. For Castlereagh stability did not exclude all change: stability necessitated coming to terms with change, while comprehending it within the larger pattern of the European order in diplomacy. But innovation was subject to the restraint of European peace and stability; and on this basis alone was intervention by the Powers to be authorized. Castlereagh drew a clear distinction between international intervention by the Powers acting for the general good, and the intervention of individual

Powers whenever they thought their own interests threatened. There would be cases when international intervention would be improper and individual intervention defensible. But even when individual intervention was right the Power directly concerned had to be prepared to act on its own responsibility. Castlereagh always appreciated the problems posed for Austria by the growth of Italian nationalism, but when in 1820 Metternich proposed that the Powers should intervene in Naples Castlereagh objected to international action, whatever justification there might be for the Austrians doing whatever they thought necessary for the defence of their own, as distinct from European, interests. He did not believe that the situation in Naples posed a threat to peace. International intervention was therefore uncalled for. If intervention were invoked irresponsibly or applied too lavishly it would cease to carry conviction. What was meant to secure the peace of Europe would be abused to the advantage of the great Powers. Metternich was anxious about the internal security of the states of Europe, and there were political as well as ideological reasons for this preoccupation: liberalism and nationalism threatened the very existence of the Austrian Empire as well as the peace of Europe. Because the existence of Great Britain was not threatened in such a way Castlereagh did not find it necessary to endow the *status quo* with the same degree of permanence that Metternich's understandable concern with the security of Austria compelled him to infer from the situation.

It was inevitable that when the Congress of Aix-la-Chapelle was summoned in 1818 to deal with the re-admission of France as a full member of the Concert of Europe Castlereagh should have misgivings about the way in which the Congress system was understood and, in his view, misrepresented. He repudiated suggestions that there was any special virtue in the *status quo* by which the principle of universal intervention could be validated. His memorandum of October 1818 gave clear expression to his unease:

The idea of an *Alliance Solidaire*, by which each state shall be bound to support the state of succession, government, and possession within all other states from violence and attack, upon condition of receiving for itself a similar guarantee, must be understood as morally implying the previous establishment of such a system of general government as may secure and enforce upon all kings and nations an internal system of peace and justice. Till the mode of constructing such a system shall be devised, the consequence is inadmissible, as nothing could be more immoral, or more prejudicial to the character of government generally, than the idea that their force was collectively to be prostituted to the support of established power, without any consideration of the extent to which it was abused.[35]

Castlereagh was as deeply disturbed by the abuse of power as he was outraged by revolutionary excesses. Such an anxiety was consistent with the whole tenor of his career. From his early years in Irish politics he had been conscious of the dangers of the abuse of power: he had seen the threats to order and social peace created by established injustices and smouldering discontent. He subjected projects for a permanent international association for the defence of the *status quo* to as searching a scrutiny as demands for the reform of the British House of Commons. He rejected any system by which Europe was to be policed by a general alliance of all European states as impracticable. Until some international agency had been devised he thought that all notions of a 'general and unqualified guarantee' should be dismissed. It would be wiser for the states of Europe to rely for their security on what he described as 'the justice and wisdom of their respective systems, aided by such support as other states may feel prepared to afford them, and as circumstances may point out and justify without overstepping those principles which are to be found in the law of nations, as long recognized and practised'.[36]

Castlereagh admitted that a universal alliance for the peace and happiness of the world had always been a matter for 'speculation' and 'hope'; but it had never been put into practice, and, in his view, 'if an opinion may be hazarded from its difficulty, it never can'. It was wiser to limit one's aims, and seek to attain realistic objectives. The treaties of Chaumont and Paris had restored Europe after a generation of French aggrandizement; they had secured Europe against the renewal of French aggression. But there were grave dangers in seeking to extend the scope of the alliance. No state could be compelled – not even France in her experiences of defeat in 1814 and 1815 – to retain its internal system of government unchanged at the bidding of the other Powers of Europe. To suggest such a mode of proceeding was humiliating for all states concerned. Even if it was argued that only legal changes were to be permitted it was impossible for other states accurately to judge the legality of procedures in any single state, or to decide whether a sufficient degree of intrigue or violence had actually taken place, thus giving them the right to interfere. There was only one sure course to take: to follow the principle which Castlereagh believed was already embodied in the law of nations: 'That no state has a right to endanger its neighbours by its internal proceedings, and that if it does, provided they exercise a sound discretion, their right of interference is clear'. He presumed that the allies had a common interest in judging such questions as and when they arose, but not before.

In response to the assertion of a general principle of intervention Castlereagh was putting forward a cautiously limited justification for intervention only in exceptional cases, when some threat to the safety and security of Europe could be established beyond all reasonable doubt. He knew that what he was expounding was open to the charge that it was imprecise, that it left too much to be decided when particular situations arose, but he was convinced that, with all its faults, his was a safer approach to the problem than the sweeping assertion of universal principles. He emphasized that the Prince Regent sincerely desired to act cordially with his allies, but that, in doing so, he was determined 'to stand quite clear in the view of his own engagements not to be supposed to have taken engagements beyond the extent and import of the treaties signed'[37]. Castlereagh had committed Britain to the Congress system, but this did not mean that Britain had yielded her right to assess the problems facing the Powers according to the criteria which the British government thought appropriate in the circumstances. Castlereagh did not forget that Britain was a European Power and that the course of events in Europe influenced British policy and affected British wellbeing. But he refused to sacrifice British interests for the sake of any abstract doctrine of legitimacy or the defence of a changeless and unchangeable *status quo*.

Castlereagh knew that his foreign policy was misunderstood and misrepresented on all sides. The Congress system inspired misgivings within the government, while radical journalists proclaimed that Castlereagh was bartering British interests for the dubious distinction of helping the autocrats of Europe to re-impose the shackles of authoritarianism upon their helpless subjects. It was argued that Britain was the accomplice of tyrants abroad, while at home the Liverpool administration was planning further inroads into traditional liberties, perhaps even plunging the country into all the degradation of a military dictatorship. All this was ignorant nonsense, but Liverpool and his colleagues knew that they had to answer for their actions to the House of Commons, and they were apprehensive about the difficulties of explaining a foreign policy whose sophistications they found it hard to understand. Liverpool, Sidmouth, Canning, Vansittart and Bathurst were all anxious, in varying degrees, about too great a commitment to regular Congresses. Canning was deeply suspicious of the Congress system in itself. He regarded it as new and questionable: it would involve Britain too closely in the politics of the continent. British policy ought to be more aloof, interfering only in the greatest emergencies, and then with commanding force.

On 20 October 1818 Bathurst explained some of the Cabinet's misgivings to Castlereagh. The ministers admitted that conferences were useful and helpful, but they preferred them to take place one at a time: they had no desire for a timetable of future conferences and they were opposed to formulations of doctrine or principle. But they appreciated Castlereagh's feelings on the matter. Bathurst wrote:

It is very natural in you to feel a strong wish that they should continue, from having experienced the advantages which have been derived by this which has taken place; but, even if we could be sure that the subsequent meetings would be equally cordial, is there any advantage in fixing beyond the next period; and we all, without exception, in the Cabinet, concur in thinking it very desirable that the next meeting should be fixed and announced . . . You will understand that the objection which I am now stating is not to the system, but to the expediency of declaring it in a circular letter.[38]

But Bathurst emphasized that Canning's misgivings were more sweeping than those of the rest of the Cabinet. Canning was anxious about anything which looked like an attempt by the major Powers to keep other states in a condition of subjection. Canning reminded the Cabinet of the unpopularity of associating with the autocrats of the continent. Such an association would give a measure of credibility to accusations that traditional English liberties were in jeopardy. Bathurst continued, 'I do not subscribe to Canning's opinion, nor did any of the Cabinet who attended. But, if this is felt by him, it is not unreasonable to apprehend it may be felt by many other persons, as well as by our decided opponents.'[39] Was it wise to take the bull by the horns?

It has often been claimed that Castlereagh was unduly disdainful of public opinion, and that he neglected to explain his policies to the House of Commons or to the public at large. But this argument can be exaggerated. Castlereagh was dubious about the capacity of the radical press and many of the more vocal of his critics to appreciate the force and the subtlety of his foreign policy. He believed that foreign policy was vulnerable to disastrous errors if it was exposed to the ignorant and wayward passions of popular emotion. No viable foreign policy could be evolved unless it was immune from the vagaries of the moods of the hour. But as Leader of the House of Commons Castlereagh knew how important it was to carry the majority of M.P.s with him. He was rightly sceptical about persuading the opposition Whigs that there was any virtue in his policies: his attitude towards them was coloured by their defeatism during the war against Napoleon. But he never underestimated the crucial significance of the country gentlemen in Parliament, the men on whose support every government depended. These men respected character more than argument, conviction more than rhetoric. They distrusted foreigners and they were suspicious of the emperors and kings of Europe. But they never forgot the overriding need of preventing another European war. They were often apprehensive about the state of affairs in France and the dangers – both real and imagined – which this posed to European stability. Though they were incapable of appreciating the skill which Castlereagh displayed in his conduct of foreign policy they shared his desire for peace in Europe, but they never grasped that some understanding with the Powers of Europe was the best way of achieving the object they had most at heart. They resented anything which suggested that Britain was being exploited by Metternich for his own ends, and as time went on they became more dubious about the Congress system, and their dislike for a policy of involvement and intervention became more and more like a fondness for isolationism.

Castlereagh recognized the force of opinion at least in its more negative sense: he knew that public misgivings imposed limits on how far he could go in his commitment to Europe, and, at the same time, a growing divergence of aim and motive separated him from Metternich and the other European leaders. Castlereagh was not fitted, either by temperament or by inclination, to take the initiative in managing public relations. Nor is it easy to see how, in the circumstances of the time, his policy could have been communicated to a public audience with real effect. The sophistication of his policy, its urbane rejection of shallow emotionalism, its disdain for the poses and postures of patriotic rhetoric, its preoccupation with equilibrium and conciliation, were not the materials for a massive exercise in over-simplification. He knew that if the system of alliances went beyond his own idea of what was justifiable there was a strong possibility that Britain would pull out. Every disagreement with his allies turned a possibility into a probability and finally a probability into a certainty.

Some historians have made much of the tragedy of Castlereagh's last years, not only with his suicide in mind, but also because of the way in which the Congress system developed, together with Castlereagh's own assessment of the utility of the system and the extent to which Britain could remain involved in it. But it is misleading to argue that the disillusionment of the years 1820 to 1822 discredited the idea of conference diplomacy. Castlereagh was not to blame for the events which gave a new twist to the meaning of the Congress system: the swing to the Right in France, the growing obsessional quality of Alexander I's outlook and the increasing determination of Metternich to use both the Holy Alliance and the Quintuple Alliance as the means of imposing his own notion of order and stability upon Europe, even at the cost of insisting that the principle of intervention had to be accepted by the Powers. Castlereagh was convinced that Britain could not remain aloof from affairs in Europe, but when Metternich became more insistent upon the implementation of policies which Castlereagh had set his face against as early as 1815, then British dissociation from certain actions was both inevitable and the expression of principles to which Castlereagh had always been attached. His attitude had been coloured by a sober pessimism. Although he believed that something of real value could be achieved through the Congress system he had never expected too much from it. Although he hoped that the Powers would remind themselves of those interests which they had in common he had never relied on idealism or the spirit of benevolence as the inspirations of policy. In 1815 he had commented on the greed and selfishness of the Powers, noting that the minor Powers were just as eager for gain and aggrandizement as the strong ones. In a letter of 4 September 1815 he had written to Clancarty:

It is curious to observe the insatiable spirit of getting something without a thought of how it is to be preserved. There is not a Power, however feeble, that borders France from the Channel to the Mediterranean that is not pushing some acquisition under the plea of the security and rectification of frontier. They seem to have no dread of a kick from the lion when his toils are removed, and are foolish enough to suppose that the great Powers of Europe are to be in readiness to protect them in the enjoyment of these petty spoils. In truth, their whole conception is so unstatesmanlike that they look not beyond their sop; compared with this the keeping together a European force has little importance in their eyes.[40]

He had always believed that a judicious appeal to intelligent self-interest was the best argument in dealing with his allies. But he knew that he could not assume that his fellow-diplomatists would habitually accept his view of what their best interests demanded. He had experienced such frustrations over the Slave Trade, but his most dramatic difference of opinion with the statesmen of Europe, represented above all by Metternich, turned on the principle of intervention, a principle which Castlereagh had always seen as dangerous and impracticable. When it became enshrined as part of the orthodoxy of European conservatism the time had come for the reappraisal of British foreign policy. The principle of intervention, as a universal remedy for the ills of Europe, and applied with rigid logic to the domestic affairs of nation states or subject provinces, had always been distrusted by Castlereagh. He had seen in it a threat to the judicious use of the Congress system and he had fought against it from the start. But although Metternich's understanding of the Holy Alliance was as much the product of events as the outcome of ideology he had seen the problems of Europe in a light rather different from that of Castlereagh, despite their common anxiety for stability and peace. Metternich could not divorce the stability of Europe and the security of the Austrian Empire from the internal affairs of other countries: his difference of opinion from Castlereagh was fundamental. Castlereagh had hoped that the experience of Congress diplomacy would convert other statesmen to his more pragmatic approach: conferences directed to the settlement of tangible problems, with strictly limited objectives, were a security for peace. But conferences attuned to the principle of universal intervention were themselves disruptive of the Concert of Europe. Castlereagh had taken this position from the beginning of his involvement with conference diplomacy. All that happened was that events disappointed his hopes and justified his pessimism.

Castlereagh believed that he was putting traditional diplomatic principles to a new use. He did not see himself as an innovator in doctrine or in theories of international relations. He tried to use experience to evolve new forms in which traditional diplomatic concepts of limited objectives, compromise settlements, and a respect for the integrity and domestic authority of the states of Europe would be given fuller expression within the context of a Concert of Powers dedicated to preserving the peace. But the preservation of peace did not mean the perpetuation of every jot and tittle of the Vienna settlement. Here was another area of interpretation and controversy in which Castlereagh's divergence from Metternich became more marked as time went by.

Castlereagh valued the notion of the Powers meeting regularly to keep the peace, but in July 1817 he was emphatic in affirming that the original limits within which the Quadruple Alliance was conceived should not be forgotten. 'The allied ministers at Paris', he wrote to Sir Charles Stuart, 'must be kept within the bounds of their original institution and not to be suffered to present themselves as an

European Council for the management of the affairs of the world.'[41] This did not mean that he was incapable of appreciating the principles upon which Metternich was acting. In the abstract, and with due caution in their application, they might even be wise and sound, he had told his brother in May 1817, but the allies had to proceed with circumspection. It was dangerous to base a policy upon 'speculative grounds which might prove fatal'. It was important to preserve the alliance and the Congress system for as long as possible, and it was necessary to give practicable and sensible aid to the régime in France, in order to assist the restored monarchy to establish itself, but nothing was to be done – 'either upon chance or upon suspicion' – which was inconsistent with the declared relations that existed between the Powers. Every development favourable to the security of Europe was to be cultivated, but it was still to be left to 'actual necessity' to determine whether some 'ascertained danger' compelled the allies to act collectively. Castlereagh feared that too broad a commitment to a policy of intervention would lead to ill-considered interference in the domestic affairs of other states. This was potentially dangerous, especially in the case of France. He consistently showed a high sense of the complexities of the situation in France and the grave difficulties facing the restored Bourbons. He never lost his initial suspicion that they ultimately lacked the judgement and the skill necessary for the proper handling of the problems of the restoration. These misgivings heightened his conviction that any bold policy of intervention along the lines advocated by Metternich would be embarrassing and disastrous from the point of view of Europe as a whole. No one had worked harder than Castlereagh to persuade the Powers to place the interests of Europe first and their own national interests second, but he became increasingly anxious about the way in which first Austria and then Russia became more committed to collective intervention as a primary resource of policy.

On 19 October 1818 Castlereagh communicated his anxieties to Liverpool, giving vent to his alarm that the Russian Emperor and his advisers were 'disposed to push their ideas very far indeed in the sense of *all the powers of Europe being bound together in a common league guaranteeing each other the existing order of things in thrones as well as in territories* all being bound to march, if requisite, against the first power that offended either by her ambitions, or by her revolutionary transgressions'.[42] Castlereagh recognized the difficulties of reconciling such sentiments either with the general tendency of British foreign policy since 1815 or with dominant opinion in Parliament. He did not have a sure confidence in the capacity of M.P.s to understand the intricacies of foreign policy but he never forgot that the government had to carry the House of Commons with it, and this would be virtually impossible if the grandiose ideas of the Russian Emperor were identified with British foreign policy and taken as the principles by which Britain's relations with her European allies were to be defined.

Castlereagh's scepticism expressed itself in his attitude towards projects for disarmament as well as in his misgivings about the policies of Austria and Russia. It was not that he failed to appreciate the value of some agreed and workable pattern of disarmament. He knew that military expenditure was the biggest single drain on the public purse: war was the gravest threat to conventional ideas of sound finance. But while other men enunciated general principles Castlereagh preferred to proceed from the particular to the general. He made no pretence of possessing that degree of universal wisdom which so often passed for omniscience. An agreement among the Powers to limit their armed forces in a certain ratio was attractive in principle, but the more he thought about the difficulties of putting such a principle into effect the greater they became. Even the preliminary question, that of agreeing some scale of force among the Powers, raised insurmountable questions of acute and complex difficulty. The length of frontiers, their varying nature, the need to strengthen defences in particular areas against especially dangerous threats to national security, the additional resources available to some Powers, but not to others, by which speedy re-armament was possible – all of these issues impressed themselves upon Castlereagh, and even if some agreed reduction in military forces was implemented it was far from clear how such a system was to be maintained. From time to time states would have to increase their armaments, however temporarily, and no one knew how this could be accommodated within any general system of disarmament. On this, as on other subjects which Castlereagh thought likely to provoke the jealousies and suspicions of the Powers, attempting to accomplish too much merely brought difficulties into view without settling them. The best course, in his opinion, lay not in attempting to reach comprehensive agreement, but for each state to disarm to the extent which it believed consistent with national security, while explaining to allied and neighbouring states the reasons for its policies. In this fashion some reduction of forces, however modest, might be achieved, and a meas- ure of mutual trust established. Castlereagh never overlooked the influence of suspicion and fear on the making of policy, but it was characteristic that he saw no universal solution to the problems which this posed.

He thought it useless to speculate on what the future might hold. Prophecy in politics was 'a very idle occupation', and this applied to schemes of intervention just as much as to dreams of world disarmament, international peace, or the brotherhood of man. General principles, whether conservative or liberal, were dubious in Castlereagh's eyes because they so often ignored the fallibility of human nature, the limited capacity of even the most intelligent and high-minded statesmen to perceive all the issues involved in certain problems and the means by which they were to be solved. He preferred to accept the fact of human fallibility, while ensuring that its worst consequences were moderated and prevented from doing excessive damage to civilized society. He was as sensitive to the limits which human vulnerability imposed on policies which he favoured as he was convinced that ideology stimulated human expectations and fanned political passions, only to bring disillusionment and frustration in its train. He was out of sympathy with demands that Britain should support liberal or constitutional régimes wherever they might appear, and equally opposed to the idea that Britain should take part in an international alliance committed to rooting out liberal or revolutionary governments wherever they were established. Neither of these attitudes helped the formulation of a foreign policy attuned to the realities of international politics.

As the situation in Spain deteriorated, and as King Ferdinand contemplated calling upon the Powers to assist him in securing his régime against the restlessness of his subjects, Castlereagh sensed that it would become more difficult for Britain to maintain a common front with her European allies. Metternich was also uneasy about the manifest political instability of the kingdom of Naples, but although Castlereagh appreciated Metternich's anxieties over unrest in Germany and Italy, since Austrian interests were threatened, he was not attracted to collective intervention in Italy. Castlereagh was also more critical of the Spanish king than were most other European statesmen. He had always been sceptical about the possibility that Ferdinand would show either insight or wisdom in his dealings with his subjects. The Spanish liberals were naïve and unrealistic and the Spanish royalists were arrogant and stupid. Castlereagh was weary of the obstinacy and pride of the Spanish and Portuguese and he thought that their intransigence had caused additional difficulties in their relations with their American colonists. In Castlereagh's opinion the situations in Italy and Spain did not justify collective intervention. There might be a case for individual Powers acting if their own security was threatened, but Britain did not seek to be identified with collective interference. Castlereagh knew that this would create problems of great delicacy in responding to Metternich and the other Europeans who were eager for firm action in the face of what they considered to be revolutionary provocation.

The Spanish crisis merely underlined all the misgivings which Castlereagh had felt about collective action. The principle that states could interfere by force as well as by exhortation in the internal affairs of other countries raised issues of moral and political intricacy. To elevate such a principle into a scheme of international policy and to make it obligatory on members of the Quintuple Alliance was objectionable and impracticable. No government such as the British, which was responsible for its policies to an elected Parliament, could tolerate such a system or have any part in it. Castlereagh believed that the sooner the doctrine of intervention, as a basis for the alliance, was denounced, the better. This did not mean that the British government ignored real threats to security and stability: at some future date some measure of intervention might be justified, but the danger would have to be 'practical and intelligible'. Castlereagh stressed that Britain would not and could not commit herself on 'any question of an abstract character'. When the balance of power in Europe was disturbed Britain would not hesitate to act with her allies in defence of international stability, but Britain was the last country in Europe which could allow abstract theories to determine her policy.

Castlereagh's memorandum on the Spanish Question emphasized this point again and again:

> We shall be found in our place when actual danger menaces the system of Europe; but this country cannot and will not act upon abstract and speculative principles of precaution. The Alliance which exists had no such purpose in view in its original formation. It was never so explained to Parliament; if it had, most assuredly the sanction of Parliament would never have been given to it.[43]

Castlereagh was applying to international questions the familiar distinction between the expression of ideas, which however distasteful in itself was permissible unless it made likely a breach of the peace, and the actual carrying out of specific actions disruptive of public order and menacing to the security of persons and property. In European terms this meant that no good would come of intervening in the domestic affairs of a country merely because the internal political situation or the forms of government which were being established were thought objectionable on principle. Whatever opinions the rulers of Europe held, however tenaciously, on the legitimacy of political institutions, each country had the right to settle its domestic problems for itself. Only when such problems posed a direct threat to European stability were they brought within the scope of international scrutiny and possible collective action. The onus lay on the Powers to establish the precise threat to the safety of Europe which a change of government in any single state posed: and here Castlereagh was thinking of tangible indications of military preparedness, acts of aggression, or denunciations of the solemn obligations implied by various treaties.

Castlereagh knew how difficult it was to generalize on this and on other questions affecting international policy. Every generalization was open to the objection that it prejudged certain issues or ignored essential factors in the overall situation. He sought to retain a firm link between taking up a general stance over particular aspects of policy and the type of action which the implementation of such a standpoint implied. He did not deny that radical principles challenged the validity of established institutions, but unless liberals in, say, Spain or Italy claimed the right to spread their doctrines to other countries by force – in the style of the French revolutionaries in 1792 – he refused to countenance any interference in the domestic affairs of sovereign states. He was acutely conscious of the difficulties of imposing political settlements from outside: foreign Powers rarely understood the finer shades of political loyalty or the motives which crucially altered the balance of political forces and the ultimate political fortunes in particular countries. The British experience in Spain and Portugal had revealed to him how difficult it was for an ally, let alone foreign Powers intervening by force, to impose policies on governments resentful of anything which resembled an affront to their pride. After 1815 Castlereagh had also seen most of his misgivings about the restored French monarchy in France justified by events. Despite the moderation and intelligence of Louis XVIII he had been unable to control the more extreme royalists. Moderates such as Talleyrand had been pushed out of public life by men whose reputations were less tarnished by history but whose insight was as defective as their principles were pure. Ferdinand of Spain was a fool: Castlereagh had little time for him or for the cause he represented. All these experiences made Castlereagh dubious about the practicability of the Quintuple Alliance acting as the watchdogs for the political probity of the states of Europe.

The Congress of Troppau saw Castlereagh urging moderation and restraint upon his allies. On 16 September 1820 he outlined his approach to his brother:

. . . With all the respect and attachment which I feel for the system of the Alliance as regulated by the transactions of Aix-la-Chapelle, I should much question the prudence, or, in truth, the efficiency, of any formal exercise of its forms and provisions on the present occasion.

If the existing danger arose from any obvious infraction of the stipulations of our treaties, an extraordinary reunion of sovereigns and their cabinets would be a measure of obvious policy; but when the danger springs from the internal convulsions of independent states, the policy of hazarding such a step is much more questionable: and when we recollect to what prejudicial misconceptions and popular irritation the conference at Pillnitz and the declaration of the Duke of Brunswick . . . gave occasion, it may well suggest the expediency that whatever ought or can be done for the general safety against the insurrectionary movements of conspiring and rebellious troops should be undertaken, after full deliberation, in the manner which will afford the least handle for misrepresentation and excitement, and which may give the effort to be made the fullest justification of a local and specific necessity arising out of the particular case.[44]

This emphasis upon local and specific necessity typified Castlereagh's anxiety to avoid broad commitments of an open-ended nature. He never forgot the experiences of the 1790s. They were fundamental to his whole manner of conducting politics. He needed no radical publicists to teach him any lessons about the errors of judgement which had so damaged the cause of legitimacy throughout the long war against the French Republic. Castlereagh recalled that Pitt had never countenanced a war of ideologies: he had always set himself firmly against any crusade based on the principles so eloquently expounded by Edmund Burke. Neither Pitt nor Castlereagh accepted that compelling rhetoric compensated for fallible judgement. Castlereagh believed in working for stability and peace, and he knew that this meant some form of international cooperation, but he never lost his sense of political reality. The heady mysteries of political philosophy never tempted him into bold gestures or obscure speculations. There was an earthy, unsentimental, shrewdly cautious quality about his policies, but the subtlety with which he tried to avoid the superficialities associated with enlightenment and the obtuseness resonant of reaction was lost on most of his contemporaries. He knew that international politics called for a mind capable of flexibility and a temperament unmoved by emotionalism. Policy was the expression, not of wordy visions, but of tangible interests and viable objectives. It was easier to talk about liberty or to denounce revolution than to formulate a policy that was sound and practicable, and since Castlereagh had little fondness for the rhetoric of Right or Left he was often misunderstood by both.

The year 1820 was characterized by upheavals throughout Europe. In Spain the King was compelled to accept a constitution, but Ferdinand appealed to the monarchs of Europe for help. Revolutions broke out in Portugal, Naples, and Piedmont. The Russian Emperor responded by urging collective action: his visionary notions of an international alliance for stability and peace were once more fired by events. Castlereagh did not flinch: 'The more Russia wishes to transport us to the heights the further we must descend to the plain.'[45] But it would not be easy to plead the cause of moderation when the allies were so convinced that international revolution was a reality, not a figment of the imagination.

Castlereagh did not attend the Congress of Troppau. His brother, Lord Stewart, was sent as the British observer. Castlereagh hoped that the negotiations at Troppau would be of a limited nature. He hoped that Metternich would exercise a restraining influence on Alexander I, who was thinking of marching Russian armies across Europe to intervene in Spain. He told his brother that whatever was decided about the Spanish crisis should be closely related to the particular needs of the situation, without 'hazarding general declarations, containing universal pledges that cannot be redeemed, and which, from the first, will be seen through and despised. Dissertations on abstract principles will do nothing in the present day, unless supported.' He doubted whether such support was right and proper on this occasion. He was opposed to making declarations which amounted to the five major Powers forming themselves into a league against the *de facto* government in Naples. Such conduct was anathema to the British government. Liverpool and his colleagues were adamant that they would not enter into any obligations of such a nature. There were several reasons for their refusal to do so. They had no wish to bind themselves to engagements which could not be justified unless the whole content of the negotiations was communicated to Parliament, and they believed that the policy of intervention would not be approved by the House of Commons. A policy of collective intervention would involve the British in the use of force, and this, in turn, would probably lead to the Neapolitans seizing British property in the kingdom of the Two Sicilies. Britain was already committed to a policy of neutrality in Naples, and there were not sufficient reasons for becoming entwined in the internal feuds of that kingdom. Britain would not be able to control all the actions of the Powers, acting collectively, but the government would be made to account for them to Parliament and this would produce political complications which were not worth risking. Even if the Powers delegated the responsibility for taking action in Naples to Austria it would be impracticable for Britain to scrutinize Austrian actions there. Every act of the Austrian army would be examined in Parliament, and this would embarrass the government in its relations with Austria. Castlereagh regarded the practical objections to collective action in Naples as insuperable, and he hoped that Metternich would see that the consequences of British participation in such a policy would be nothing less than alarming. Anglo-Austrian relations would be embittered by such an involvement.

But Castlereagh did not deny that if Austrian interests in Italy were threatened by what was happening in Naples it would be proper for them to intervene on their own initiative and on their own authority. But it would not then be a matter for the Powers. Nothing that had occurred in Naples came within the stipulations of the Quintuple Alliance as Castlereagh understood them. Castlereagh took this stance despite his recognition that his allies believed the revolution in Naples to be 'pregnant with danger and of evil example'. The revolution had been the work of disloyal troops and a secret sect, whose object was the subversion of existing governments in the Italian states and the creation of a unified Italian state. But the degree to which such objectives bore upon the interests of the member-states of the Quintuple Alliance varied. There could be no more dramatic contrast than that between the attitudes of Austria and Britain in this instance. The Austrians believed that the defence of their own interests in Italy compelled them to adopt measures to restore legitimate government in Naples. But Britain was not threatened, either directly or indirectly. Nothing that had been said in Parliament could possibly justify British intervention in Neapolitan domestic politics. It was possible to acquiesce in Austria's own act of intervention, but it would still be necessary for Britain to be satisfied that Austria had had no objectives of aggrandizement, and that she was not seeking, under the pretence of defending legitimacy, to establish her own supremacy in Italy in a sense which went beyond existing treaty arrangements or which threatened the Italian states. Her actions would have to be seen as being related to the protection of her own legitimate interests in Italy and nothing else. Only in this fashion would Austrian intervention be defensible and it would have to be evident to everyone that no formal action had been taken on behalf of the Quintuple Alliance as a whole. Britain might condone Austria's conduct, but she did not intend to be publicly associated with it. 'We desire to leave Austria unembarrassed,' Castlereagh wrote, '. . . but we must claim for ourselves the same freedom of action.'[46] He believed that Austrian interests would be best served if she understood the British position and admitted its validity.

Castlereagh's deep distrust of King Ferdinand of Spain became more pronounced as the years went by. Shortly before his death he told Mrs Arbuthnot that the King of Spain's behaviour had been shameful and that the Spanish people were showing great forbearance in dealing with him. He was mindful of the protests which Spanish liberals had made against any joint action by the Powers, and he was unmoved by pleas from Ferdinand for combined intervention by the allies on his behalf. Castlereagh thought that the Powers would have to think very carefully before embarking on a course of action which might have the deplorable consequence of encouraging 'all the crowned heads of Europe to expect aid from them in those perilous situations in which they are or may find themselves involved'. He rejected any suggestion that the allies should save kings from the consequences of their own folly, incapacity or wilfulness.

Fallacious hopes may seriously augment their danger by relaxing their legitimate and natural efforts either to maintain their own power by their own means (an effect perhaps already apparent in the facility with which all the recent revolutionary changes have been submitted to), or to accommodate themselves with good faith and before it is too late by some prudent change of system to the exigencies of their peculiar position.[47]

There was a greater degree of elasticity of mind in his thinking here than has often been supposed. Metternich was irritated by what he considered Castlereagh's deplorable ambivalence. Castlereagh was capable of saying that he liked to see evil germs destroyed even when he could not publicly approve the deed. In May 1820 he boasted to Metternich of the progress made in the struggle against radicalism in England: 'the monster still lives, and shows himself in new shapes; but we do not despair of crushing him by time and perseverance'.[48] It was this type of statement which impelled the Austrian ambassador to say that Castlereagh was like a great lover of music who found himself in church: he wished to applaud but he could not do so. But Castlereagh never lost sight of the need to humour his allies, even when he disagreed with them. He and Metternich disagreed about the policy of intervention and the purpose of the Quintuple Alliance, but they shared a common anxiety for the peace of Europe and in order to facilitate Anglo-Austrian collaboration Castlereagh was capable of touching up the Liverpool administration's record in dealing with domestic disturbances in order to convince Metternich that despite their disagreements they shared a concern for stability and order.

However, Castlereagh could not give indiscriminate approval to the régimes of post-Waterloo Europe. He knew that many of the restored monarchs and princes owed their thrones, not to the transcendent rightness of a principle of legitimacy, but to a nice calculation of what was politically viable. He had accepted legitimacy as a useful expedient, but it could not be cited in condonation of behaviour which was inhumane, unjust, and tyrannical. It was only logical that he should recognize that in certain circumstances it was judicious to come to terms with change, and that in certain situations monarchs would be better advised to accept the reforms desired by their subjects than to call upon the Powers to save them from their own ineptitude. Castlereagh believed that each country had the right to find its own way forward and to evolve, in the light of its own experience, the institutions of government best suited for its needs. This implied that if, in some countries, the chief requirement was the defence of the constitution against those who were planning insurrection or riot, in others measures of cautious reform were just as legitimate and if they were properly handled they would make a valuable contribution to the peace and stability of Europe. Castlereagh always differentiated between countries such as France and Holland, and the situation in Spain and the states of Germany or Italy. It was ironic that those countries where the régime was repugnant to him – Spain, Portugal and Naples – should also be those whose radicals inspired him with as much mistrust as their legitimate monarchs. But misgivings such as these only strengthened his determination to prevent any British involvement in a universal policy of collective intervention.

Castlereagh believed that in dealing with the situation in Naples Metternich had made a grave mistake in defining it as a European rather than an Austrian question. Had Metternich emphasized the particular dangers which the Neapolitan revolution held for Austrian interests in Italy he would have had just as much sympathy and would have avoided raising the ticklish question of collective action. It would have been better if Metternich had merely asserted the potential threat to every government in Italy which a government based on nationalist principles, and associated with the Carbonari, presented, rather than arguing that every government in Europe was menaced by events in Naples. Castlereagh believed that a more limited approach would have carried more conviction with British public opinion: Metternich had ruined his case by overstating it. A carefully restrained justification for limited Austrian action would have been preferable to 'embarking himself on the boundless ocean on which he has preferred to sail'. Castlereagh could not refrain from commenting, 'Our friend Metternich, with all his merit, prefers a complicated negotiation to a bold and rapid stroke.'[49]

It was inevitable that the decisions made by the Congress at Troppau, which approved and supported Austrian action in Naples but which also authorized Austria to act on behalf of the Powers while claiming a universal right of intervention whenever it was deemed necessary, should call forth a negative response from Britain. The British Circular of 19 January 1821 summed up the British case, communicating to all the Powers of Europe the thinking which Castlereagh had already made clear to his brother and to his colleagues in the government. The British government did not disguise its disapproval of the revolution in Naples, but such disapproval was not tantamount to advocating a policy of interference. The British repeated that they recognized that other Powers, particularly Austria and the Italian states, would assess their own interests differently from those of Britain. The British had no intention of prejudging the issue or of denying to states their legitimate right to take the actions they thought necessary for their own security. But the British were looking for the assurance that when intervention was contemplated it was not being undertaken for purposes of aggrandizement or for the subversion of 'the territorial system of Europe, as established by the late treaties'. The boundaries agreed upon at Vienna had the sanction of the Powers and of the nations of Europe generally. But this sanction did not automatically extend to every domestic institution of government. At the same time Britain was not condemning all acts of intervention:

It should be clearly understood, that no government can be more prepared than the British Government is, to uphold the right of any state or states to interfere, where their own immediate security, or essential interests, are seriously endangered by the internal transactions of another state. But, as they regard the assumption of such right, as only to be justified by the strongest necessity, and to be limited and regulated thereby; they cannot admit that this right can receive a general and indiscriminate application to all revolutionary movements, without reference to their immediate bearing upon *some* particular state or states, or be made prospectively the basis of an alliance. They regard its exercise as an exception to general principles, of the greatest value and importance, and as one that only properly grows out of the circumstances of the special case; but they, at the same time, consider, that exceptions of this description never can, without the utmost danger, be so far reduced to rule, as to be incorporated into the ordinary diplomacy of states, or into the institutions of the law of nations.[50]

Castlereagh believed that Metternich was wrong to try to convert a properly recognized discretionary power into a regular agent of collective diplomacy. At the same time, however strained relations had become and however much British policy had diverged from that of her partners in the alliance, it was hoped that the 'difference of sentiment' would not undermine 'the cordiality and harmony of the Alliance on any other subject, or abate their common zeal in giving the most complete effect to all their existing arrangements'. But for Castlereagh the phrase 'existing arrangements' had as much weight as the references to cordiality. He had always supported the Quadruple and Quintuple Alliances. In some ways they were his creations more than any other single diplomatist's. But he had consistently argued that the alliances were for definable objectives and for limited purposes. Far from being drawn into an ever-widening web of continental commitments Britain had accepted precise responsibilities for valid and attainable ends. Castlereagh rejected the vague principles expressed in the Tsar's Holy Alliance, and he knew that, if the more grandiose principles embodied in the Holy Alliance were ever associated with the Quintuple Alliance and the Congress system, the Concert of Europe would be questioned in England and all the more difficult to defend in Parliament. It was especially galling to find his allies distorting the purpose of the Alliance and thereby making it easier for his critics at home to denounce his foreign policy in general. He had no wish for Britain to slip into isolationism, but the strain of maintaining the European commitment became greater with every year that passed, and at a time when his European allies ought to have shown restraint they were becoming more extravagant in their conduct.

Castlereagh vehemently disapproved of the Troppau Protocol, which proclaimed the belief of Austria, Prussia, and Russia that a general right of intervention stemmed from the system of alliances. Castlereagh was infuriated by the behaviour of his allies. He had shown sympathy with the predicament in which the Austrians found themselves in Italy, despite his belief that the troubles in Italy did not constitute a threat to the peace of Europe. But now he felt that he was being subjected to pressures which betrayed a total lack of understanding of the British point of view. The British government had consistently sought to dissuade the other Powers from defining the doctrine of intervention in universal terms. Castlereagh felt compelled to remind his allies that the Powers had originally committed themselves to renewed cooperation and regular conferences for reasons of self-defence against any possible renewal of French aggression. The treaty of November 1815 had stated that the Powers would deliberate together to concert the means of securing their own safety in the event of another revolution in France. But the assertion of the principle of intervention went far beyond this. The Powers were making innovations in international practice which Castlereagh believed to be in violation of established international law. Worst of all, the right of intervention – asserted as a general principle of politics – was an obstacle to the intelligent handling of difficult and dangerous situations. On 16 December 1820 Castlereagh assured his brother that 'the extreme right of interference between nation and nation can never be made a matter of written stipulation or be assumed as the attribute of any alliance'. The British government objected to the fundamental principle of the protocol, by which the Powers were made responsible for scrutinizing the internal transactions of independent states. The doctrine of general intervention destroyed all independent action and what Castlereagh described as 'all wholesome national energy' within the smaller states. Every country ought to depend on its own resources for the solution of domestic problems. The British government would not and could not take upon itself 'the moral responsibility of administering a general European police of this description'.[51]

Castlereagh's distrust of the principle of intervention had now gone further than in his state paper of May 1820. He believed that systematic intervention would stimulate those developments which it was intended to destroy. The revolutions of 1820 had not been comparable to the French Revolution of 1789. There had been no attempt to spread the principles of revolution by force of arms or to change the frontiers of Europe. But if the Powers insisted upon exercising the right of intervening in domestic politics Castlereagh argued that this would have grave implications. The peoples of countries subjected to intervention would be tempted to imitate the example of the French in 1792:

The apprehension of an armed interference in their internal affairs may excite them to arm, may induce them to look with greater jealousy and distrust than ever to the conduct of their rulers, in short, may accelerate the progress of republican principles and perhaps lead to the destruction even of the semblance of monarchical institutions within these states. What hope in such case of a better order of things to result from the prudence and calm deliberations among a people agitated by the apprehensions of foreign force, and how hopeless on the other hand the attempt to settle by foreign arms or foreign influence alone any stable or national system of government!

Castlereagh urged his allies to refrain from an experiment which was controversial and the effects of which – at a time of 'moral and political ferment' – 'no human foresight can estimate and no combination of powers may be able to control'.[52]

On 17 December Castlereagh reminded his brother that the House of Hanover could not maintain the principles on which the House of Stuart had forfeited the British throne. He was sadly coming to the conclusion that Austria, Russia, and Prussia were destroying the alliance on which so many of his hopes had rested. They were taking the initiative in making assertions which went far beyond the terms of the alliance, and they were responsible for perverting the Congress system.

It now rests with the three Courts to decide whether they choose to contend against the dangers of the times under separate banners: the choice is with them, not with us: they may contend upon the case as we propose without laying down disputed principles. We cannot adhere to their doctrine, and if they will be theorists we must act in separation upon matters not specifically provided for by treaty, which seems an odd option for them to make in the present state of Europe.[53]

Castlereagh believed that in their very anxiety to preserve established institutions in Europe the rulers of Austria, Russia and Prussia were jeopardizing all that they held most dear. He knew that they would regard Britain as the Power which was at odds with its allies, but he remained convinced that the onus for destroying the Congress system as a security for peace – as distinct from an agency for international repression – rested with Austria, Russia, and Prussia. Although the Congress of Troppau was adjourned to meet at Laibach, and though in the summer of 1822 preparations were being made for another Congress at Verona, Castlereagh had little doubt that the assumptions upon which his own commitment – and that of Britain – to the practice of Congress diplomacy had been based had been shattered by events and undermined by the obstinacy of his allies. It was a sad end to a great experiment.

What was all the more galling for Castlereagh was his awareness that the Russian Emperor was capable of violating all the abstract principles of international conservatism whenever he judged it to be in Russian interests to do so. The Greek Revolt exposed all the potential dangers of the extension of Russian influence in the Near East. The noble protestations of principle emanating from Metternich and Alexander were prone to evaporate when calculations of national self-interest were brought to bear upon the dogmas of conservatism. Metternich believed that the preservation of the Ottoman Empire was essential for the preservation of the Austrian Empire. It was ironic that the traditional foe of the Habsburgs should now be seen as an insurance against instability in the Balkans and a barrier to Russian expansion towards the Mediterranean. But Metternich was too familiar with the twists and turns of history not to appreciate the way in which yesterday's enemies become tomorrow's friends. Metternich could not allow an exception to be made to the rule affecting his attitude towards those who rebelled against established and legitimate authority: he was unmoved by sentimental pleas that because the Greeks were Christians their rebellion against the Sultan should be condoned, perhaps even encouraged, by the Powers of Europe. The principle of nationality was especially dangerous in the Balkans, and especially ominous for Austria's dealings with her Slav subjects. Alexander was bound to look at the situation differently. In a vague sense Russia saw herself as the heir to the Eastern Roman Empire: it was tempting to revive ideas of Moscow as the third Rome. Piety, sentiment and national prestige combined to fire visions of Russia as the liberator of the Greeks, with a Christian Power re-established in Constantinople, and Russia as the patron of Greek Orthodoxy and the focal point of a Christian *imperium* in the Balkans. Dreams such as these were attractive to a man of Alexander's mystical disposition. He was untroubled by the contradiction that, while in central and western Europe he was the defender of traditional forms of government against insurrection and revolt, in Greece he stood forth as the defender of an oppressed Christian people and the spokesman for a nationalism as pervasive as it was ambivalent and as disturbing as it was appealing to liberals everywhere.

Metternich was distressed by Russian unreliability on the Greek rebellion. Despite their disagreements Metternich and Castlereagh were once more drawn together by the peculiar problems raised by the eastern question. Their sober assessment of national interests compelled them to defend the Turkish Empire against internal disruption and the threat of Russian intervention on the side of rebels and revolutionaries. Neither Castlereagh nor Metternich had any illusions about the Turks. They were appalled by Turkish atrocities, and they recognized how ramshackle the structure of the Turkish Empire had become. But they saw the Greek revolt as posing dangers to the equilibrium in Europe: they could not risk the expansion of Russian power in the eastern Mediterranean.

The Greek crisis saw Castlereagh seeking to exploit the language of counter-revolution to dissuade the Russian Emperor from throwing the weight of Russian might into the struggle on the side of the Greek insurgents. It was convenient to claim that the spirit which was active in the Greek rebellion was the same spirit which had motivated revolutions in Spain, Portugal and Italy and which had distressed the Tsar so much. But the situation was made all the more complex because the Turks behaved in ways which gained much sympathy for the rebels, permitting them to cloak their designs under emotions of general benevolence.

Castlereagh therefore attempted – with pardonable exaggeration – to impress upon Alexander the dangers to the internal stability of Russia if the Greek revolt succeeded. The principles of revolution would spread: the southern provinces of the Russian Empire would be infected. Castlereagh stressed that more than local issues were at stake, but he did so to prevent the Tsar from intervening in Greece: nothing that he said muted British opposition to the principle of intervention. Castlereagh was using the ideology of conservatism to thwart Russian intervention. The Russian Emperor had to see the threat to his own dominions, a threat posed by a conspiratorial rebellion led by foreign adventurers rather than being the spontane-ous eruption of Greek idealism that so many fondly imagined it to be. In any other country bordering on Russia the Tsar would have seen the danger. He could not afford sentiment and romanticism to blind him to the threat posed by the rebellion in Greece. He had to be convinced of the need to oppose the common enemy with all the authority at his command. Quarrels between Russia and Turkey were subordinate to the primary need to preserve some semblance of order in Greece. The unusually extreme language which Castlereagh used to bring the Tsar round reflected his anxiety to prevent any Russian intervention in Greece, under any pretext whatsoever. Castlereagh knew that once Russian forces were committed in Greece – whether to support the legitimate government or, as was more probable, to defend the Greek Christians – it would be difficult, perhaps impossible, to get them to withdraw. He did not assume that the Russians would model their actions on the example of

Austria's intervention in Naples. Once the Russians moved into Greece they would become involved in hostilities between the Turks and the Greeks. It was necessary to stop the Russians from doing anything which would prevent the Turks from restoring order and putting down the revolt. Only in this way would the needs of internal stability and the general tranquillity of Europe be satisfied.

But this did not mean that the Greeks were to be abandoned to every indignity which the Turks might choose to inflict. Castlereagh argued that the Powers would be well advised to support the Turks as the rightful government, while extending their protection to the Greeks once order had been restored. Once the Greeks had given up open resistance to legitimate authority then the Powers would be able effectively to intervene, not on political grounds, but for reasons of common humanity.

Castlereagh had no particular affection or respect for the Ottoman Empire. In some ways it was an excrescence upon Europe. It had been guilty of acts of barbarism and it held out little prospect of significant improvement. But its destruction would create a dangerous vacuum in the Balkans. Castlereagh was sceptical about the chances of creating a stable body of states from the dismembered corpse of the Turkish Empire. It was much more likely that if Turkish power in Europe were destroyed Russia would establish her own hegemony in the Balkans. This would threaten British interests in the Mediterranean and the very existence of the Austrian Empire. The risks of conniving in the destruction of Turkey were too great to be borne. Turkey was no more than 'a necessary evil', but he advised Alexander against intermeddling in 'the endless and inextricable mazes of Turkish confusion'.[54]

Despite his caution Castlereagh was not without a measure of sympathy for the Greeks. He confessed that if a statesman were permitted to regulate his conduct by 'the counsels of his heart instead of the dictates of his understanding' he would naturally seek to free the Christian subjects of Turkey from bondage. The Greeks were descended from a people 'in the admiration of whom we have been educated'. But the first duty was to provide for the peace and security of Europe and the stability of the Balkans. Vague notions of humanity and improvement could not be allowed to seduce the British or other European governments from their clear duty to preserve order. They could not encourage or support the Greek insurrection, and it would be especially improper if a remote chance of eventual self-government tempted the Powers sympathetic to the Greeks to throw the political system of Europe into confusion.[55] Yet this was likely to happen if the Russians intervened on behalf of the Greeks and successfully propagated their influence in the Balkans. A dispute over Russian expansion towards Constantinople or over schemes for a Russian protectorate over the Greek Christians, whether these remained under Turkish rule or were given some measure of independence, would destroy the alliance on which Castlereagh still hoped to erect an acceptable method of facilitating European peace and security.

His aims in the Greek crisis were simple, though he showed considerable skill in seeking to achieve them. He had first to attempt to prevent an open conflict between Russia and Turkey, with all that this implied in dealing with the possibility of Russian intervention in Greece. He had to procure agreement on the necessity of recognizing the legitimacy of Turkish authority and seeking to re-establish it, at least to some extent. At the same time he worked for the amelioration of the condition of the Greeks and the easing of the horrors of war. Above all, he sought to enforce a policy of strict non-intervention by the Powers. This was, in the circumstances, the approach which was least destructive of international understanding and harmony. Unilateral Russian intervention was the gravest threat to peace, and in all that he did Castlereagh attempted to avert such a possibility.

It was ironic and yet appropriate that after their differences over Spain and Naples Castlereagh and Metternich should act closely together in the final months of Castlereagh's life. After his death the Greek question took a more serious and different turn. Canning came to believe that since the Turks could not restore order it was advisable for the Powers to intervene collectively, firstly to prevent Russian intervention without international scrutiny, secondly to establish a kingdom of Greece, and thirdly to limit it carefully, while ensuring the continuation of the Turkish Empire by compelling the Sultan to make concessions which he was powerless to deny. It is a matter of speculation whether Castlereagh would have followed a similar policy had he lived. But what may be emphasized is that Canning acted as much from a shrewd calculation of the balance of interests in the Balkans as from any idealistic sympathy with the Greek cause.

Castlereagh never lost his suspicion of Russian designs in the eastern Mediterranean. They seemed to him to be as dubious as Russian hegemony in eastern or central Europe, and in some ways his deepest anxieties during the post-war years were related to the policies of the Russian Emperor, rather than those of Metternich. Despite his disagreements with Metternich and his dislike of the policy of intervention Castlereagh regarded Austria as a Power which was seriously interested in stability: there was a common purpose, even though there were dissensions about the best means of securing equilibrium in Europe. But the unpredictable policies of Alexander I meant that Russian foreign policy was capable of being disruptive of European stability. Castlereagh did not forget that Alexander had invented the Holy Alliance and that he was always eager to project it in cosmic terms. Metternich believed that revolution should be suppressed wherever it appeared, and that this was the best insurance for both the Austrian Empire and the peace of Europe. Whatever terminology he used his primary objective was the defence of Austrian interests in a genuinely conservative sense. But Alexander lurched from one enthusiasm to another. He was a liberal and an autocrat, a visionary and an imperialist.

But while the Emperor's temperamental instability made him difficult to deal with, Castlereagh never doubted that Russian interests would finally dominate Russian policy. Wherever Russian armies marched Russian power would be manifest, and its impact would be permanent, not temporary. The fate of Poland was a warning of the manner in which Alexander exploited sentiment and power politics in the cause of Russian aggrandizement. Although Russia was the most repressive and reactionary of the major Powers she was also an element making for disturbance and displacement in the balance of power in Europe. Castlereagh's critics usually overlooked these considerations. Those who naïvely believed that the Turkish Empire could be speedily dismantled, and a free Greece set up, writhed under what they erroneously regarded as Castlereagh's frigid lack of imagination. But in his assessment of the likely consequences of the collapse of Turkish power in the Balkans he was more imaginative than his critics. He knew that nothing is more abhorrent to powerful nations than a power-vacuum, and that power contains its own temptations, regardless of the ideology used to validate it. He remembered that oppressed peoples could themselves become oppressors when they acquired the power to do so, and that nationalism was by no means synonymous with freedom for minorities or a respect for the rights of subject peoples. Others consoled themselves with the thought that a new ideology might inspire men with higher motives in their political behaviour: Castlereagh preferred to argue that international relations demanded a policy which minimized the disruptive effects of power by avoiding the wilful creation of situations in which the temptation to use force would arise.

Castlereagh never judged events by some previously articulated ideology. He had certain assumptions, most of them resonant of the fundamental principles of eighteenth-century statecraft, and these had been enriched and amended in the light of the experience of the French Revolution and the precepts inculcated by Pitt. But he believed that each case was unique to itself: each situation had to be assessed on its merits, and the diplomatist had to have a keen eye for the particular factors in any situation which made that situation different in some degree from all others. He was dubious of any approach which ignored the particular in order to affirm some convenient but deceptive generalization. He dealt in a world of matured experience and tangible realities: he had a permanent dislike for universal truths as guides to political conduct.

It was not surprising, therefore, that the opponent of revolution in Greece and Naples sympathized with the Spanish colonists in their struggle against Spain. Castlereagh had a low opinion of King Ferdinand, regarding him as a political idiot whose sterile incompetence merely added to the threat of revolution and the risk of international conflict. But the problem of the independence of the Spanish colonies was an especially ticklish one. Three types of recognition presented themselves for consideration. Firstly there was the concession of *de facto* recognition, which Castlereagh believed already virtually existed by 1822; secondly there was the possibility of a more formal recognition by diplomatic agents; and thirdly there was *de jure* recognition. *De jure* recognition presumed a certain right to the title of legal government and this was bound to militate against the rights of the former régime. Castlereagh was reluctant to see Britain commit herself to *de jure* recognition. He hoped that the two parties in the dispute might settle their quarrel over the question of sovereignty without the interference of outside parties, however well disposed these might be. But he did not overlook the problem of how long it was possible to act as if the colonial governments had been given *de facto* recognition without translating this into diplomatic practice and allowing the technicalities of international law to be brought into line with political convenience and day-to-day practice.

The dispute between Spain and her colonies created additional complications for the Powers when they were debating the possibility of intervention in Spanish domestic affairs. Castlereagh hoped to use British influence to persuade the Spaniards that they would benefit by coming to terms with their former colonists. But he could not assume that the other Powers would be convinced of the rightness of the British approach to the problem and it was therefore important

H

for Britain to be free to act as she saw fit according to circumstances. Castlereagh was prepared to contemplate recognizing the independence of the Spanish-American republics. It was a possibility which became more likely with every month that passed. But he would never have exploited the situation, as Canning did, to strike a pose and cut a figure. The chances are that the outcome of British policy would have been similar, but the method, if not the timing, would have been different. In essentials Canning's policy towards Spanish America differed little from that of Castlereagh. But the manner in which he conducted it dramatically reflected the contrast between the two men: a contrast of style and personality rather than of fundamental conviction. Both were preoccupied with the defence of British interests, though Castlereagh was repelled by the histrionic gestures which Canning, perhaps rightly, saw as part of the practice of diplomacy. But, as Sir Charles Webster stated in his classic study of Castlereagh's foreign policy, had Castlereagh lived 'it would have been more clear to posterity that the independence of the Spanish colonies had been won and maintained by the enterprise and heroism of the South Americans themselves'.[56]

Castlereagh's desire for good relations with the United States also influenced his handling of the Spanish question, and his conduct of British policy in both north and south America reflected a desire for conciliation, for the assertion of British interests while maintaining a policy of growing understanding. His insight into the relationship between Britain and her own former colonies made him hope, despite the bleak prospect, for some similar advance in understanding on the part of the Spanish government. The image of the icy apostle of universal reaction is nowhere more false, more shamelessly inaccurate or more wilfully misleading than when applied to Castlereagh's sophisticated and judicious attitude towards American questions. Castlereagh never lost his sense of the complexity of human behaviour, the mixture of motives which impels men to act. His Irish experience had made him sceptical of arrogant claims by one interest or party to the monopoly of truth. In other men the Irish tragedy inspired bitterness, vindictive self-righteousness, an incapacity to separate imagined wrongs from real grievances, but Castlereagh recognized that there were legitimate interests in Ireland for the British and the Irish, for the Anglicans, Catholics and Presbyterians. Similarly, throughout the years when he was responsible for the direction of British foreign policy, he appreciated the mixture of rights and wrongs in every clash of interest, and, however complex or bewildering this was, it was nevertheless the duty of the diplomatist to seek to resolve such conflicts, not in a spirit of applying absolute truths, but in the hope of procuring some measure of harmony from competing dissonances.

The Congress of Verona would have exposed growing tensions between Castlereagh and his allies even if he had not committed suicide, but this is not to say that his whole work collapsed in his personal tragedy. Castlereagh had hoped that the Congress system would preserve the peace of Europe. Though Congress diplomacy came to be used for ends which he did not approve, and though he was driven by events to take up a more independent stance, this did not mean either that the experiment had not been worth trying or that he would have been unable to adjust to a new situation. However much the alliance was under strain Castlereagh and Metternich had had much in common on the Greek question, and there were therefore possibilities for a measure of cooperation, even if the extent of harmony shown at their final meeting in Hanover must not be exaggerated. The difference between the two men was that Metternich was compelled, by the logic of the position in which he was placed and the nature of the empire whose interests it was his duty to secure, to assert that the principle of revolution was in itself a threat and to claim that intervention was the only sure means of preventing disorder and disaffection from spreading. Castlereagh, chiefly because of the peculiar circumstances influencing Britain's role as a great Power, regarded European peace much more in terms of equilibrium between the Powers, with revolution or liberalism or nationalism only becoming of international significance when a change of régime brought with it some likelihood of aggression or a breach of the settlement of 1815.

Castlereagh did not see foreign policy as the means by which some eternally valid international structure was to be maintained for all time. Adaptation and change were acceptable, even if revolution was undesirable in itself. There were times when he believed that judicious reform and sober constitutional innovation might prevent the onset of extremist principles, with all that they implied of chaos and disorder. It was possible for some continentals to discern in the principle of non-intervention a cloak for the security of British interests and the pursuit of a policy of growing isolationism while still masquerading as being concerned for European stability and balance. But Castlereagh strove to avoid having to make a choice between the defence of British interests (which he was bound to regard as his primary responsibility) and the preservation of equilibrium in Europe. He believed that it was impossible adequately to achieve the first objective without attaining the second. He never allowed Britain to lose her freedom of action, but he never gave up his conviction that Britain had a role to play in Europe, and he believed that British interests could not be divorced from the balance of power in Europe. British interests could not and would not be preserved merely by pretending that Europe did not exist or that European problems and conflicts could be ignored in a mood of complacent isolationism. Britain could not let the rest of the world go by: everything that had happened since 1792 had impressed this indelibly upon Castlereagh's mind. Britain could neither impose her will on Europe nor insist that her opinions prevailed on those questions which were more germane to the interests of Austria, Prussia, Russia and France. But this did not mean that Britain had no legitimate role to play in Europe: Austria and Britain had common interests in resisting Russian aggrandizement, and the Congress of Vienna had shown that Britain had certain interests in common with France. Events could change the balance of interests, new developments would compel British policy to take new directions, but if Britain withdrew from Europe she would eventually find that her interests were being threatened by forces which were outside her control, but which she would ignore at her peril.

Castlereagh never expected permanence as the outcome of all that he sought to achieve. He worked for limited ends, and he knew that the means to hand were often defective and unreliable. But this did not mean that the politics of necessity were a failure: peace, however limited and however fragile, was the consequence of constant vigilance, a keen-eyed determination to turn even bad fortune to good account and to wrest from the vulnerable uncertainty of human affairs a measure of stability and a period of repose. On these terms his achievement was a very considerable one, and the manner in which he conducted British diplomacy was a model of realism, restraint, sobriety and a humanity related to attainable political aims rather than attuned to the passions of idealism.

Throughout the years when Castlereagh struggled with the intractable problems of foreign policy he was also involved in the day-to-day business of domestic government. As Leader of the House of Commons he had a special responsibility for carrying legislation through Parliament and for winning the confidence of the House of Commons on the more controversial issues of the day. So dominant was Castlereagh's personality in the Commons that many radical critics regarded Liverpool's administration as in many ways Castlereagh's government. This did scant justice to the skill and intelligence of Liverpool, but it helps to explain why Castlereagh became so hated. He had to defend measures such as the suspension of Habeas Corpus and the Six Acts, as well as damping down criticism of the magistrates after the Peterloo affair in 1819. Nevertheless, as Miss Joyce Marlow has commented, 'Why Castlereagh was quite so hated is now a little difficult to appreciate.'[57] Castlereagh's reputation may possibly be cited as one example of the validity of Oscar Wilde's famous statement that nothing succeeds like excess: ferocious abuse was showered so relentlessly upon Castlereagh that its abundance was taken as evidence of its truth.

But nothing is more misleading than historical legend, especially one engendered by the romantic mythology of revolution. The striking thing about Liverpool's government was not that it believed, from time to time, that there was a risk of revolution but that it usually kept its head in a situation of unprecedented difficulty. The men governing England were as baffled by the onset of industrialism as were the victims of the factory system. When judged by contemporary standards Liverpool, Castlereagh and Sidmouth did not act with extravagance, malice or undue harshness. They lacked the machinery of government necessary to intervene in economic matters, even if they had believed it wise to do so, and it should not be forgotten that their radical critics were just as resentful of governmental intervention. Tom Paine had stated that government was like dress, the badge of lost innocence, and radicals assumed that the more governments interfered the more they would do so in the interests of some privileged section of society. Liverpool and his colleagues were as hesitant about any extension of the powers and scope of government as were their critics. Liverpool had a belief in 'the gradual effect of the general policy of the government', but this implied a reluctance on the government's part to do anything which could be described as an innovation or as an extension of its powers. Far from being eager to impose their will on the people the government hoped that it would not have to take unprecedented or novel action. Its confidence lay in the gentlemen of England, the country gentlemen and the magistrates, who were bound to know more of what was happening in their local community than ministers in far-away London. Overwhelmed by the pace of change, exhilarated by commercial success and industrial inventiveness, and yet apprehensive about the social consequences of the new technology, the government was convinced that the answers to these new problems lay outside the scope of politicians. Liverpool was fond of saying that trade and industry should be allowed to find their own level, and he was convinced that government interference did more harm than good. There was no doubt in his mind that the greater part of the miseries which men had to endure were 'at all times and in all countries beyond the control of human legislation'.[58] Castlereagh's own position was similar. In 1819 he denied that distress and unemployment could be removed by parliamentary interference: 'time alone would bring effectual remedy'.[59]

But this did not mean that the ministers were unmoved by human suffering. Where their attitude differed dramatically from that of the mid twentieth century was in their reliance on voluntary agencies to alleviate distress and hardship. They looked to the churches and the various charitable societies for the chief contribution to the amelioration of the condition of the poor. In pre-industrial England, with its small towns and village communities, this approach had had much to commend it, but the process of industrialization was rendering it more and more inadequate. Yet even Sidmouth, often regarded as one of the most insensitive members of Liverpool's Cabinet, had sympathized with the keelmen on Tyneside during the troubles of 1819, arguing that it was necessary for the owners to meet the justifiable grievances of the men. In 1820 he stated that he was delighted that the owners had shown that they appreciated the propriety and justice of keeping faith with the keelmen.

What did cause the government considerable anxiety was the danger that distress and unemployment would be exploited for political purposes. There was no lack of compassion for the tribulations which economic recessions, rising prices, and erratic trade imposed on the mass of the people, but there was a determination to deal severely with attempts to use these misfortunes for political ends. Yet even here the government was in the position of checking symptoms rather than removing causes. The appalling distress of the years 1815 to 1819 drove many men to despair; it was not surprising that anger and frustration should vent themselves in political agitation and radical movements. But even here it was difficult for Liverpool and his colleagues to know what was really going on. They lacked a modern police force, and they shared all the conventional prejudices of the age against the employment of the army to maintain public order. Although the soldiers were the most impartial and the most efficient force available for the control of crowds they were usually called in only when everything else had failed and when the situation had already deteriorated. The magistrates relied on the yeomanry, but it was the inexperience and incompetence of the yeomanry which were responsible for the Peterloo Massacre in 1819.

The government also had to use spies – of whom Oliver was the most notorious. But the distinction between an informer, a detective, a spy and an *agent provocateur* was hard to maintain even when it could be defined. The information gained by the government in this way was unreliable, but, as Castlereagh himself explained, Oliver had been sent out in 1817 merely to find out what the state of the country really was.

If Liverpool and the other ministers of the Crown were unsure of the extent to which disaffection had gripped the country, historians still debate the reality or illusion of the alleged revolutionary threat in England in the years between Waterloo and Peterloo. At one time it was fashionable to argue that Liverpool's government erred in over-reacting to events, exploiting all the resources of the law to crush what was never more than a sporadic outburst of local discontent. Now it is sometimes argued that the revolutionary tradition in Britain was more pervasive and more powerful than was once supposed. Even the unfortunate Jeremiah Brandreth, the leader of the pathetic Pentrich Rising in 1817, is elevated to 'heroic stature'. The problem is that it is difficult to assess the evidence on which appreciations of a revolutionary movement are based. Secret oaths, vows of vengeance and slaughter, dark tales of men drilling in military formations, plans for the distribution of pikes and firearms: men talked wildly about such things, and government spies and informers eagerly fed such rumours back to the Home Office. What is curious is the failure of the revolutionaries to carry into effect any sustained campaign of direct action, if such a plan ever existed. Furthermore, if there was a real danger of revolution, Liverpool and his colleagues could hardly be blamed for taking all the precautions necessary to secure property and prevent insurrection. Although the sequence of events – from the Spa Fields Riot and the March of the Blanketeers through to the Pentrich Rising and Peterloo and, as a last lurid climax, the Cato Street Conspiracy – seems continuous, at first sight it was much more the result of coincidence than coordination. Liverpool had no wish to act with unnecessary violence: although Brandreth and two others were hanged at Derby on 7 November 1817, a fourth man, George Weightman, was reprieved because of his youth and previous good character. It was important to show that high treason carried the penalty of death, for both the common people and the nobly born, but there was a general reluctance to spill blood, although contemporary opinion believed capital punishment to be appropriate when acts of violence or offences against person or property had been committed for the furtherance of political objectives. After the execution of Thistlewood and four of his accomplices in the Cato Street Conspiracy, public opinion was revolted by the decapitations which took place after the men were hanged: they were the last traitors to suffer by the axe in England.[60]

Peterloo has long been the subject of mythology, but recent work has re-opened questions of the extent to which the government was responsible for what happened, and even of the conventional notion of what took place at St Peter's Field in Manchester on 16 August 1819. Peterloo was certainly not the culmination of a premeditated policy of bloodthirsty repression on the part of Liverpool, Sidmouth and Castlereagh. Professor Donald Read has trenchantly summed up the matter as follows: 'Peterloo, as the evidence of the Home Office shows, was never desired or precipitated by the Liverpool Ministry as a bloody repressive gesture for keeping down the lower orders. If the Manchester magistrates had followed the spirit of the Home Office there would never have been a "massacre".'[61] Indeed, although the ministers dutifully defended the Manchester magistrates, they had misgivings of their own. Liverpool thought that the behaviour of the magistrates had been injudicious, and he assured Canning that while he thought the conduct of the magistrates 'justifiable' the course which they had pursued was not 'in all its parts prudent'.[62] But there was no doubt in Liverpool's mind that, despite the outcry and the way in which the opposition was seeking to make the most of the affair to discredit the government, there was no alternative but to support the magistrates. To refuse to do so would erode the foundations upon which the maintenance of law and order rested.

Castlereagh defended the magistrates, but he did so with more intelligence and discrimination than his enemies gave him credit for. As so often he was the victim of misrepresentation. He had spoken in the Commons of glorying in the share he had had 'in protecting men who had saved the country from the base attempts which evil-minded persons had made to subvert the constitution'. But his words referred to the precise charges which had been levelled at the magistrates of being guilty of murder: if the Whigs really thought so, then Castlereagh argued that they should take appropriate legal action instead of keeping the subject 'afloat as a topic of inflammatory declamation'.[63] But it was easy for such language to be misapplied, and for men to talk as if Castlereagh had gloried in the bloodshed of the day. As so often, Castlereagh won the battle for the mind of the House of Commons but lost the struggle for the popular voice.

Public order was not the only problem with which Castlereagh had to busy himself as Leader of the House of Commons. He was involved in the sordid and grotesque episode of Queen Caroline, when the Liverpool government sought, rather shamefacedly, to satisfy King George IV's prejudices against his wife. The ministry's relationship with George IV, whether as Regent or King, was a highly sensitive one, and Castlereagh frequently acted as the chief mediator between George and his ministers. Like the rest of the government Castlereagh believed that there was no alternative but to go along with the Bill of Pains and Penalties but the investigation into the Queen's private conduct had to be dropped and the government's reputation suffered when the Bill was abandoned. The failure to procure evidence for a divorce did not endear the ministers to the King: the government suffered, first for raising the subject and then for dropping it. The campaign against the Queen had also been especially unpopular in London, where Whigs and Radicals had been able to exploit opinion against the government: despite their humiliation Liverpool and his colleagues sensed that it was expedient to defer to popular feeling on the issue, however much this annoyed George IV. Castlereagh had been too optimistic about the prospects of carrying the Bill; later he admitted the seriousness of the situation and the potential embarrassments it held for the government. Again, whatever the rights and wrongs of the situation, it was Castlereagh who was closely indentified with the affair because he was the government's chief spokesman in the Commons. The stresses of handling the House of Commons probably contributed to the mental collapse which led to his suicide. But, despite his occasional misjudgements, Liverpool regarded him as irreplaceable, and expected him to continue to shoulder the burdens of the Foreign Office and the Leadership of the House of Commons.

It should not be forgotten that in dealing with the Commons Castlereagh lacked the resources which eighteenth-century ministries had taken for granted, while he was unable to invoke the disciplinary procedures of an organized party. Liverpool lamented that he did not have at his disposal the means by which his predecessors had managed the House of Commons. It was all the more important, therefore, that his ministry should have a Leader in the Commons who was capable of winning the confidence of backbenchers. Castlereagh possessed this gift in abundance. He was no dazzling orator, but his speeches carried weight and conviction. Even those which seem least impressive to posterity – on such matters as paper money in 1817 or the dangers of insurrection in 1819 – were attuned to the mood of the House and best calculated to win its support.

But Castlereagh was no more inclined than Liverpool to take the initiative in building up a nationally organized political party, and they were content to allow a considerable degree of freedom to their colleagues. This was an understandable attitude, given the political circumstances of the time, but it added to Castlereagh's difficulties in dealing with the Commons. In 1822 at the close of the parliamentary session he expressed his total exhaustion: he said that he wished never to go through another session like it. He was never immune from attacks in the House, and outside it opponents denounced the government in general, and Castlereagh in particular, in language that was often vile and scurrilous. Castlereagh was not insensitive to such attacks, and, though he bore them with remarkable patience, they wounded him deeply.

Defiance was one of his characteristics, though it would be going too far to say that he took a delight in outraging opposition in the Commons by what seemed to be cold indifference or frigid arrogance. What to one man looks like courage appears to another as obstinacy or pride. But among Castlereagh's contemporaries there was never any doubt about his courage. They knew that, as well as saving young Henry Sturrock from drowning, he had taken the initiative in piloting a schooner safely to the Isle of Man, after the ship had been caught in a storm after putting out from Portaferry. He had also been attacked by robbers while returning from a day's shooting in the Wicklow Hills, but, after shooting one of his assailants, he had succeeded, with the help of a young man who had come to his aid, in apprehending his three attackers. During the Irish rebellion he had throughout behaved with exemplary bravery. He had been cool, unruffled, and self-controlled. His political courage sprang from one of the deepest instincts of his being.

But there was an imaginative, possibly even an introspective, side to his nature which many of his friends missed. Sir Walter Scott heard a strange story from Castlereagh's own lips at a supper party in Paris in 1815. The company had been impressed, even disturbed, by the seriousness with which Castlereagh told the tale. One night, while he was serving with the militia, he had been roused from sleep by a sense of ominous foreboding. Gazing into the fire he saw the apparition of a naked boy, 'the Radiant Boy' as Castlereagh called it – an apparition which Irish folk-lore took to be an omen of violent death. As it approached the phantom grew into a hideous giant, with glaring eyes and a bloody wound on its brow. Castlereagh confronted the ghost in an attitude of defiance. It shrank in size and disappeared. He never forgot the incident: it had impressed itself too deeply upon his consciousness. Perhaps it reflected a strain of introversion, even of anxiety, which was little seen in his public life or even in his dealings with his family and friends.[64]

His unpopularity may also have preyed upon him more than he realized, though there were times when he laughed about it. On one occasion, when walking down Parliament Street arm in arm with Sidmouth, Castlereagh heard the groans and hisses of the crowd. 'Here we go, the two most popular men in England,' Sidmouth commented wryly. Castlereagh replied, 'Yes, through a grateful and admiring multitude.'[65] But when Castlereagh visited Ireland with George IV he was pleasantly surprised by the geniality of his reception. He happily told his wife that everything had gone off perfectly, and when he was cheered in the streets of Dublin he could not refrain from remarking, 'I am grown as popular in 1821 as unpopular formerly, and with as little merit; and of the two, unpopularity is the more convenient and gentlemanlike.'[66]

But in the summer of 1822 his friends began to notice signs that his self-control was breaking down. There were instances of lapse of memory, which were most unusual for him. He became moody and petulant, in contrast to his habitual courtesy and charm. He talked of being quite worn out, and in one conversation with George IV he expressed fears that he was to be arrested on the same charge as the Bishop of Clogher. The King was deeply distressed. He had come to respect Castlereagh and he sought to reassure him. But when the King told Castlereagh that he was suffering from delusions and a bout of depression following overwork, the Foreign Secretary broke down and wept: 'I am mad. I know I am mad. I have known it for some time, but no one has any idea of it.' He talked of a conspiracy against him. There was no doubt that he was gravely ill.

Mr Montgomery Hyde has argued that Castlereagh was probably the victim of a plot to entrap him into a situation which could then be exploited for the purposes of blackmail.[67] It would seem that he yielded to the soliciting of a young woman, but when he accompanied her back to her room he was astonished to find that the prostitute was a boy dressed as a woman. Accomplices rushed into the room, and Castlereagh was compelled to yield to blackmail. The evidence for such a sequence of events is far from conclusive, but it is possible that something of this sort happened. The case of the Bishop of Clogher was a particularly notorious one in the summer of 1822, and it might well have brought Castlereagh's fears to a head. The bishop had been caught in a London tavern, engaging in homosexual acts with a guardsman. The scandal had been the talk of the town for some weeks. Whatever may be the truth in Castlereagh's case, there is no doubt that he associated his own disgrace with that of the bishop, though Mr Montgomery Hyde refutes suggestions that Castlereagh had actually committed a homosexual offence. There will always be a degree of mystery surrounding his end, but a combination of overwork, feelings of guilt associated with blackmail, and a fear of some public disgrace as grievous as the bishop's, destroyed his mental balance. He had once talked earnestly with his doctor about the precise location of the jugular artery and the most efficient means of severing it. On 12 August 1822 he cut his throat, carrying out the deed with skill and precision. On 20 August he was buried in Westminster Abbey, close to the remains of his hero, Pitt.

The tragic end of Castlereagh's career cannot detract from the essential consistency and selfless integrity which marked his public conduct, from his first beginnings in Irish politics to the distinguished climax represented by his years as Foreign Secretary. He was always able to tackle the great issues and to see beyond the narrow confines of insularity, both in its Irish and in its British form. His capacity to learn from experience and to acquire the more subtle skills of the politician's craft was apparent from his early years as a member of the Dublin Parliament. His desire to combine Irish reform with a strengthening of the British link was a distinctive and remarkable stance for a young man to take, and though what many contemporaries regarded as his greatest achievement, the passing of the Irish Act of Union, has proved to be transient, this does not detract from the political insight and courage which transformed initial defeat into victory. Castlereagh was not to blame for the failure of the Union to fulfil the hopes which Pitt had pinned upon it, and though he would have regretted its demise he was too much of a realist to expect any constitutional arrangement to be permanent. Transience was one of the facts of political life. Even the conservative, seeking to preserve all that was best in the traditional system at a time of urgent and unprecedented change, recognized that a measure of change was necessary if the constitution was to be preserved. Castlereagh's commitment to Catholic emancipation was evidence of the way in which he was willing (if one might adopt a famous phrase of Professor Michael Oakeshott)[68] to explore the intimations of a received pattern of political behaviour. He was able to distinguish between the essentials of the constitution and the form which it took under the pressure of events. Sceptical though he was of the validity of abstract speculation his understanding of historical experience, and his shrewd awareness of what was unique in the nation's political development, ensured that he was no frightened defender of the *status quo*, seeking to preserve forever a frozen and unchangeable pattern of institutions. Similarly, though Castlereagh sought to moderate the pace of innovation, and though he was dubious about the suggestion that liberalism and nationalism were themselves either universally applicable throughout Europe, or the infallible solutions to inherited difficulties, he was not insensitive to the appeal of nationalist emotions or the delusory attractiveness of liberal principles. All that he sought to do was to relate them to the political realities of the time, the demands of the balance of power and the overwhelming need throughout Europe for a period of repose.

Fundamental to the development of Castlereagh's political outlook were his Irish experience and the example of Pitt. It was in Ireland that his scepticism about idealism as a political force for good was reinforced by the tragic experience of the rebellion of 1798, and it was in Ireland that he first learned of the complexities of political motivation, of the way in which a clash of interests defied simple-minded categorization, and of the perplexing tendency of human affairs to elude the precise definitions of speculative thought. Pitt typified all that was best in the practice of politics: a judicious capacity to assess conflicting forces, a willingness to adapt policies to the realities of the situation, a formidable administrative skill, a preference for attainable objectives, an ability to combine a respect for the constitution with intelligent reform. Castlereagh lacked Pitt's mastery of the orator's art, but in other respects he was a statesman of a similar temperament and he was endowed with similar abilities. Castlereagh, like Pitt, did not see the French war in ideological terms, but he did not shrink from the burdens of the conflict. Amidst misrepresentation and abuse he pressed on with the tasks of organizing the military machine, and it is significant that historians have seen in him a great War Secretary.

His place in the Pittite tradition was central. Pitt bequeathed to his successors a unique style in administration: it was in office, and through the trials of war, that the new Tory party was born. The impact of the French Revolution and war had ensured that constitutional reform was regarded with scepticism by the majority of English politicians, but in commercial and financial matters Castlereagh and Liverpool and their colleagues were responding to new ideas, and, so far as Castlereagh was concerned, he did not object to constitutional reform, providing that it sprang from a judicious assessment of the facts of each particular case, and if it could be shown to be a fulfilment of the constitution, not a speculative innovation. This was precisely the type of argument he used to justify Catholic emancipation, and though he was opposed to widespread parliamentary reform he was willing to accede to cautious disfranchisement and restrained redistribution on a strictly limited basis: in this, as in other matters, he was willing to listen to the House of Commons, which was one reason why he was such a remarkable parliamentary manager. He was no more a dogmatic reactionary in domestic matters than he was an advocate of international intervention on the model favoured by Metternich. Disorder had to be curbed, especially when it had political implications, but however perplexed Castlereagh was by the social problems of the time there is no evidence to suggest that he lacked compassion for those in need, or that he was other than appalled by human suffering. His concern for peace and his belief in social order were both strengthened by his memories of the suffering he had seen in Ireland in 1798. Unlike many of his detractors he had a keen personal awareness of what the horrors of civil strife, revolution and war meant.

His ability to maintain an intelligent balance of forces when framing policy was typified by the fact that the man who was the chief architect of the allied victory in 1814 was also an advocate for a moderate peace. His desire to defeat Napoleon did not obscure his anxieties about Russian policy in eastern and central Europe. His commitment to Congress diplomacy and the Quadruple Alliance did not make him a convert to the Holy Alliance. His realization that British policy implied a concern for European interests did not lead him to ignore other areas of vital significance, as his liberal and far-sighted policy towards the United States demonstrates. Of course there were times when he struggled to resolve paradoxes and contradictions – as over the Greek Revolt, for example – but this was part of the inevitable turmoil of international politics, a reflection of the intractable nature of human affairs.

But this ability to sense the subtleties in a given situation made it impossible for Castlereagh to adopt the simple-minded attitudes which his critics desired. His career demonstrates the superficiality of any division of the politicians of the time into 'progressives' and 'reactionaries'. His combination of a sincere Anglican faith with a willingness to rebuild the ruined Catholic chapel at Strangford at a cost of £500 typified the way in which he transcended many of the prejudices of the age. And since he still suffers from the accusation of being a reactionary it is worth pointing out that he took an interest in education – whether Wellesley's plan for a college at Fort William or in patronizing the Belfast Academy or in sympathizing with plans for a university to be established in Ulster. The advocate of the Union helped to set up the Dublin Gaelic Society, and even used his influence to secure the release of its secretary from prison, where he had been locked up for debt. Even when he felt compelled to support firm measures to secure public peace he was always eager to alleviate distress and exercise the prerogative of mercy whenever circumstances justified doing so.

It is, therefore, as a man of his time that Castlereagh must be judged, and when he is assessed by the standards appropriate in making such a judgement he emerges as a more sophisticated and more attractive figure than the icy reactionary of radical legend. Except for parliamentary rhetoric he possessed all the skills necessary for success in contemporary politics. He reflected the contemporary devotion to the constitution, the prevalent belief that politics was the art of reconciling conflicting interests, the conventional assumption that, once the national finances had been stabilized and secured, the conduct of foreign policy was the primary purpose of government. In both domestic and foreign politics his achievements were real, but he well knew that they were vulnerable to the erosions of time, and because later generations infused a different order of priorities into their political expectations it was all too easy for Castlereagh's achievements to be undervalued and for his political conduct to be grievously misunderstood. But the Act of Union can now be seen as a serious and impressive attempt to grapple with the forbidding complexities of the Irish problem, not as a mere exercise in bribery and corruption, while final victory over Napoleon, and the attainment of a peace settlement which provided Europe with half a century of peace, can be appreciated as the fulfilment of those political skills which Castlereagh showed throughout his career, not the accidental product of chance or coincidence.

Restraint allied to insight, perception attuned to political realism, imagination disciplined by intellectual control, conviction matured by experience – these were the secrets of Castlereagh's achievement, and they represented a rich flowering of the eighteenth-century political tradition, as it had been refined and practised by Pitt. The aims for which politicians laboured were limited, but they were not negligible. Castlereagh did not seek to discover a political Utopia: he preferred the modest satisfactions of experience to the wanton delights of the unknown. But parliamentary government, social order, civil harmony and international peace are not ignoble objectives for the politician's art, and it was to these that Castlereagh devoted his life and his gifts. A love of liberty, as represented by the English constitution, and a devotion to the welfare of England and Ireland guided his political conduct, and both merit the imaginative understanding of posterity, not the vindictive condemnation inspired by shallow enthusiasm or misguided zeal.

REFERENCES

Chapter 1: Myths and Realities (pages 1–25)

1. H.Martineau, *A History of the Thirty Years Peace*, vol. I, pp. 385–8.
2. *The Creevey Papers* (ed. H.Maxwell), vol. II, p. 44.
3. ibid., vol. II, pp. 42–3, Creevey to Miss Ord, 14 August 1822.
4. *The Greville Memoirs* (ed. L.Strachey and R.Fulford), vol. I, pp. 52–3.
5. Wellington to Lady Salisbury, 5 June 1836, cited in J.A.R.Marriott, *Castlereagh*, p. 341.
6. *Memoirs and Correspondence of Viscount Castlereagh* (ed. Londonderry), vol. I, p. 128.
7. ibid., vol. I, p. 133.

8. R.Rush, *A Residence at the Court of London* (London, 1845), p. 120.
9. A.Cecil, *Metternich*, p. 103.
10. S.Bamford, *Passages in the Life of a Radical* (London, 3rd edition, 1967), vol. I, ch. XVII.
11. J.W.Croker, *Correspondence and Diaries* (ed. L.J.Jennings), vol. I, p. 219.
12. *The Journal of Mrs Arbuthnot* (ed. F.Bamford and the Duke of Wellington), vol. I, p. 180.
13. *Memoirs and Correspondence of Viscount Castlereagh*, vol. I, p. 180.
14. F.H.Hinsley, *Power and the Pursuit of Peace*, p. 202.
15. For Sidmouth and the strikers, see N. McCord, 'The seamen's strike of 1815 in north-east England', *Economic History Review*, 2nd series, vol. XXI, no. 1, 1968.
16. *Passages in the Life of a Radical*, vol. I, pp. 147–8.
17. For Peterloo, see D.Read, *Peterloo: The Massacre and Its Background*, and R.Walmsley, *Peterloo: The Case Re-opened*.
18. H. Fairlie, *The Kennedy Promise* (London, 1973), p. 364.
19. R.Glover, *Peninsular Preparation*, p. 254.

Chapter 2 : The Irish Union (pages 26–99)

1. H.Montgomery Hyde, *The Rise of Castlereagh*, p. 38.
2. See John W. Derry, *The Regency Crisis* (Cambridge University Press, 1963), and J.Ehrman, *The Younger Pitt*.
3. *The Rise of Castlereagh*, p. 65, R.Stewart to the Earl of Moira, 21 July 1790.
4. ibid., p. 77, Camden to R.Stewart, 23 January 1791.
5. ibid., p. 78.
6. Sir A.Alison, *The Lives of Lord Castlereagh and Sir Charles Stewart*, vol. I, pp. 13–14.
7. *Charlemont Correspondence* (Historical Manuscripts Commission, London, 1891), R.Stewart to Camden, 11 November 1791.
8. J.A.R.Marriott, *Castlereagh*, pp. 40–41, and *The Rise of Castlereagh*, pp. 92–5, R.Stewart to A.Haliday, 27 February 1792.
9. *The Lives of Lord Castlereagh and Sir Charles Stewart*, vol. I, p. 23, R.Stewart to Camden, 25 September 1793.
10. ibid., vol. I, p. 21, R.Stewart to Camden, 3 April 1793.
11. For R.Stewart's views see his letter to Bayham, 17 September 1794, *The Lives of Lord Castlereagh and Sir Charles Stewart*, vol. I, pp. 24–6, and *The Rise of Castlereagh*, pp. 113–14.
12. *The Rise of Castlereagh*, p. 115, Haliday to Charlemont, 27 August 1794.
13. ibid., p. 127.
14. For a good summary of Castlereagh's constituencies and official appointments, see A.Hassall, *Viscount Castlereagh*, pp. 235–6.
15. *The Rise of Castlereagh*, pp. 160–61.
16. ibid., p. 163, Castlereagh to Pelham, November 1796.
17. ibid., p. 251.
18. *Memoirs and Correspondence of Viscount Castlereagh* (ed. Londonderry), vol. I, p. 219, Castlereagh to Wickham, 12 June 1798.

19. ibid., vol. I, p. 414, Castlereagh to Wickham, 29 October 1798.
20. ibid., vol. I, pp. 393–4, Clare to Castlereagh, 16 October 1798.
21. ibid., vol. I, p. 404, Elliot to Castlereagh, 24 October 1798.
22. See G.C.Bolton, *The Passing of the Irish Act of Union.*
23. *Memoirs and Correspondence of Viscount Castlereagh*, vol. II, pp. 35–6.
24. G.C.Bolton, in *The Passing of the Irish Act of Union*, p. 108.
25. *Memoirs and Correspondence of Viscount Castlereagh*, vol. II, p. 133, Castlereagh to Portland, 25 January 1799.
26. *Report of the Speeches Delivered by Viscount Castlereagh in the Debate on the Regency Bill* (Dublin, 1799); *Belfast News-Letter*, 16, 19 April 1799; *The Rise of Castlereagh*, p. 322.
27. *Memoirs and Correspondence of Viscount Castlereagh*, vol. II, pp. 274–5, Castlereagh to Portland, 14 April 1799.
28. ibid., vol. II, p. 369, Castlereagh to Portland, 5 August 1799.
29. *The Rise of Castlereagh*, p. 348.
30. E.R.Norman, *A History of Modern Ireland*, p. 43.
31. *Memoirs and Correspondence of Viscount Castlereagh*, vol. III, p. 327, and *The Lives of Lord Castlereagh and Sir Charles Stewart*, vol. I, p. 125, Castlereagh to Camden, 18 June 1800.
32. *Cornwallis Correspondence* (ed. C.Ross, London, 1859), vol. III, p. 294, and *The Lives of Lord Castlereagh and Sir Charles Stewart*, vol. I, p. 127.
33. *Memoirs and Correspondence of Viscount Castlereagh*, vol. IV, pp. 8–12, and *The Lives of Lord Castlereagh and Sir Charles Stewart*, vol. I, pp. 129–31, Castlereagh to Pitt, 1 January 1801.
34. *Memoirs and Correspondence of Viscount Castlereagh*, vol. IV, p. 12, Castlereagh to Pitt, 1 January 1801.
35. ibid., vol. IV, p. 40, Castlereagh to Cornwallis, 9 February 1801.
36. ibid., vol. IV, pp. 225–9, Castlereagh to Addington, 21 July 1802.
37. ibid., vol. IV, pp. 392–400. Probably composed in 1801.
38. ibid.

Chapter 3: The Legacy of Pitt (pages 100–144)

1. For Castlereagh's view of the relative political situations of Britain and France, probably written in March 1802, see *Memoirs and Correspondence of Viscount Castlereagh* (ed. Londonderry), vol. V, pp. 35–7.
2. For Castlereagh's assessment of the situation, see his paper printed in ibid., vol. V, pp. 62–70.
3. ibid., vol. V, pp. 78–80, Castlereagh to Hawkesbury, 19 August 1803.
4. See R.Glover, *Britain at Bay*, pp. 47–50.
5. *Memoirs and Correspondence of Viscount Castlereagh*, vol. V, p. 124, Castlereagh to Nelson, 27 October 1805.
6. ibid., vol. V, p. 127, Castlereagh to Collingwood, November 1805.
7. For the Elbe expedition, see Castlereagh's memorandum of 21 October 1805, ibid., vol. VI, pp. 25–9.
8. ibid., vol. VI, p. 88, Castlereagh to Cathcart, 23 December 1805.
9. *Britain at Bay*, p. 148.

10. *Despatches of the Duke of Wellington* (ed. G.Gurwood, London, 1835–8), vol. IV, pp. 18–19.
11. *Memoirs and Correspondence of Viscount Castlereagh*, vol. VI, pp. 365–6, Castlereagh to the Duke of Manchester, 4 June 1808.
12. ibid., vol. VI, p. 454, Castlereagh to Wellesley, 26 September 1808.
13. ibid., vol. VII, p. 89, Wellesley to Castlereagh, 17 June 1809.
14. ibid., vol. VIII, pp. 87–8.
15. ibid., vol. VI, p. 247. Memorandum undated.
16. ibid., vol. VI, p. 285, King's Instructions to Chatham.
17. Spencer Walpole, *Life of Spencer Perceval* (London, 1874), vol. I, p. 296, and J.A.R. Marriott, *Castlereagh*, p. 134.
18. C.Barnett, *Britain and Her Army 1509–1970*, p. 258.
19. D.Gray, *Spencer Perceval*, pp. 381–2.
20. *Parliamentary History*, vol. XIX, pp. 986–1011.
21. *Despatches of the Duke of Wellington*, vol. VII, p. 502.
22. See E.P.Thompson, *The Making of the English Working Class*, and N.McCord, 'Some limitations of the Age of Reform', in *British Government and Administration: Studies presented to S.B.Chrimes*, ed. H.Hearder and H.R.Loyn (Cardiff: University of Wales Press, 1974).

Chapter 4: The Years of Achievement (pages 145–232)

1. H.W.V.Temperley and L.Penson, *Foundations of British Foreign Policy*, p. 11.
2. ibid., p. 20.
3. Sir Charles Webster, *The Foreign Policy of Castlereagh, 1812–1815*, p. 110, Castlereagh to Cathcart, 15 December 1812.
4. *Memoirs and Correspondence of Viscount Castlereagh* (ed. Londonderry), vol. IX, p. 31, Castlereagh to Cathcart, 6 July 1813.
5. *The Foreign Policy of Castlereagh, 1812–1815*, pp. 160–61, Castlereagh to Cathcart, 18 September 1813.
6. *Memoirs and Correspondence of Viscount Castlereagh*, vol. IX, p. 75, Castlereagh to Aberdeen, 13 November 1813.
7. ibid., vol. X, p. 26, Castlereagh to Sir H.Wellesley, 10 May 1814.
8. ibid., vol. X, p. 18, Castlereagh to Bentinck, 7 May 1814.
9. Bradford Perkins, *Castlereagh and Adams*, p. 2.
10. ibid., p. 200.
11. ibid., p. 202.
12. ibid., p. 212, Castlereagh to Stratford Canning, 7 August 1820.
13. ibid., p. 304.
14. *Memoirs and Correspondence of Viscount Castlereagh*, vol. X, p. 77.
15. ibid., vol. X, p. 92, Castlereagh to Sir C.Stewart, 14 August 1814.
16. ibid., vol. X, pp. 93–4, Wellington to Castlereagh, 18 August 1814.
17. ibid., vol. X, pp. 144–5.
18. ibid., vol. X, p. 173, Castlereagh to Wellington, 25 October 1814.
19. ibid., vol. X, p. 174, Castlereagh to Wellington, 25 October 1814.
20. ibid., vol. X, p. 175, Castlereagh to Wellington, 25 October 1814.
21. ibid., vol. X, p. 235, Castlereagh to Liverpool, 4 January 1815.
22. *The Foreign Policy of Castlereagh 1812–1815*, p. 379.

23. *Memoirs and Correspondence of Viscount Castlereagh*, vol. x, p. 206, Castlereagh to Wellington, 21 November 1814.
24. *The Foreign Policy of Castlereagh, 1812–1815*, Castlereagh to Clancarty, 29 April 1815.
25. *Memoirs and Correspondence of Viscount Castlereagh*, vol. xi, p. 15.
26. *The Foreign Policy of Castlereagh, 1812–1815*, p. 471.
27. H. Nicolson, *The Congress of Vienna*, p. 260.
28. *Memoirs and Correspondence of Viscount Castlereagh*, vol. xi, p. 105, Castlereagh to Rose, 28 December 1815.
29. ibid., vol. xi, p. 255, Castlereagh to Cathcart, 28 May 1816.
30. J. A. R. Marriott, *Castlereagh*, p. 275.
31. Sir A. Alison, *The Lives of Lord Castlereagh and Sir Charles Stewart*, vol. ii, pp. 607–18.
32. Sir Charles Webster, *British Diplomacy 1813–1815*, pp. 382–4.
33. ibid., p. 385, Liverpool to Castlereagh, 3 October 1815.
34. H. Kissinger, *A World Restored*, p. 316.
35. *Foundations of British Foreign Policy*, p. 46.
36. ibid.
37. ibid., p. 45.
38. *Memoirs and Correspondence of Viscount Castlereagh*, vol. xii, p. 56, Bathurst to Castlereagh, 20 October 1818.
39. ibid., vol. xii, p. 57.
40. W. Alison Phillips, *The Confederation of Europe*, p. 138.
41. *The Foreign Policy of Castlereagh 1815–1822*, p. 71, Castlereagh to Sir C. Stuart, 22 July 1817.
42. ibid., p. 148, Castlereagh to Liverpool, 19 October 1818.
43. ibid., p. 240.
44. *Memoirs and Correspondence of Viscount Castlereagh*, vol. xii, p. 312.
45. *The Foreign Policy of Castlereagh 1815–1822*, p. 279; *Foundations of British Foreign Policy*, pp. 48–63.
46. *Memoirs and Correspondence of Viscount Castlereagh*, vol. xii, pp. 312–17, Castlereagh to Sir C. Stewart, 16 September 1820.
47. *The Foreign Policy of Castlereagh 1815–1822*, p. 299, Castlereagh to Sir C. Stewart, 4 December 1820.
48. *Memoirs and Correspondence of Viscount Castlereagh*, vol. xii, p. 259, Castlereagh to Metternich, 6 May 1820.
49. ibid., vol. xii, p. 341, Castlereagh to Sir C. Stewart, 5 January 1821.
50. *The Foreign Policy of Castlereagh 1815–1822*, pp. 322–3.
51. ibid., pp. 303–4; *The Confederation of Europe*, p. 210 ff.
52. *The Foreign Policy of Castlereagh 1815–1822*, pp. 304–5.
53. ibid., pp. 305–6.
54. *Memoirs and Correspondence of Viscount Castlereagh*, vol. xii, pp. 403–8, and *The Lives of Lord Castlereagh and Sir Charles Stewart*, vol. iii, pp. 164–7, Castlereagh to the Tsar, 16 July 1821. For Castlereagh's views on the Greek Question and Russian intervention, see his letters to Sir Charles Bagot, 14 December 1821, *Memoirs and Correspondence of Viscount Castlereagh*, vol. xii, pp. 444–6, and 27 July 1821, *The Foreign Policy of Castlereagh 1815–1822*, p. 360.
55. J. A. R. Marriott, *Castlereagh*, p. 324.
56. *The Foreign Policy of Castlereagh 1815–1822*, p. 436.

57. J.Marlow, *The Peterloo Massacre*, p. 44.

58. *Hansard*, vol. XLI, p. 497.

59. For a discussion of Castlereagh's attitude to economic questions, see C.J.Bartlett, *Castlereagh*, pp. 183–5, and *The Lives of Lord Castlereagh and Sir Charles Stewart*, vol. III, pp. 21–2.

60. For what might be called the revisionist view, see E.P.Thompson, *The Making of the English Working Class*, though I lean to the interpretation presented in R.J.White, *Waterloo to Peterloo*.

61. D.Read, *Peterloo: The Massacre and Its Background*, p. 207.

62. C.Yonge, *Life and Administration of the 2nd Earl of Liverpool* (London, 1868), vol. II, p. 410, Liverpool to Canning, 23 September 1819.

63. R.Walmsley, *Peterloo: The Case Re-opened*, p. 387.

64. H.Montgomery Hyde, *The Strange Death of Lord Castlereagh*, pp. 35–6.

65. H.Martineau, *A History of the Thirty Years Peace*, vol. I, p. 339.

66. *The Strange Death of Lord Castlereagh*, p. 125.

67. ibid., pp. 151–8.

68. M. Oakeshott, *Rationalism in Politics* (London, 1962), pp. 125–6.

SELECT BIBLIOGRAPHY

In preparing this study I have consulted the
Castlereagh Papers which form part of the Londonderry Collection now
deposited at the Durham County Record Office, but much significant
Castlereagh material is printed in *Memoirs and Correspondence of
Viscount Castlereagh* (edited by his brother Charles, Third Marquess of
Londonderry, 12 vols., London, 1848–54). The chief source of Castlereagh
material is at Mount Stewart in Northern Ireland, but some of the most
interesting documentation for the earlier part of Castlereagh's life is
printed in H. Montgomery Hyde, *The Rise of Castlereagh* (London, 1933),
which is an indispensable book. The same author's *The Strange Death of
Lord Castlereagh* (London, 2nd edition, 1967) is of substantial interest.

C.J.Bartlett's *Castlereagh* (London, 1966) is especially good on the diplomatic aspects of Castlereagh's career. Sir Charles Webster's *The Foreign Policy of Castlereagh* (2 vols., London, 2nd edition, 1963) and the same author's *British Diplomacy 1813–1815* (London, 1921) are fundamental. Sir A.Alison, *The Lives of Lord Castlereagh and Sir Charles Stewart* (3 vols., London, 1861) is prolix and lacks proportion, but it contains much information and is of value if used carefully. There is much material relating to Castlereagh in the Second Duke of Wellington, *Supplementary Despatches and Memoranda of the Duke of Wellington* (15 vols., London, 1858–76). Some important documents are printed in H.W.V.Temperley and L.Penson, *Foundations of British Foreign Policy* (London, 1938).

Among biographies A.Hassall, *Viscount Castlereagh* (London, 1908) and J. A. R. Marriott, *Castlereagh* (London, 1936) are worth reading. I.Leigh, *Castlereagh* (London, 1951) is more concerned with personality than with policy. H.Kissinger, *A World Restored* (London, 1973) is a perceptive study of Metternich and Castlereagh. J.W.Fortescue, *British Statesmen of the Great War* (Oxford, 1911) is sympathetic to Castlereagh. For Castlereagh and the United States see Bradford Perkins, *Castlereagh and Adams* (Berkeley and Los Angeles, 1964). For the period of the Congresses W. Alison Phillips, *The Confederation of Europe* (London, 1920), Sir Charles Webster, *The Congress of Vienna* (London, 1934) and H.Nicolson, *The Congress of Vienna* (London, 1945) have different emphases. For some of the broader implications of international relations F.H.Hinsley, *Power and the Pursuit of Peace* (Cambridge, 1963) has much illuminating comment.

Irish issues are best served by consulting E.R.Norman, *A History of Modern Ireland* (Harmondsworth, 1973) for a stimulating and controversial introduction, and then going on to T.Pakenham, *The Year of Liberty* (London, 1969), E.M.Johnston, *Great Britain and Ireland 1760–1800* (Edinburgh, 1963) and G. C. Bolton, *The Passing of the Irish Act of Union* (Oxford, 1966). For the French Wars Sir Arthur Bryant's trilogy, *Years of Endurance* (London, 1942), *Years of Victory* (London, 1944) and *The Age of Elegance* (London, 1950) remain vivid reading. C.Barnett, *Britain and Her Army 1509–1970* (Harmondsworth, 1974) places military matters in a broad perspective. R.Glover, *Britain at Bay* (London, 1973) and the same author's *Peninsular Preparation* (Cambridge, 1963) are important contributions towards a fuller comprehension of Castlereagh's achievements at the War Department.

Books on Castlereagh's contemporaries are too numerous for a complete listing but it is worth directing attention to the following: D.Jarrett, *Pitt the Younger* (London, 1974); J.Ehrman, *The Younger Pitt: the Years of Acclaim* (London, 1969); J.W.Derry, *Charles James Fox* (London, 1972); P.J.V.Rolo, *George Canning* (London, 1965); H.W.V.Temperley, *Life of Canning* (London, 1905); H.W.V.Temperley, *The Foreign Policy of Canning* (London, 1925); W.Hinde, *George Canning* (London, 1973); D.Gray, *Spencer Perceval* (Manchester, 1963); W.R.Brock, *Lord Liverpool and Liberal Toryism* (Cambridge, 1941); Lady Longford, *Wellington: The Years of the Sword* (London, 1969) and *Wellington: Pillar of State* (London, 1972); P.Guedalla, *The Duke*

(London, 1931); Sir A. Bryant, *The Great Duke* (London, 1971); P. Ziegler, *Addington* (London, 1965); N.Gash, *Mr Secretary Peel* (London, 1961); Duff Cooper, *Talleyrand* (London, 1932); J.F.Bernard, *Talleyrand* (London, 1973); A.Cecil, *Metternich* (London, 1933); A.Palmer, *Metternich* (London, 1972); I.Butler, *The Eldest Brother: The Marquess Wellesley 1760–1812* (London, 1973).

For some political and social issues the following should be consulted: M.Roberts, *The Whig Party 1807–1812* (London, 1939); A.Mitchell, *The Whigs in Opposition* (Oxford, 1967); G.I.T.Machin, *The Catholic Question in English Politics* (Oxford, 1964); R.J.White, *Waterloo to Peterloo* (London, 1957) and *Life in Regency England* (London, 1963); F.O.Darvall, *Popular Disturbances and Public Order in Regency England* (London, 1934); E.P.Thompson, *The Making of the English Working Class* (London, 1963); D.Read, *Peterloo: The Massacre and Its Background* (Manchester, 1957); J.Marlow, *The Peterloo Massacre* (London, 1969); R.Walmsley, *Peterloo: The Case Re-opened* (Manchester, 1969); H.Martineau, *A History of the Thirty Years Peace* (4 vols., London, 1877).

The diarists and memoir-writers of the period throw much light on social and political life and, in certain cases, on Castlereagh's personality. They exist in a number of editions and the following may be recommended: *The Journal of Mrs Arbuthnot* (ed. F.Bamford and the Duke of Wellington) (2 vols., London, 1950); *The Creevey Papers* (ed. H.Maxwell) (2 vols., London, 1903); *The Croker Papers* (ed. B.Pool) (London, 1967); J.W.Croker, *Correspondence and Diaries* (ed. L.J.Jennings) (3 vols., London, 1884); *The Greville Memoirs* (ed. H.Reeve) (8 vols., London, 1875–87); *The Greville Memoirs* (ed. L.Strachey and R.Fulford) (8 vols., London, 1938).

INDEX